BUCKINGHAM PALACE

As President of Save the Children, I know how much the Fund relies upon the energy and abilities of so many different individuals to help raise the funds necessary to enable our vital work, in the UK and overseas, to continue. In the case of Gordon King, it is his talent as an artist that has proved so invaluable to Save the Children's fundraising effort.

In 1992 Save the Children launched the Birmingham Children in Cities Appeal to help improve the quality of life for children living in cities around the world. Asked by a member of the organising committee if he would be prepared to help, Gordon King readily agreed and subsequently produced twelve splendid paintings, all, appropriately, depicting children. These were subsequently made into limited edition prints which were sold individually and also into Christmas cards and the proceeds made a substantial contribution to the £700,000 eventually raised by this imaginative Appeal.

This book is a fitting tribute to the life and work of Gordon King to date. It chronicles his career as an artist from its earliest stages and reflects the quality and diversity of his paintings. I have no doubt it will prove a source of enjoyment to art lovers everywhere.

Anne

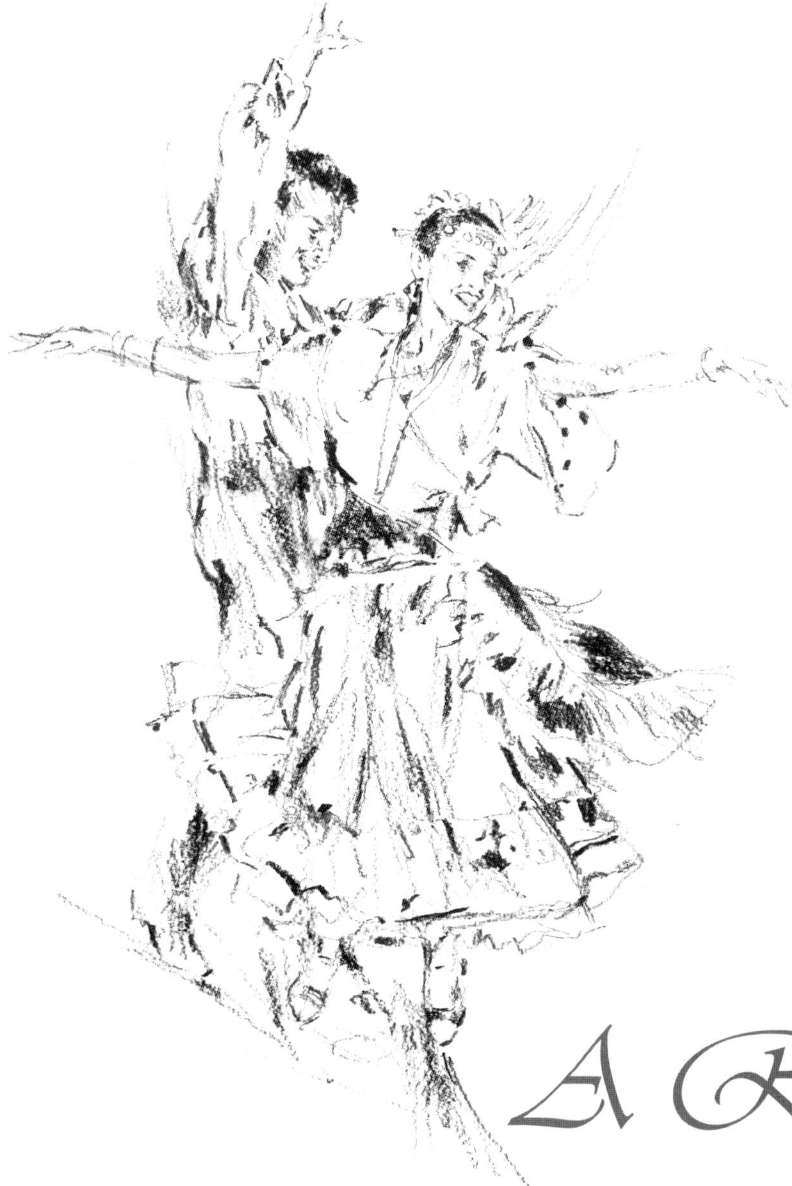

A Romance with Art

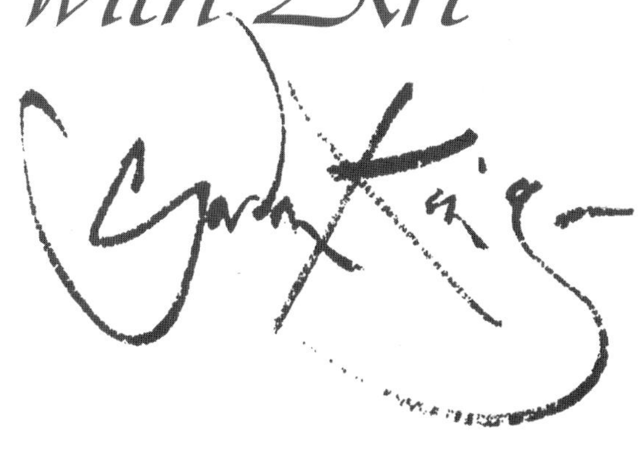

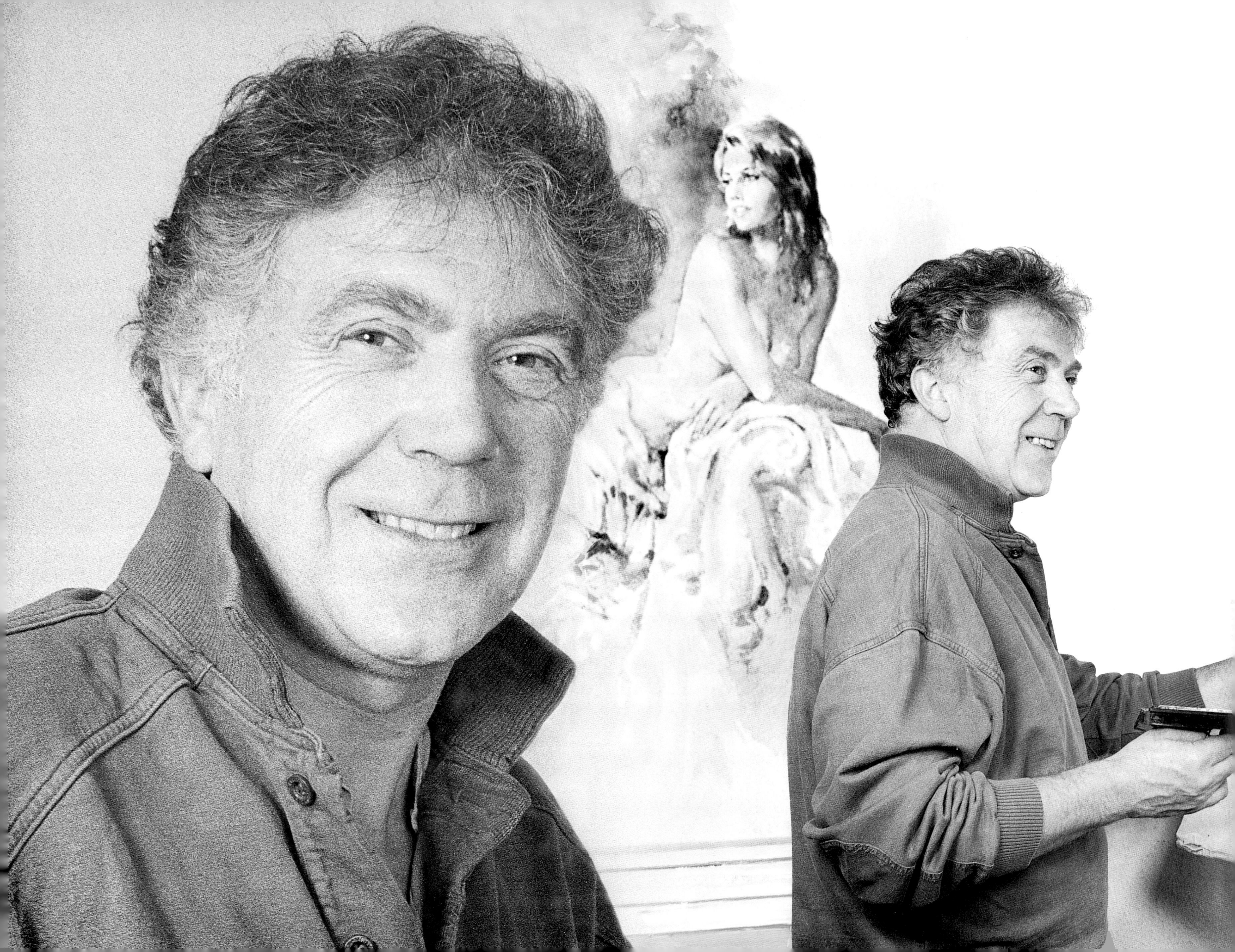

A Romance with Art

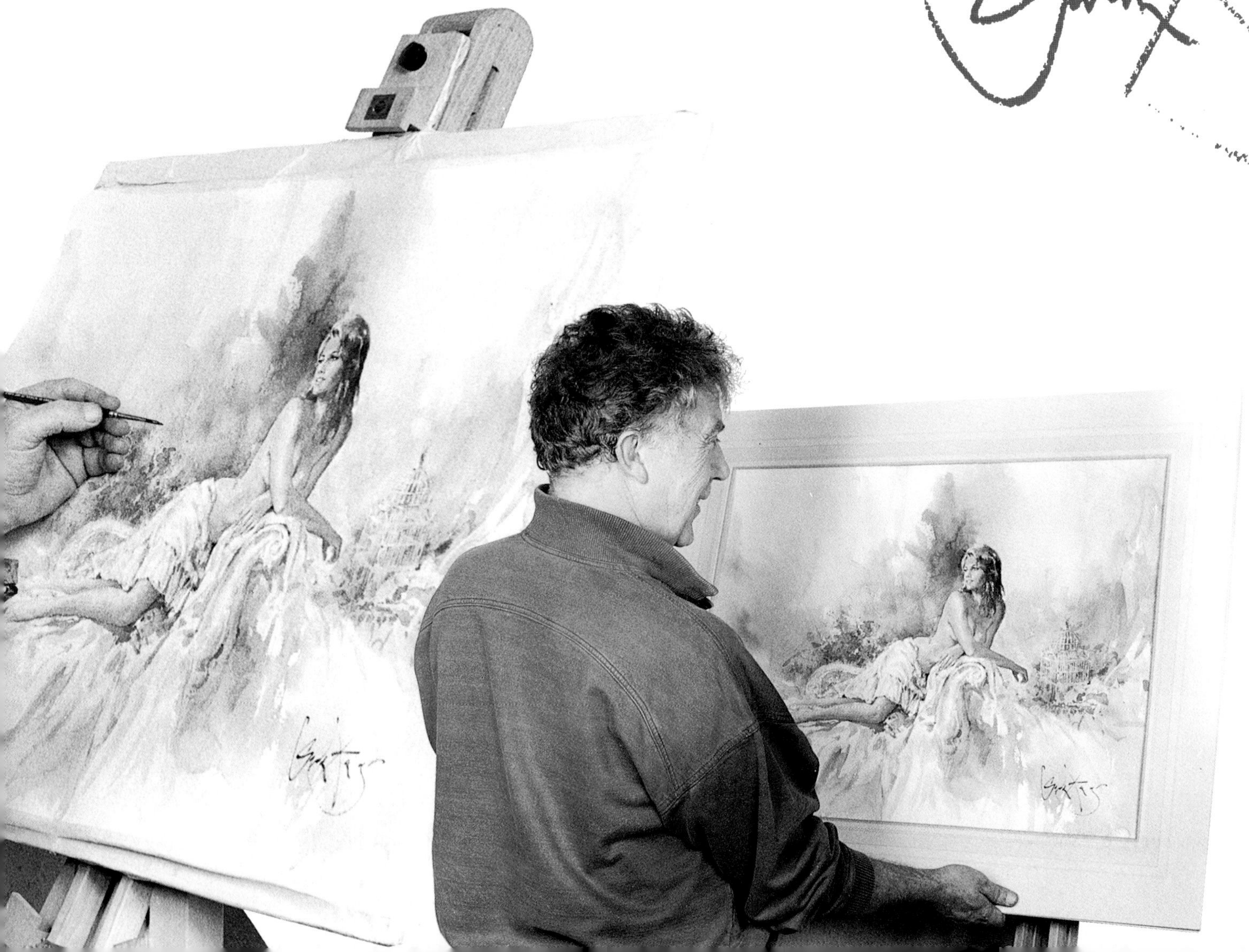

Photographs by John Simcock

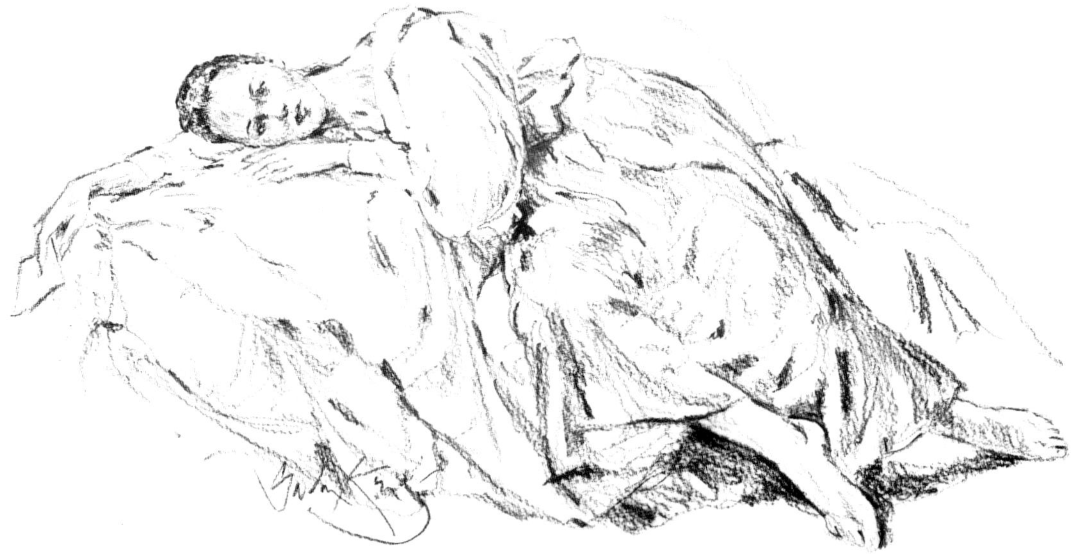

A Romance with Art

Gordon King has for the last 20 years been regarded as one the country's most popular contemporary watercolourists. His paintings have been admired and collected at numerous national and international exhibitions. King's ability to portray his subjects with a delightful delicacy and atmosphere has earned him considerable acclaim throughout the art world. His work has been produced as best selling limited editions and fine art prints the former being highly collectable. His early "Flower Girl" paintings became instantly recognisable with the classic "My Fair Lady" published in 1984 becoming one of the country's best selling fine art prints.

In recent years the breadth of the artist's subject matter has been admired with his paintings depicting a diversity of subjects including sport, culture and travel. King has been involved with several charities. His paintings have been donated for auction and reproduced in the form of both limited editions and greeting cards, sales of which have benefited the "Save The Children Fund'.

"A Romance with Art" is the artist's first illustrative book tracing the history of Gordon King's paintings and featuring a wide collection of work from the last 20 years many paintings will be recognised by collectors nationwide, many have been reproduced as limited edition prints. The book has been long awaited and we are sure will be enjoyed by all.

First Published in Great Britain in 1995 by Washington Green Publications.

Designed by Gordon King and Jonathan Kearns. Typeset by DuoDesign Ltd.
I would also like to express my thanks to Agfa Gevaert for donating the film and Horsell Anitic for donating the printing plates. Mondial Silk supplied by Robert Horne Paper Co. Limited.
Colour origination by Culver Graphics Litho Ltd, Lane End, Bucks. Printed in the UK by Hill Shorter.

British Library Cataloguing in Publications Data
Gordon King - A Romance With Art

ISBN 0 9525833 0 5

PUBLISHED BY

WASHINGTON GREEN PUBLICATIONS

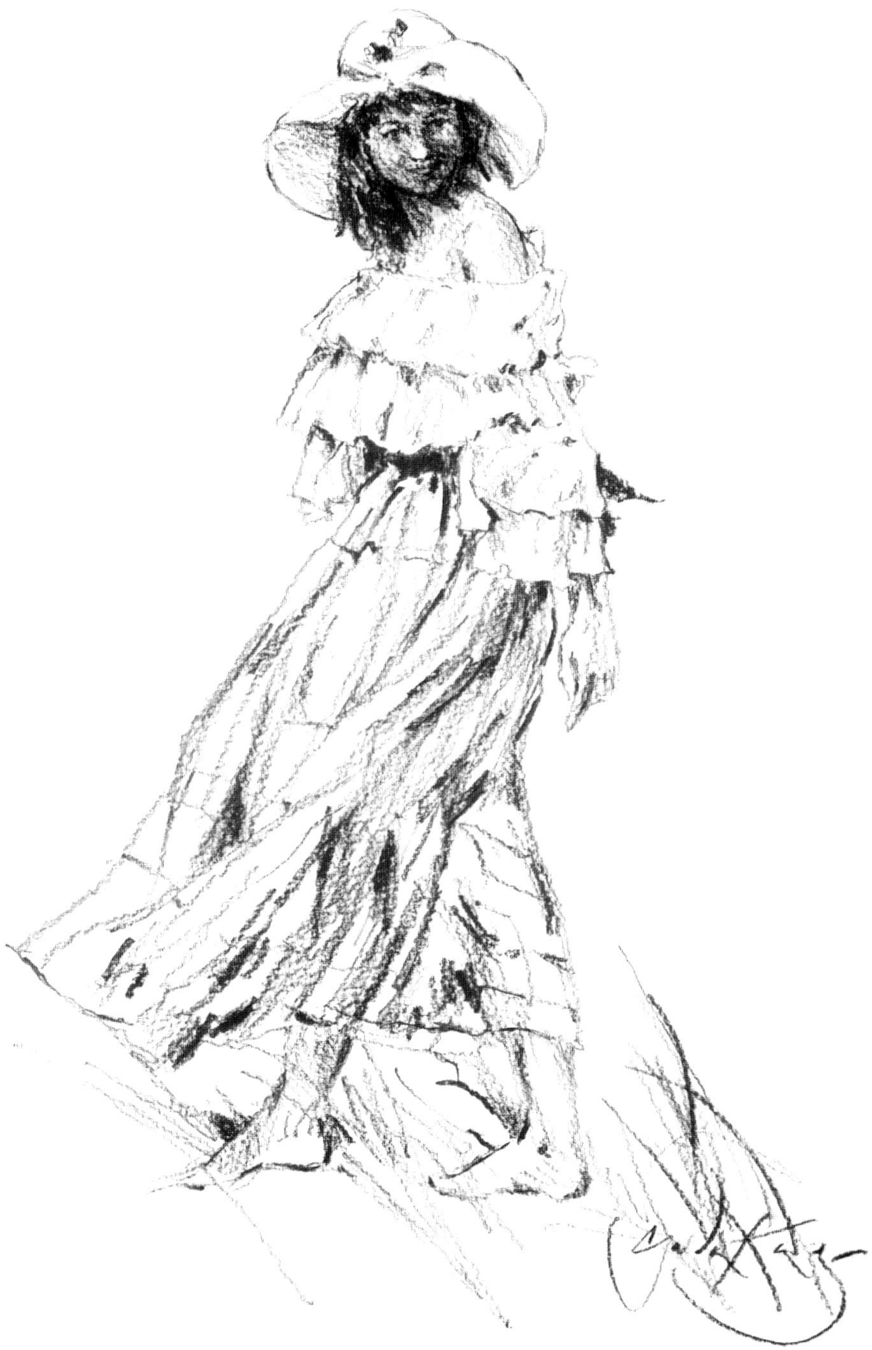

Contents

Acknowledgements

My love and thanks go to Mary and her faithful word processor, for her patience in putting my rambling words and scribbles into a readable script, as well as being a sounding board and a second pair of eyes for all those design and text decisions that were needed, alongside Jonathan Kearns of Washington Green who always seemed totally unflappable in seeing the whole production through.

My thanks also go to my family and friends who have contributed in some way to this project, especially:

Bob & Carol Barrie, Gloria Hunniford, Chris Kemp, Janet King, Robert & Linda King, Roland Miller, Ray & Carol Rice, John Stringer & Rosemary Gizzy, Clive & Kay Thomas.

Gordon King, Chalfont St Peter, 1995.

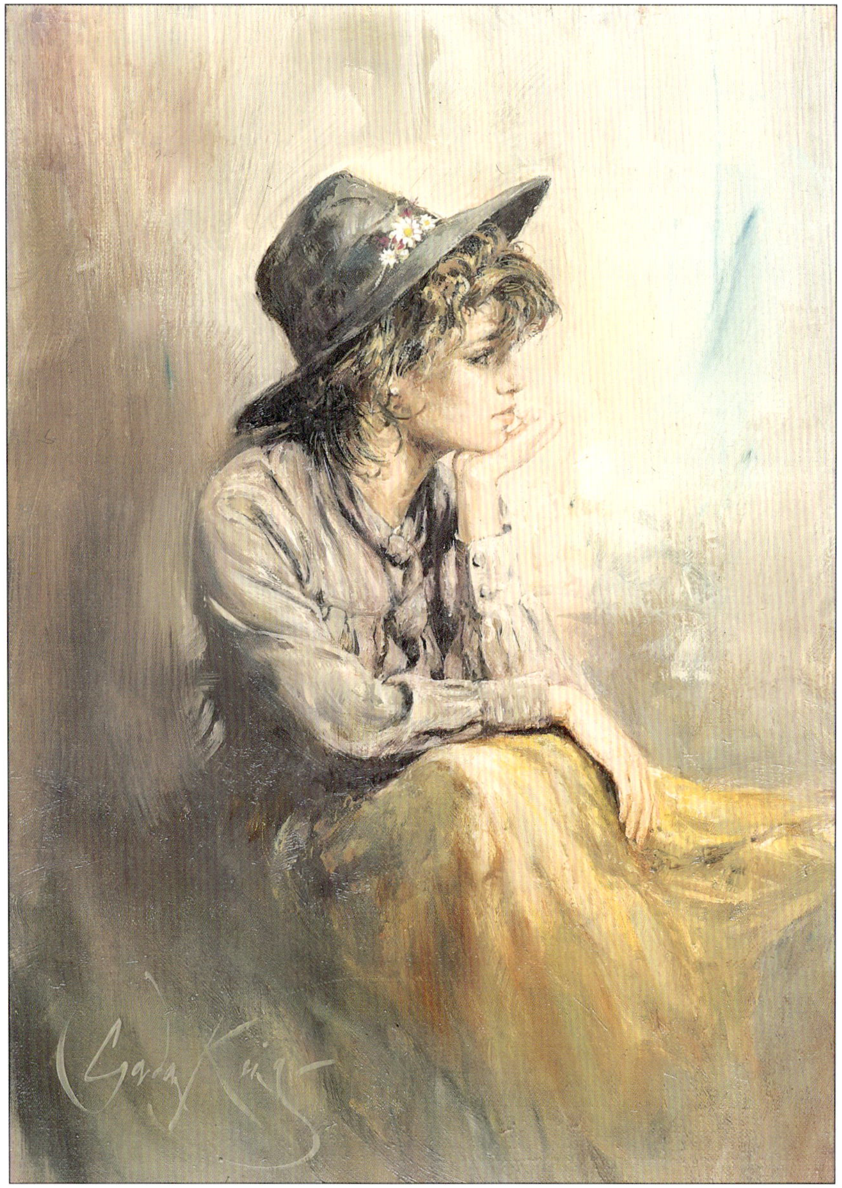

HIDDEN THOUGHTS (OIL)

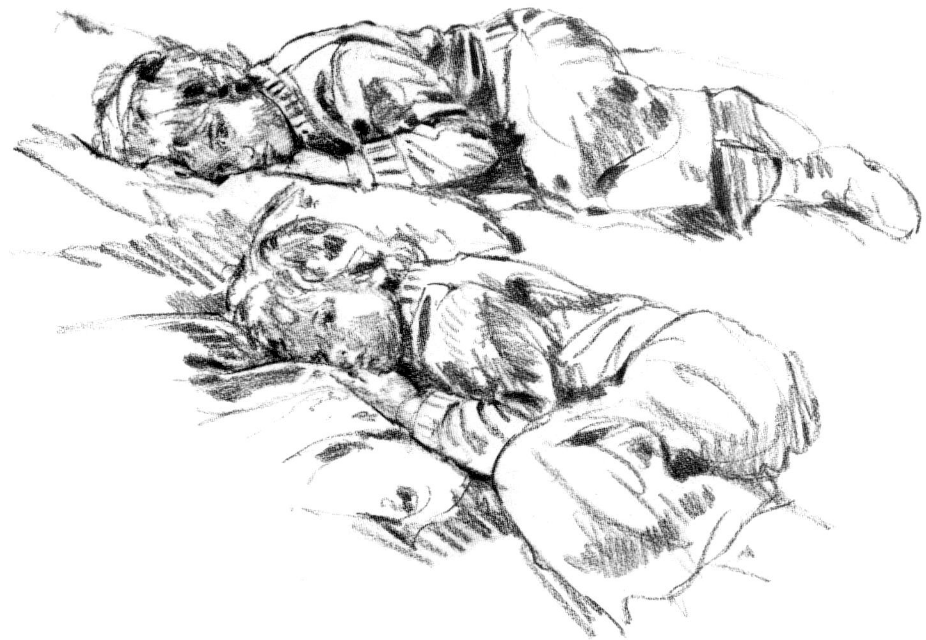

Introduction

Art, to me, is a very basic expressive talent. In its simplest form it is a direct statement which communicates to others without the need for any deep understanding of academic learning. I have always invested a lot of emotion in my work and I hope this comes through, reflecting not only the image in the painting, but something of my personality as well.

In writing this book I am grateful for the opportunity it provides for me to reach out to the many people who have bought my paintings and prints over the years. I've always enjoyed meeting them and one thing they all seem to have in common is the kind of questions they ask: When did you start?, Where do you get your inspiration?, Where do you find all those girls?, Are they all your daughters?, (God forbid!), and the eternal 'How long does is take to do a painting?'.

The first part of the book is an autobiography, drawing together the main strands of my life which have influenced the development of my career. I have been painting and drawing for as long as I can remember and hopefully will continue to do so for many years to come.

The second part is a visual journey through the various subjects I have painted over the years. Although the girls have been the dominant subject over the last decade, I have also spent many hours capturing the excitement of special events and memories from my travels. Hopefully the images selected for inclusion, both old and new, provide an interesting and fair reflection of my overall work.

I have always felt very privileged to be able to do something that I love to earn my living, and if I can give an ounce of pleasure to others in the process I feel highly rewarded. In a way it seems unfortunate that as an artist's paintings become more popular, the price of the work goes up and fewer people are able to own the originals. But that's where the prints come in - a way of spreading the work of one man's hands to a wider public. I owe a great deal to all those who have supported me over the years and would like to take this opportunity to thank them all. I still feel passionate about my work. When I am painting, I'm in a world of my own - nothing outside can touch me. It really is a romance with art.

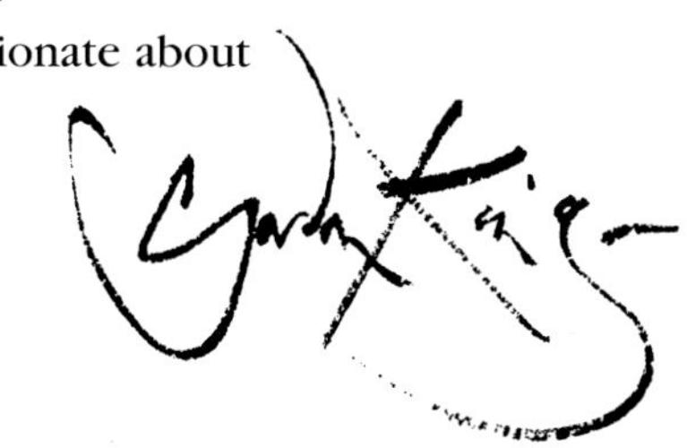

The Story So Far...

EARLY MEMORIES - SCOTLAND

It has always seemed totally natural for me to draw. I can't remember precisely when I first picked up a pencil or a crayon but drawing has been second nature to me for as long as I can remember.

My first visual memories go back to the sea and the beaches of the east coast of Scotland. Kinghorn, where I lived, was a small holiday resort in Fife near Kirkcaldy. There was a lovely bay with golden sands and rocks washed smooth and clean by the ebb and flow of the tide. A short walk took us to the harbour with its fishing boats and lobster pots and we often used to go and watch the boats come in with their catch. It was a delightful place to be. The Flying Scotsman used to roar right through the centre of the village and my sister and I would stand on the bridge waving frantically to the driver and the people on the train. At that stage I wanted to be an engine driver when I grew up!

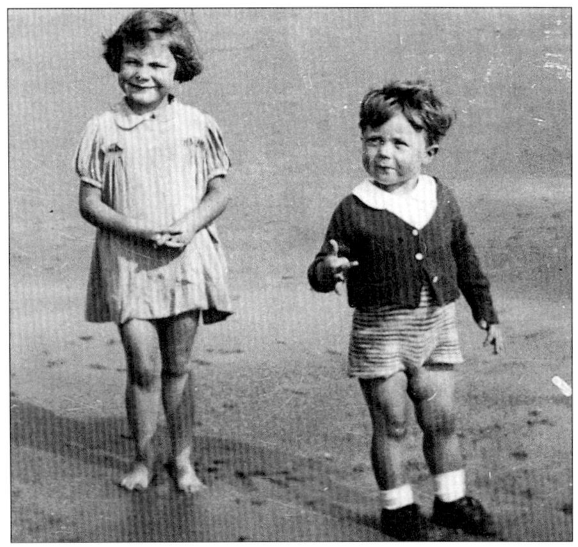

With my sister on the beach.

On Sundays after church the local pipe band would arrive and I'd watch spellbound as they marched up and down surrounded by that wonderful swirling sound. On these occasions, of course, I wanted to be a bagpipe player when I grew up! At one point I did try to learn the chanter but, much to the relief of my family, I didn't find it at all easy and gave up fairly rapidly.

Although the war was on it didn't seem to affect us much as children. Occasionally we would see enemy aircraft flying across the sky on sorties over Rossyth Dockyards and one day I saw a mine that had been washed ashore - a large rusty globe with spikes sticking out which had been cordoned off for safety. The beach was our playground in those days and generally it was rather an idyllic life.

It came as quite a shock to discover later on that I wasn't actually Scots at all, but had been born in London on June 6th, 1939, just before war broke out. My Scottish father, Reuben James King, came from Kirkcaldy and was the son of Captain King - Commodore Skipper of the East Coast Shipping Line. He was in the confectionery business and moved to England in the early 30's where he met my mother, Vera Rosa Newport, the daughter of Sidney Newport who ran a furniture business in Reading. They married and set up home in Mottingham Gardens on the outskirts of London where my sister and I were born.

When war was declared my parents were faced with something of a dilemma. My father had started his working life as an apprentice shipwright in the Naval Dockyards at Rossyth and this was one of the industries that was now desperate for qualified workers to help them meet the war effort. After much deliberation he decided to leave his job in London and return to his native Scotland.

So it was that when I was 6 months old and my sister Janet (known as Jean to the family) was three, we made the long journey up to Scotland in our faithful Austin 7. After staying with my Uncle Jack in Kirkcaldy for a while, my father bought a bungalow overlooking the sea in Kinghorn where we were to spend the next few years.

The local surroundings with its boats and beaches were an important part of my early life and these were the subjects I drew from an early age. When I started school at the age of four, my first sketch books were full of very disciplined little drawings in coloured chalk or pastel which, according to my sister, were always recognisable images even at that early age.

Unfortunately, I suffered from frequent bouts of bronchitis which meant I was at home much of the time so my drawing became quite therapeutic in some ways being something I could do even when I wasn't feeling well.

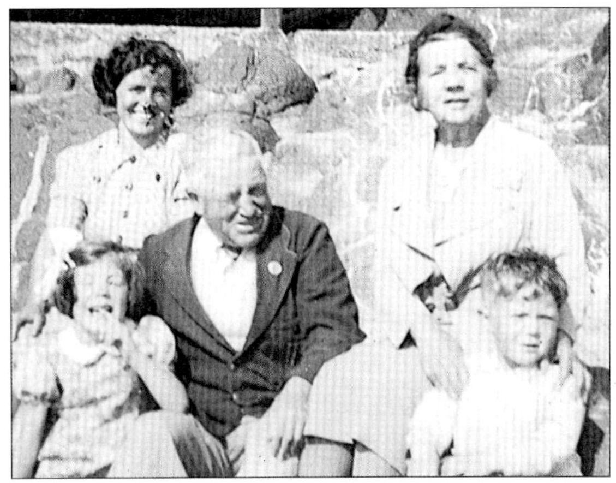
With my mother, sister and grandparents in Scotland.

When I was five years old I remember going to buy my first real artist's materials on my own - I wanted to get myself a new pencil rubber with my pocket money. Walking down the hill to the shops by the harbour I felt very adventurous as I went in and made my purchase. However, when I arrived home and proudly showed off my new acquisition, I discovered that it was a typewriter rubber and absolutely no use to me at all!

My grandparents used to journey up by train from Reading to visit us for their annual holiday and my memory of them at that time was of a rather grand Edwardian couple having wonderful picnics on the beach and playing bowls with my mother at the Bowls Club which was just across the road from our house.

Soon after my 7th birthday it was our turn to make the journey from Scotland to Reading as my parents decided to return to England and take advantage of the fact that my grandfather had a vacant flat above his furniture shop, S.H. Newport & Son, in Caversham Road which was to become our new home.

Life changed very rapidly. We had moved from the natural beauty of Scotland to the built up area of Reading and overnight my playground changed from the beaches of the Fife Coast to the grassy banks of the River Thames. At the local primary school I swapped my kilt for a pair of short trousers, and found myself in a class of English children for whom the strong Scottish accent which I then possessed was something of a novelty. I very soon became known as "Scottie" and this nickname was to stay with me throughout my schooldays.

SCHOOLDAYS IN READING

My grandfather's shop was a marvellous cavern of a place for me. The apartment which became home for us was in the two storeys above the shop with a flat roof which extended quite a long way out across the area below which was used as the store room and workshops.

Part of the second-hand furniture business involved buying up the contents of houses. I would wander down and look at all these treasures - fascinating bric-a-brac, beautiful antiques and lots of paintings. The post-war period of the late 40's was a time of change when it was fashionable to discard the old and buy something new. It was the era of utility furniture, which wasn't particularly well designed or even well made but it was new and looked modern and that's what seemed to matter. But I loved the old things and every collection that came in was a feast for my eyes.

One day my grandfather had come back with an exotic collection of stuffed animals in glass cases which he donated to my primary school as an educational aid and I remember how proud I felt as I helped him carry them into the classroom. Around the walls was a colourful freize illustrating the legend of Hiawatha. Sitting at my rickety old school desk I used to find myself gazing at it in a world of my own thinking I'd like to do something like that for myself. It really inspired me to come up with my own ideas and paint my own pictures.

Every Saturday the family would go to the local library to choose our books for the week. Mine were invariably about art and most of my spare time was spent browsing through them, totally absorbed, admiring the wonderful paintings and techniques of so many different artists.

Next door to the library were the offices of our local newspaper, the Berkshire Chronicle, and one day we noticed that they ran a weekly art competition. The first time I decided to have a go the subject was 'A clipper ship in full sail' - the kind of ship which my seafaring grandfather once sailed. My father had always enjoyed art, his own father having been an accomplished artist, and he gave me a lesson in shading the sails, helping me to create the feeling that they went round in a curve and that the wind was blowing through them. My first lesson in shape and movement. The painting was entered for the competition and a few days later I was notified by the newspaper that I'd won. The prize was in savings certificates but the real highlight for me was going to the Berkshire Chronicle's offices the following Saturday to see the winning paintings displayed in their window with mine right in the middle.

After this early success I entered the competition on numerous occasions and much to my delight kept on winning. However I eventually received a rather plaintive letter from the newspaper asking if I minded not receiving any more prizes because they felt I'd won it too many times and they wanted to give someone else a chance!

The River Thames played quite a large part in my life at that time providing a new source of excitement and inspiration for me. I had always enjoyed swimming with my father who was a founder member of Reading Swimming Club, so we used to swim regularly in the river and also had fun with our canoe. The banks of the river provided an unexpected new source of art materials - I used to dig out the clay to use for modelling as I enjoyed making things almost as much as I enjoyed drawing and painting. I made all sorts of puppets, from marionettes to hand-puppets, and even made my own Ventriloquist's dummy. The fascination lay not in performing but in the sheer intricacy and movement involved in getting the limbs and mouth to work. But most of all, the river became a wonderful subject for me to paint, then and now.

The first serious river painting I did was when I was 10 years old. The School had entered me for a prestigious national competition sponsored by the Art Group Gainsborough for which I did a painting in watercolour of the boats moored around the island in the middle of the River Thames at Caversham, emphasising the mirror image of the boats in the reflections on the water. Every detail was crystal clear in my mind, after all I played there nearly every day, and this was probably one of the most important lessons I learned as an artist - the importance of painting what you know.

The winning paintings were to be displayed in Foyles Art Gallery in London and when we heard that I had won the competition for my age group the whole family made the journey to the City where we combined our visit to the Gallery with a visit to one of the West End theatres. To see my painting displayed in the show alongside others from all over the world gave me a tremendous buzz and as I looked at the other prize-winning paintings it occurred to me that many of them were of other subjects that I too liked to paint, particularly horses. I remember wondering whether they had been painted by children who had horses of their own. If they, too, were painting what they knew.

It was about this time that my love for sport began and I added football and cricket to my swimming activities. I was particularly keen to become a footballer, preferably for Scotland, and my first football strip, made for me by my mother, was the blue shirt and white shorts of the Scottish team.

Unfortunately I still had frequent bouts of illness which kept me at home and off the sportsfield, but I was always able to turn this to advantage by using the time to paint even though life at home was going through quite an upheaval with the arrival of a baby brother. Robert was a delightful addition to the family. From the moment he was born I thought he was very special and found myself feeling very responsible and protective towards him.

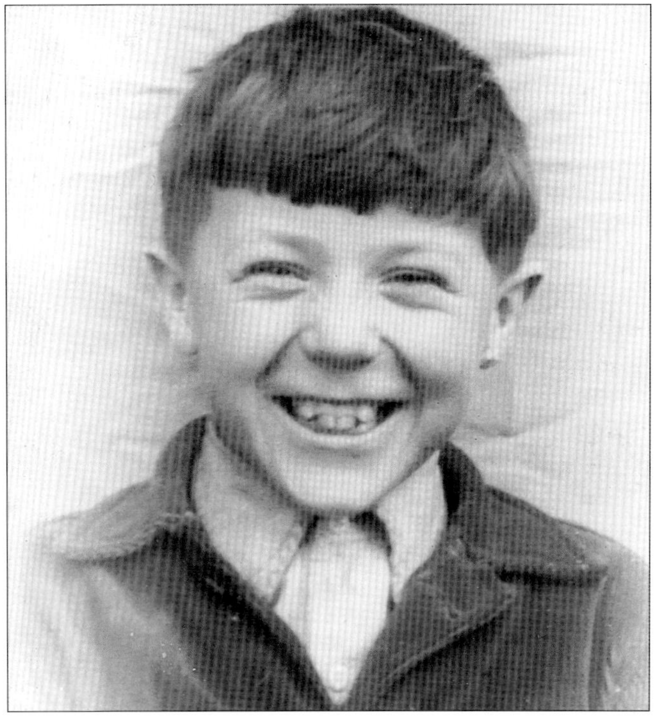
At primary school.

Soon the day came when I had to say goodbye to the primary school. I'd had a lot of fun taking part in the school Open Day by dressing up as a pavement artist, complete with blue beret, and doing some chalk drawings in the playground. As people walked by I rattled my plate vigorously in front of them trying to persuade them to part with some money for the school. I was very commercial about this, eagerly wanting to raise as much as I could - something that I've done many times since for a good cause.

My final contribution was an enormous mural all round the main hall and I found myself confidently looking forward to even more exciting projects which would hopefully be forthcoming at the secondary school which was just across the bridge on the other side of the river.

SECONDARY SCHOOL

Caversham Secondary School was a relatively modern building. It was built in the late 1920's and in comparison with E P Collier School, my primary school, which was an old Victorian monster of a place in red brick, this was delightful with its large windows, purpose built gymnasium and a well-equipped art room. My art teacher was a charismatic gentleman called Mr. Burgess who was a member of the Magic Circle in his spare time and used to delight us all by practising his magic tricks on the class. He was also a thespian with the local amateur dramatic society. A real character. I remember my first meeting with him when I told him, perhaps a little precociously, that I wasn't really used to painting in the powder paints that were on offer - I preferred oils!

Mr. Burgess took all this in his stride and in fact gave me a very quick break. The school was renowned for its plays and drama and he gave me the opportunity to paint the backdrop for a production of Treasure Island. I went home that night, visions of clipper ships and the Spanish Main going round in my mind, and worked on a rough outline. The scene I came up with was a typical harbour view with square rigged ships alongside the quay with fishermen's nets and lobster pots scattered about and when I showed him the next day he was impressed enough to tell me to go ahead with it. I had never worked on such a large scale before but I thoroughly enjoyed the challenge and I loved the excitement of being on the stage with everyone during rehearsals. The atmosphere was brilliant and I felt this should be my life, it was so terrific.

The production and my backdrop were a great success and the local paper came along and took a photograph which appeared the following week alongside an excellent review. From then on I became the official artist and programme designer for all the school plays.

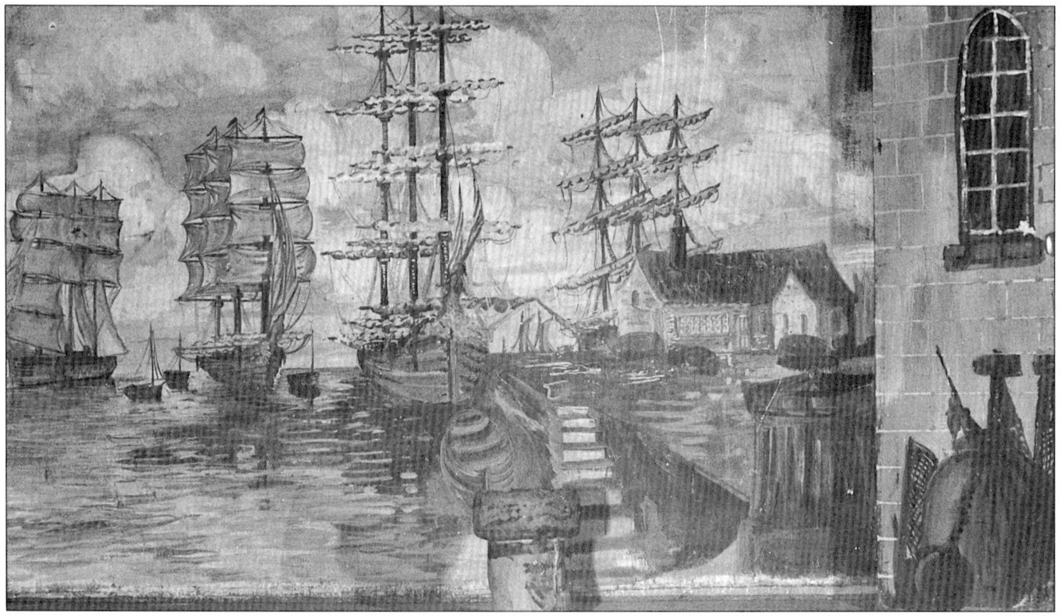

The backdrop for the School Play - Treasure Island.

Mr. Burgess continued to give me tremendous encouragement to the extent that I was singled out from the rest of the art class with my own working area and always seemed to be involved in some project or other, including designing and illustrating the school magazine. I've never forgotten one particular lesson he gave me when I was about 12 years old. I was painting a scene with a foreground figure of a young lady wearing a long dress. He clearly wasn't happy with what I'd done and told me emphatically that I had to imagine what was underneath the dress! At the time it was enough to make this innocent pre-adolescent youth blush to his fingertips but, in retrospect, it was a useful lesson. The feet at the bottom of the dress had to bear some relationship to the head and shoulders at the top - mine obviously didn't! A case in point for any figurative artist having at least an elementary knowledge of anatomy.

My creative skills also followed me into the woodwork lesson where, instead of using rulers and set squares to make neat joints for stools and tables as instructed, I confidently attacked a piece of wood with a chisel, sculpting it into the shape of a footballer to make a base for a lamp. I can still see the look of horror on the teacher's face!

My sporting activities were very much to the fore at this time although there was a certain amount of conflict with Mr. Burgess over this as he felt sport was an unwelcome distraction from my painting activities. However I was determined to continue with all of them - cricket, tennis, swimming and my big love which was football. I played for the school, where I was Captain of the school team, and subsequently proudly played for the Reading & Berkshire Schoolboys. I can laugh now at the fact that I think I was the only one in the team not to be signed by Reading Football Club. Obviously my future was not to be in professional football!

At home, my grandfather had soon recognised my abilities as a sign writer and often asked me to do some work for the shop designing tickets for the summer sale and special offer labels. One of my other early jobs entailed lettering the butcher's bike. It was a black bicycle with a large basket on the front and my task was to paint "Stephen's Butchers" on each side.

When I was about fourteen I began my first professional instruction in graphic design and art. A family friend, Mr. Griffin, ran the Art Department of Huntley Bourne & Stevens, the company that made all the tin boxes for Huntley & Palmer's biscuits in Reading. Mr. Griffin agreed to let me go over to see him every Saturday morning when he set me specific tasks doing lettering and designs for the top of biscuit tins.

These sessions provided me with excellent instruction from an early age which was a great help in raising the standard of my work and extending my creative abilities. It also led to the offer of several jobs from local businessmen, one of them being for Wall's Carnival Stores, a fascinating shop specialising in everything from theatrical costumes to magic tricks, who asked me to paint a number of life-size characters and clowns for their displays. Next door to Wall's was my local Fish & Chip shop and as there was a national potato shortage at the time, they asked me to do a poster for them telling their customers that they could only buy chips if they bought fish as well. I painted a small boy sadly holding a single chip and, much to my delight, was paid in chips - to this day I still love chips with everything!

My schooldays were generally happy days for me. By 1954, when I was 15 years old and in my final year, I was appointed Head Boy, came top of the form (my favourite academic subjects being history and geography), and was also Captain of the football and cricket teams.

It was at this time that I was awarded the Coronation Prize which was given to celebrate the Coronation of Queen Elizabeth II. All the schoolchildren in Reading were eligible to be entered by their schools in recognition of an individual pupil's overall achievement. The prize was a book of my choice and I opted for an American publication on Life Drawing which was specially embossed with the Queen's Head. It was presented to me by the Mayor of Reading and caused quite a stir when he looked through it and found it was full of drawings and photographs of nude women!

MY FIRST JOB

Lengthy discussions took place with the whole family about my future. As Mr. Griffin was still giving me weekly lessons in graphic design and lettering, it was generally presumed that I would join him at the studio of Huntley Bourne & Stevens to undertake a 5 year apprenticeship as a lithographic artist. However, fate played its part when the time came for me to apply as it transpired that they would not have a vacancy until the following year. Filled with consternation we had to look elsewhere.

After further discussions, Mr. Griffin suggested that I apply to join the studio of Granthams of Reading, the largest advertising agency in the area. This I did and as soon as I received a date for the interview my mother insisted on taking me shopping to buy my first suit. I was not happy. Every suit I tried on made me feel more uncomfortable and self-conscious but the more I sulked the more my mother came into her own. She knew exactly what she was looking for and eventually found it - a brown suit on the bargain rail at Burtons which she decreed would be just right! I thought it made me look rather old but I knew when I was beaten and grudgingly agreed that it would probably do.

My interview was with a Mr. Buchanan, the Managing Director, an ebullient larger-than-life character, married to an ex-showgirl, and I felt confident that it went quite well. This was confirmed by the arrival of a letter a few days later offering me a job in the studio at 30 shillings a week. I was delighted but no more so than my mother who clearly felt my success was entirely due to that brown baggy suit!

The first day of my new job dawned on a sunny September day and I reported to the Head Office of Granthams in Fleet Street, Reading, as instructed, only to be immediately sent round to the studio part of the Agency which was housed in a 3-storey building next door to the Black Horse Pub opposite Reading Station. It was a walk of just under a mile and, little did I know it then, but I would be running frantically along that route in many a panic situation in the future.

The Reception and Accounts Department were in the basement and the

Office and the Studios on the next two floors. A tall ex-wartime Petty Officer, Steven Doughty, was the Studio Manager, an accomplished figurative artist and illustrator who was desperately trying to keep a roof over his head and pay his way at the bar of the pub next door. Other artists seemed to come and go at random, mostly women, usually very pretty, a requirement of the fair sex apparently.

When I arrived I was briefed on my duties which were basically to make the tea, run errands, take messages and do the filing - not a forte of mine then or now! I was more than a little disappointed to find that there wasn't even a working area for me but fate was again going to play its part and strangely enough it was indirectly my love of football that was going to put this right before too long.

At the time I was a very keen member of Caversham Boys Club and I played football in their team on Saturdays. The National Association of Boys Clubs ran a Poster Competition which I entered and when it was announced that I had won, Mr. Buchanan at the Agency was notified that a photographer was to be sent to the studio to photograph me at work. When he arrived, however, he was horrified to find that I didn't even have a work space. I managed to make quite a play of this and a hastily assembled area was created for me with a board and materials where I could pose for the photograph which later appeared in the Association's magazine. Mr. Buchanan was impressed - especially when the Association of Boys Clubs gave the contract to the Agency to print the poster. I was really pleased that my design was going to be used throughout the country but more important still at that stage was the fact that I had started to be noticed - and I had a place of my own to work!

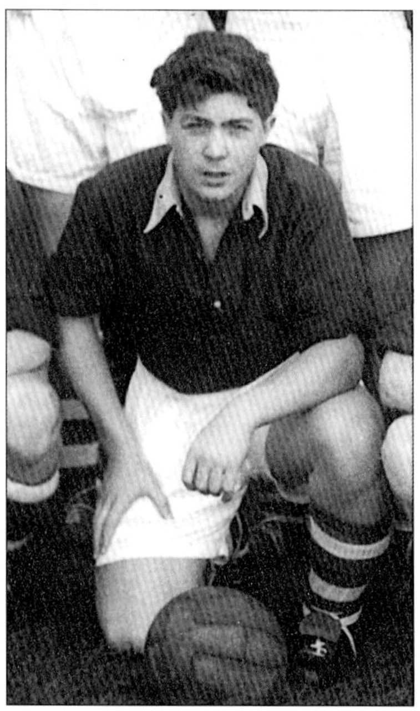

In the football team.

I cycled everywhere in those days so I usually went home for my lunch and worked on my latest paintings. In the evenings I would work on them again, burning the midnight oil, and on many a night my mother would order me to bed in the early hours of the morning. I was quite obsessional about painting and drawing, desperately wanting to emulate some of the artists of the day. I used to carry my sketchpad everywhere and would often find myself in the local coffee shop sketching the characters I saw around me.

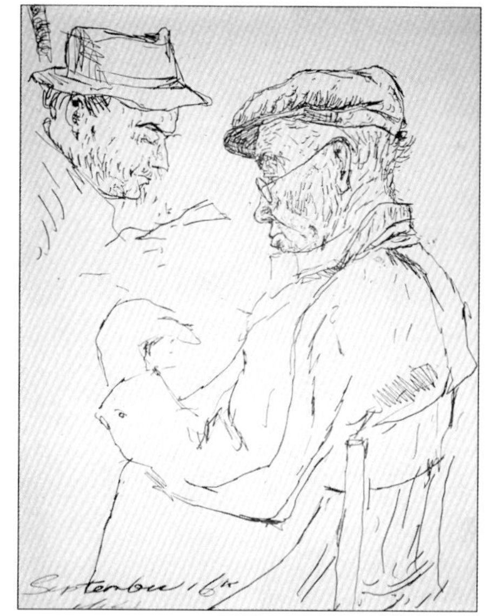

Lyons Coffee Bar.

On a short camping holiday to Zanborg in Holland I visited some of the galleries in Amsterdam, including the Reich Museum where I saw Rembrandt's "Nightwatch" in all its splendour. I found it very inspiring and came back wanting to paint more than ever.

In due course it was arranged for me to attend life drawing classes at the Post-graduate Art School at Reading University on a day release basis. I will always remember my first day - Mr. Doughty sent me off with a pad of hard shiny paper and a hard pencil saying menacingly "You'll get no help from the materials - your drawing will have to stand on its merits!" A tough lesson but a good one.

Attending night school and day release classes meant I was working very hard, at one stage 5 nights a week. Also the Boys Club appointed me the Berkshire representative for the NABC so I had a few interesting ventures with them meeting such people as the Duke of Gloucester, Roger Bannister and a stalwart of the Association, Frankie Vaughan, who had just had a hit record called "Green Door".

At the studio I was thankfully able to give up the filing before too long to work full-time on artwork. My abilities in painting and drawing figures had been recognised so when Steven Doughty left to go freelance I became the main figurative artist in the studio. The advertising world was booming. In those days photography was rarely used. Most advertising was in black and white and figurative art was considered to be the elite of illustration. A friend of mine, Lee Taylor, who had been working for one of the other agencies in Reading, joined our team and we had lots of fun together. We were both avid fans of "The Goon Show" and were always talking 'goon' language. The in-places to go at the time were jazz clubs and coffee bars and I felt really with-it in my green corduroy trousers and suede shoes.

Although things were going well on the work front, at home it was a different story. Sadly, a couple of years earlier my grandparents had passed away within a few weeks of each other. My mother inherited the house at 160 Caversham Road and we had moved into this very tall building with huge rooms and a strong air of Victorian austerity about it. It was a strange feeling moving into a house that I felt I knew so well but somehow didn't feel like home.

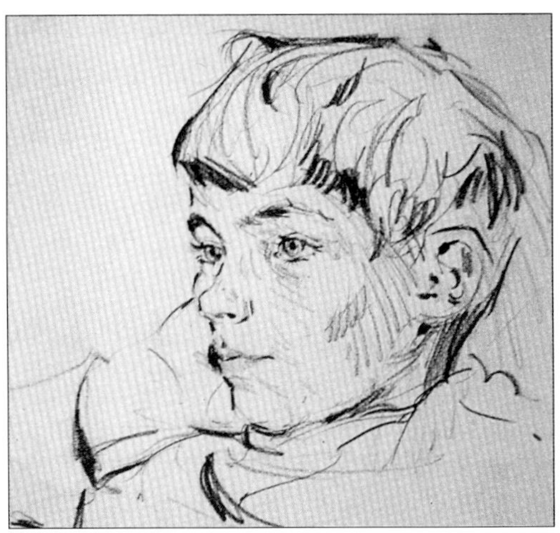

Sketch of my brother.

Now it was my mother who was desperately ill. It was a very sad time. I went away for a couple of days with Lee, travelling up the river in the canoe with our camping gear, playing at Tom Sawyer and Huckleberry Finn, but tragically I arrived home to find that my mother had suffered a relapse. The cancer had won. I was distraught. My father who had slept on the floor by her bed downstairs in the front room was heartbroken. Young Robert was only 8 years old and my sister and I rallied round him as much as we could. I was just 18 when my mother died. I grew up overnight.

THE YOUNG ILLUSTRATOR

In and out of the studio, I was always talking and dreaming about the London scene - especially Carlton Studios, the most famous, revered by any aspiring artist. Under its banner were International Artists, the main agency of the time, who had artists such as Roland Hilder, John Piper and Felix Topolski on their books. I would drool over their specimen sheets and could recognise each individual artist's style at a glance.

One day I happened to notice that Carlton were advertising for trainee figurative artists and were interviewing prospective applicants over a 2 week period. I couldn't possibly let such an opportunity go by, the chance to join my dream studio, so I put my specimen book under my arm and went off to London, full of optimism and determination.

The studio was in Portman Square, a lovely Georgian building, alas no longer there. My interview the following week was with Mr. Phipps, the Head of Carlton, it was my first lesson in being put in my place - on the bottom rung of the ladder - but they were at least interested in me. They operated an indenture system which was quite common in those days, whereby three young artists would be taken on for training on a three year cycle. I had to go for a second interview with my father present for the contract to be signed. My salary would be halved and it would be a long way to travel, but this, for me, was a dream come true.

The three budding artists who joined Carlton on that day were Eric Roe, Harry Jelly and myself. Eric was a Londoner, very confident and enormously talented and Harry, equally talented, was a Welsh lad from the valleys who had just finished his National Service.

The sheer size and vibrancy of the Portman Square Studio was a far cry from Reading. It was very light and airy, right at the top of the building, overlooking the rooftops of London. The competition was intense and Mr. Phipps ruled with a rod of iron. With his critical eye hovering constantly over our shoulders, the atmosphere was quite Dickensian in many ways. But although it was extremely hard work we felt privileged to be working in such an environment with so many talented artists around us.

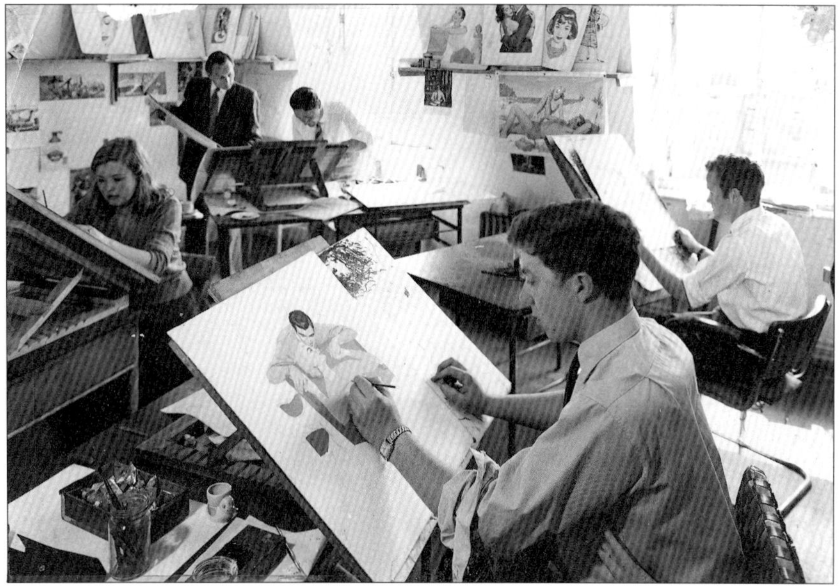

In Carlton Studios.

We found ourselves doing work for most of the top advertising agencies and magazines of the time so there was always plenty of challenging work about. My burning ambition now was to be a successful magazine illustrator and many a lunch-hour would be spent in Selfridges' magazine department, browsing through the American Journals admiring the work of Norman Rockwell, Joe Bowler and Frank McCarthy. I desperately wanted to be like them.

At weekends I worked on my specimen paintings - lots of freedom and exciting colour, painting in gouache on Whatman board - that was the medium then. Never oils.

In September of that year I went with some friends to the new Modern Jazz Club in Reading. A new face appeared in the group - a dark haired girl from Wales called Marguerite. When the music finished we all made our way to the local coffee bar for the customary expressos and chat. Marguerite was 17, just out of secretarial college, and I was attracted by her flashing blue eyes and confident personality. We soon started going out together and I'll always remember our first date going to the cinema to see Kirk Douglas portraying Vincent Van Gogh in the film "Lust for Life". Much as I enjoyed it I'm glad to say I've never had the least inclination to cut my ear off! At other times we used to spend our evenings at Marguerite's house listening to a collection of old 78 records - Bing Crosby's rendering of 'The Folks who Live on the Hill' was a special favourite of the time. Since the death of my mother it had seemed rather lonely at home but Marguerite came from a warm, happy family who made me feel very welcome.

Unfortunately, just as our relationship was beginning to blossom and my work at Carlton was going from strength to strength, the rug was suddenly pulled from under my feet by the arrival of a small buff envelope through the letterbox...

SIGNALMAN KING

It was 1959 and the buff envelope that dropped through the letterbox contained my call-up papers. I was horrified. I had naively been under the impression that being under a training contract would exempt me from doing

National Service. But the unthinkable had happened and in March of that year my instructions were to report to Catterick Camp, Yorkshire, for basic training in the Royal Signals.

I travelled up with a lad I knew from my old football team. It was an emotional journey as we talked, sometimes tearfully, about the loved ones we were leaving behind and our fears and uncertainties of what lay ahead. We were both about to start a completely new life in uniform.

My arrival at Catterick was followed swiftly by a breakdown in my health and an unfortunate bout of pneumonia. However, after a few weeks in a military hospital I eventually completed my basic training and then had to make the first major decision of my Army career - which trade did I wish to pursue? When I looked at the various jobs available in the Royal Signals, the decision was very simple. It didn't take long to come to the conclusion that being a Draughtsman was about the only thing that would suit me so I confidently entered 'Draughtsman' against my first, second and third choice. When I went in front of the Selection Officers with my completed preference form, the powers-that-be seemed to think this showed good use of my initiative and duly sent me to 2TR Squadron, Royal Signals to commence training - as a Draughtsman.

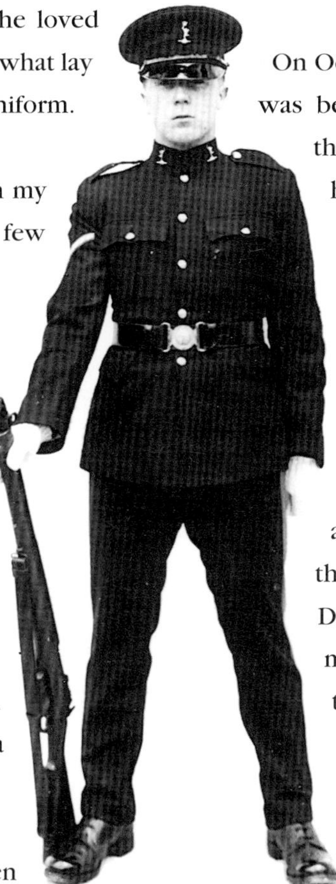
On Parade.

I hadn't realised until I started the course that all draughtsmen weren't the same. There were Jig and Tool Draughtsmen, Architectural Draughtsmen, Engineering Draughtsmen, Electrical Draughtsmen and so on. All the others on the course had been working in this capacity before their call-up whereas I had to rely on what little training I had received at school for my technical drawing skills. However one skill which few of the others needed was to be able to draw freehand and this was where I was in my element. Tasks such as sketching a gun emplacement, drawing up a poster for the squadron dance and lettering of all kinds, were second nature to me and gave me quite an advantage. In the event, I managed to get by although my electrical diagrams may well have caused mayhem if actually used!

On October 8th, 1959, I received my posting. I could hardly believe that I was being ordered to report to Paris! Somehow or other I had come through to top the course giving me a choice of postings and when I had seen Paris as an option, the artist in me absolutely dived at it. Not only would it be an exciting place to spend a couple of years but it was classified as overseas so I would get extra money for being there and I would still have the chance of getting home periodically.

With my kit bag over my shoulder I set off to Paris arriving at the Gard du Nord Station late in the evening where I was met by some army lads with a 3 ton truck. They had been to the Paris Motor Show that night and were picking me up on their way back. My posting as a Draughtsman was at the SHAPE Headquarters in Fontainebleu, 20 miles south of Paris, so it was a bumpy journey along the motorway to my final destination.

Fontainebleu was beautiful with its famous chateau and Napoleonic buildings, the barracks dating back to the days of the Great Emperor, all surrounded by the forest in its colourful Autumn coat. It was a welcome change after the bleak surroundings of Catterick Camp. I joined 50 other Royal Signals personnel who were stationed there, mostly teleprinter operators, all housed in one block on an American Army base. With the dollar being used as currency on the camp, it actually felt more like being in America than France in many ways.

I had about a month to wait before taking up my duties so I used the time to paint a mural in the Corporals' Mess. I had painted one while I was at Catterick Camp called "A Sergeant's Paradise" and when I mentioned this to my new comrades they were immediately enthusiastic about having one of their own. The mural depicted some of the screen goddesses of the time - Marilyn Monroe, Bridget Bardot etc., life-size at floor level, smiling seductively. They were very scantily dressed with a rather Hawaiian background if my memory serves me right. It proved very popular and even one of the Generals came to approve.

After a few weeks I had to report to Le Madeleine Chateau, a Security Headquarters about 5 miles away from the base. It was a beautiful building, sloping down to the River Seine with landscaped lawns, shuttered windows and large balconies, so it really was a pleasure to board the Army bus in the mornings and travel the 5 miles through the forest to the Chateau.

I was given my own office with a balcony, a security room, a large drawing board and several files which, needless to say, I soon put into disarray. My main function as a Draughtsman was basically to draw up rather mundane electrical diagrams - not my forte at all and somewhat uninspiring. However there were relatively few to do as NATO only had two main exercises each year for which these diagrams were needed, mainly as instructional charts.

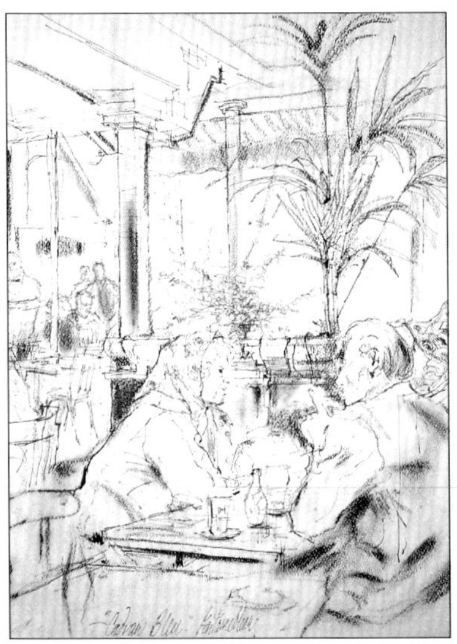

Fontainebleu cafe - from my sketchbook.

My boss was an American Colonel with the other officers in our group being mainly French and a few Germans. I was made up to Corporal King and, being the only British soldier there, found myself being nicely fussed over by the nine French typists in the room next to me so life was really quite pleasant.

At weekends I would visit Paris with my sketchpad, drawing and painting the local scenes. I loved the cafes and barges on the River Seine and I felt wonderfully free.

On one of our regular nights out, we met some of the American G.I.'s. One of them, Richard, turned out to be the Service Club artist. He had been a props man at the San Francisco Opera Company and soon recruited me as his assistant after showing me the facilities at the base Service Club. I was impressed at how well the U.S. looked after their men. Richard was the first to admit he was out of his depth doing posters and backdrops for the Club shows and when he realised this was right up my street he happily let me do most of the work, eventually letting me take over completely.

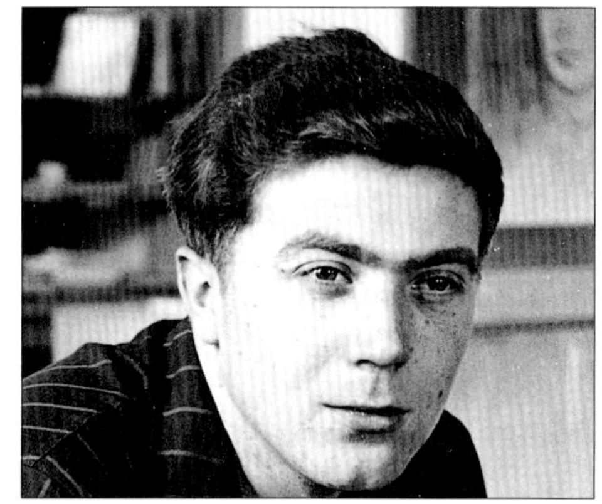

In the Service Club.

Every soldier seemed to know exactly how many days he had left to demob and most of National Service seemed to be spent trying to make sure the time passed as quickly as possible. I had made a lot of friends through the Service Club and even sang in the Church Choir. It was a great social life. The Service Club had a full-time instructor in the Art Department which was superbly equipped with a photo lab, painting facilities, silk screen printing, etc.

Every Thursday night the Club organised a dance for the troops. They would put up a sign on the Champs Elysees alongside a bus with "Fountainebleu Base" on the front and it would quickly fill up with young girls, mostly blonde

Swedish au-pairs, who would arrive at the Camp Base at about 6 o'clock in the evening. We gave them hamburgers and chips, a mass exercise in catering, in return for which they were persuaded to dance with the troops before being returned to the Champs Elysees. They were always very successful evenings.

At Christmas I was asked to decorate the International Officers Club which I did with huge paper sculptures using enormous sheets of coloured paper to depict various Christmas themes. It was a good 2 or 3 weeks work but I was given complete freedom to do what I wanted so it was a lot of fun and everyone was pleased with the results. I also produced some silk screen Christmas Cards which were so free and abstract in design that when I sent them home to friends and family they were really quite horrified but they proved to be quite popular on the camp.

The last few months of my time in France flew by and in no time at all I was getting ready to return to England. Just before leaving I put on a small exhibition in the Service Club to sell some of the many paintings and cards I had done during my time there. I was fortunate to have been with such a friendly group of people and, just before I left for England, they put on a special farewell party for me.

Returning to Catterick Camp for my demob was a salutary experience. Suddenly I was back in the real British Army and realised what a good time I'd had in France and how I'd avoided all that rather tough discipline I might have had with other postings. I remember a slight feeling of unease as I was about to rejoin civilian life, not quite knowing what would happen next.

On the positive side I was really looking forward to being back with Marguerite again. We had become engaged during one of my home leaves in the middle of a long, hot summer, sitting on the grass under the trees of Hyde Park. It had been very romantic. Then we managed to have two more brief periods together during my National Service, once when I returned home for Christmas and New Year to welcome in the swinging 60's, and the other when we had a holiday with our friends, Chris & Yvonne Kemp, touring the Cote D'Azur in a battered old van.

Just before my 22nd birthday, Marguerite and I were married, and we set up home together in a large rented one-room flat in Ealing Broadway. I could already see myself as a freelance artist, illustrating for all the major magazines, so I looked to the future with total confidence which was just as well because, in no time at all, Marguerite was pregnant.

When I returned to Carlton Studios, they had moved away from Portman Square and were now in a mews off Marble Arch which had a totally different feel about it, not having the elegance of the old place. I found myself sharing a studio with Chris Harrison, the still life artist, but my old mates, Eric and Harry had both completed their contracts by then. Suddenly it felt as if I was way behind.

I began to realise that the relative freedom of my two years in the Army had changed me as an artist. I was a much freer person now. I hadn't had the restriction of someone like Mr. Phipps looking over my shoulder, telling me what to do and how to do it. Everything at Carlton had to be the way they liked it, and this made it quite difficult for me to settle down. The time was right for me to start thinking about working for myself.

I decided to join Harding & Giles, a well established agency which handled both artists and writers. Michael Fenton, the owner, was a pleasant man with a nice smile, not particularly forceful but confident he could get me some freelance work. Slowly the additional work began to come in which I did after I came home from the studio, setting up my easel in the corner of our one big room. It was a bit chaotic but didn't seem much of a hardship because it was what I wanted to do. Then, out of the blue, I had a stroke of luck. "Women's Own" magazine bought two of my specimen illustrations. This was a real breakthrough but suddenly I realised with horror that I would get a credit when they were reproduced. All very well except that my contract clearly decreed 'no freelance'. Panic set in. I'd come to a crossroads much earlier than expected and the only way out seemed to be to leave Carlton and take my chance as a full-time freelance.

After discussing this with the agency, who seemed to think it was a reasonably good idea, I remember storming into Mr. Phipps' office, (well actually I probably crept in) announcing that, because I was married and my wife was pregnant, I had decided it would be best if I went freelance. He looked down his nose at me in total disbelief and said "What rubbish!"

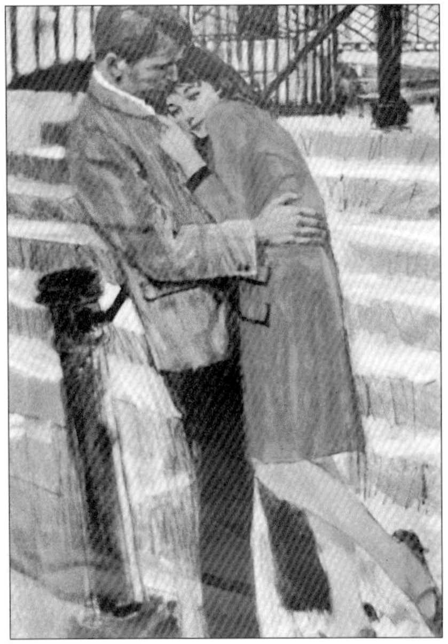

Illustration for 'Women's Own' magazine.

GOING FREELANCE

When I left Carlton Studios we hardly dared spend anything to begin with while I struggled to get myself established. Mr. Phipps' attitude had given me something to prove and my anxiety level was high but I was determined to succeed as a freelance artist.

Most of my work was going to come through Michael Fenton at the agency together with one or two studio contacts I had built up myself but it was not until some time later when John Dale joined the agency as one of their reps. that the future began to look a little less daunting. John had been at Carlton Studios and knew my work well; it didn't take him long to prove himself a success with the main advertising agencies and this started the ball rolling with an ever increasing flow of work coming my way.

My main ambition was still to do story illustrations for the major magazines and, spasmodically, I had the chance to do this with one or two full colour paintings for "Woman" and "Women's Own" magazines. But, initially, most of my work consisted of small advertising jobs illustrating children with products, book covers and picture book illustrations. I was always very adaptable and turned my hand to anything in the figurative line. One particular commission was for Oxo with a long running weekly series of advertisements promoting the famous cube with a particular cut of meat. This was the first time I used my whole family as models - the King family became the Oxo family.

Life as a freelance proved fruitful and I was busy rushing up to London several times a week collecting and delivering work. Any spare time I had was spent working on my specimen paintings to show prospective clients my style and technique.

Then, when I was 23, "Women's Own" gave me my first real break: a serial commission of six paintings. I was one of the youngest illustrators they had ever given a full serial commission to and I remember being invited into the prestigious boardroom of IPC to meet the Managing Director. The drinks cabinet was opened and I was briefed on the commission over a glass or two of whisky. I went home with a copy of the manuscript under my arm feeling elated.

The advantage of working for a magazine with such a large circulation was that their budget was always very generous. This allowed me to choose some of the top models from the main photographic agencies of the time to enable me to portray such romantic notions as love and passion with couples embracing, kissing, gazing into each other's eyes, etc.

During the next decade photography gradually came into its own with people like David Bailey very much to the fore. Artists suddenly found themselves with major competition.

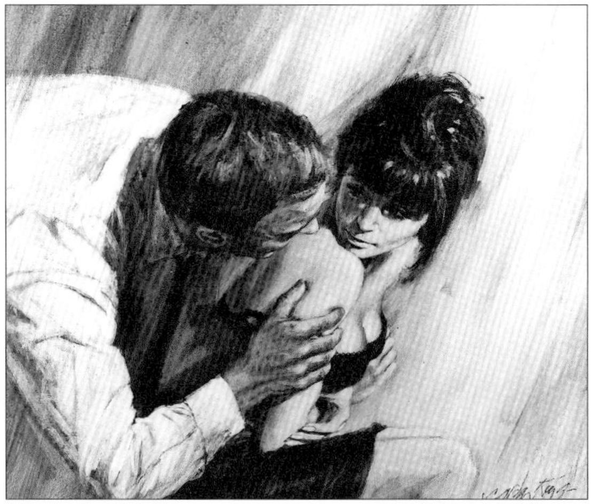

Paperback book cover.

Throughout the 60's I worked with most of the major book publishers as there was a strong demand for good illustration in the paperback book market. My very first commission in this line was from Corgi books - a J.B. Priestley book called 'Shapes' - for which I remember painting a man smoking a pipe with various abstract shapes coming out of it and floating up into the air. I also worked on illustrating children's books and any advertising jobs that came at spasmodic intervals. Family, neighbours and friends were all persuaded to model for me as the workload increased.

I was kept so busy with agency work that the chance to paint just for the sake of painting was fairly rare during this period. It was a fulfilling and challenging time for me until tragically, in 1969, the agency went into a sudden downhill spiral. Unknown to me, Michael Fenton had got himself into severe financial difficulties. The clients had paid him but he couldn't pay me. It was a dreadful shock and I felt terribly let down. Michael Fenton had to give up the agency and fortunately the new owners took on the debt which was gradually paid off over the next two years. It was a traumatic period for me, one I would never forget, and it made me quite cynical about money and agents.

Throughout this period I was lucky enough to get tremendous help and support from my family. Louise, my daughter, had been born in March, 1962, just as I was about to go freelance. We moved to a larger 3-roomed apartment but unfortunately it was right beside the railway line and the milk train woke us up at 3 a.m., every morning which, with a small baby also waking us up in the early hours was no fun at all. So we decided to use the money I had saved up during my Army days together with a loan from my father and buy our own house. We had no car, hardly any furniture and very little money, but at least we had the shell of a house in Eskdale Avenue, Northolt, which was within walking distance of the local tube station for me to get to London.

A couple of years later after our second child, Richard, was born, as my freelance work was going well we decided to move again before the children went to school. I had always wanted a studio with a view and as Northolt was not a great place for views we decided to look further out into the countryside. We were now the proud owners of a brand new Cortina Estate de Luxe, so we drove around for a few weeks and eventually found what we were looking for - a house on a hill. It was a charming old house in the village of Chalfont St. Peter in leafy Buckinghamshire. In 1966 we moved in with Louise and Richard and began a fairly extensive building programme, extending and modernising our new home, including my new studio which was on the first floor with a large picture window overlooking the Misbourne Valley - I had my view!

We enjoyed living in the Chalfonts and soon became part of the community there. I started to play tennis, badminton and squash regularly and before long we had a large circle of friends.

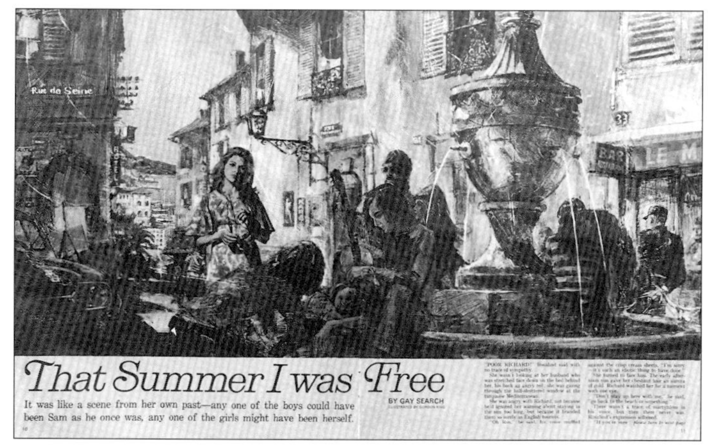

Illustration for 'Woman' magazine.

In 1969 our third child, Fraser, was born. He had a mass of curly blonde hair and immediately joined his older brother and sister in modelling for me. Sometimes I painted them for fun as they looked so cute but I also used them much of the time in my regular work as they were readily available models. The cry would go up: 'Stop everything I've got to pose for dad' and this became a way of life for them. They were always willing, if sometimes a little reluctantly, and they were a great asset in my work.

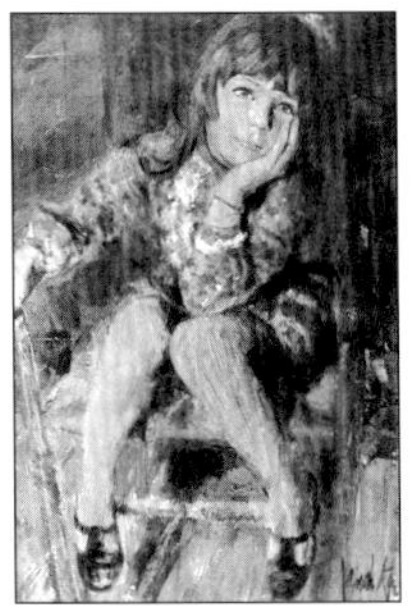
Louise.

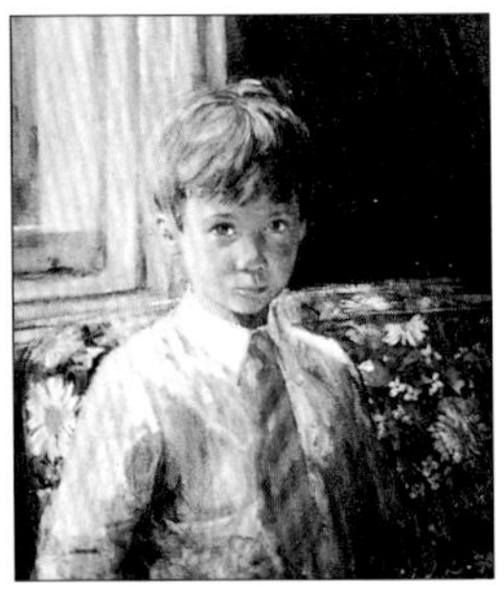
Richard.

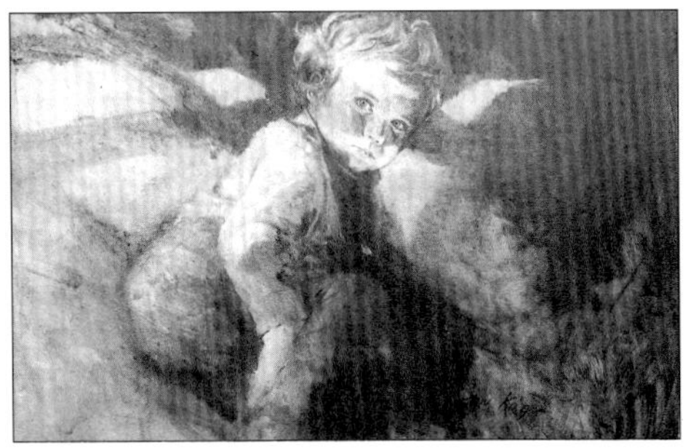
Fraser.

After the nerve-wracking problems I had experienced with the agency and the extreme crisis of confidence which followed, I decided to start looking for other directions in my work. I wanted to make sure I would never again be totally dependent on my agency work to earn a living. The only event that managed to raise my spirits at this time was on the home front. Much to our delight, after many years on his own, my father had decided to marry again so we had good reason to celebrate on this front at least.

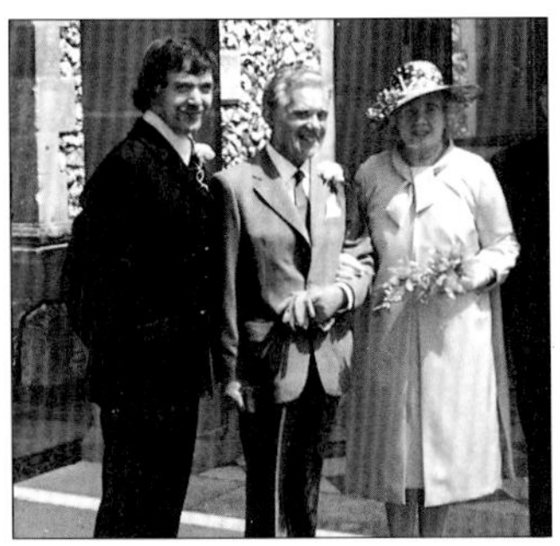
With my father and Margaret at their wedding.

I decided to show some of my paintings to a local gallery and this turned out to be quite encouraging when they managed to sell a few and even succeeded in getting me some local publicity with one of the paintings being reproduced in the local paper. This brought about a further boost to my confidence when I began to receive commissions for portraits, mostly of children.

Over the next decade I found myself wearing two hats, with the paintings and portrait commissions on one side and the illustrations on the other. In some ways my paintings were just a continuation of my magazine illustrations both in technique and medium but the content was far freer and far more personal. Sometimes the restriction of working to the rigid brief of a London Art Director had felt like being in a straitjacket. I loved the freedom of painting for myself - it was more relaxing, much more fulfilling and I was never short of inspiration.

In 1970, as more and more of my paintings, mainly of the children, were being shown in galleries locally - in Windsor and around the Chalfonts - a small gallery opened in Chalfont St. Peter called Nucleus. They planned to show original paintings and also introduce limited edition prints. The gallery opened with a small exhibition of my work and Sid James, the 'Carry On' actor, agreed to perform the opening ceremony in return for which I was to do an oil painting of his daughter's horse walking across the stream which ran through his garden in the nearby village of Iver.

For the opening I drew a small sketch of Sid's smiling face and had copies made for him to sign and give away. The queue went all the way down the High Street of Chalfont St. Peter and I would like to have thought that they were all coming to see my paintings but unfortunately I had to acknowledge that the majority of them were coming to meet Sid James and get his autograph. He had, after all, just been nominated "the most recognisable person in Britain."

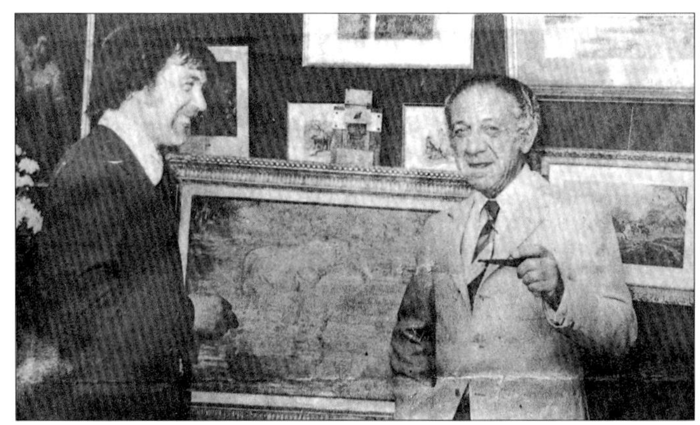
With Sid James at my Exhibition in the Nucleus Gallery.

Nucleus then gave me the opportunity to do the first prints of my work in partnership with a production company. I came up with 'The Four Seasons' which seemed really original at the time. (I subsequently discovered that just about every artist has done something on this theme!) The paintings were of nudes on horseback with the colour and background reflecting the mood of the four seasons. We felt optimistic as the advertisement appeared in the national press but, once again, my trust was misplaced - the production company experienced financial difficulties, so the venture was only a modest success but on the positive side, the four original paintings fetched the highest price ever for my work at the time and were subsequently featured on a BBC television programme called 'Collectors World' in a special feature about Limited Edition prints.

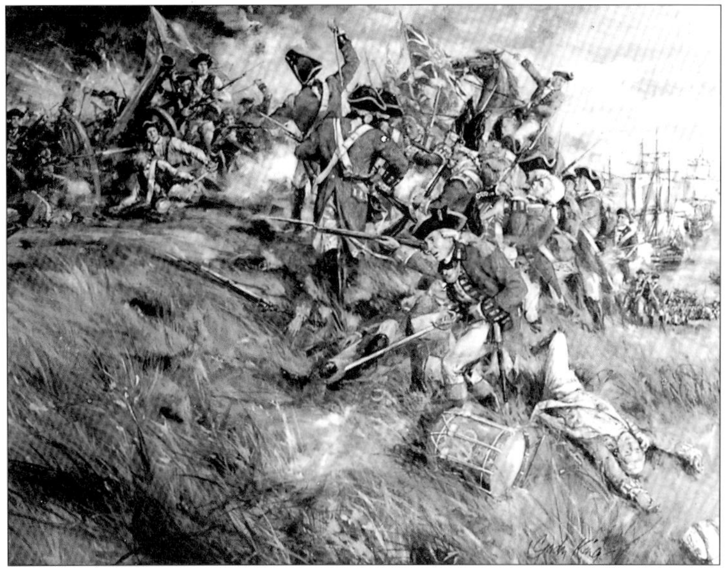
Battle of Bunker Hill.

I refused to be too downhearted about the print venture and my confidence was restored a little when Gulf Oil of Chicago commissioned a large oil painting of the Battle of Bunker Hill, asking for a British artist's perspective. After several fascinating days immersed in research at the British Army Museum in Chelsea, checking out the uniforms and weaponry, I thoroughly enjoyed working on the painting which was subsequently released as a print for the American market.

In 1975, I decided to have my first attempt at the Royal Academy Summer Exhibition and submitted a large oil painting of the winning Shire Horse at the Wembley Arena. Such was my confidence that I got quite a shock when it was rejected!

The following year I tried again with a rather yellowish looking painting of a man selling flowers in South Molton Street, London. I was into one-colour looking paintings then, everything seen through a haze of colour. As an illustrator I had always been versatile, often experimenting with different techniques, and certainly this one seemed to work because the painting was accepted but unfortunately not hung due to lack of space. Several of my paintings were accepted over the next few years but, much to my disappointment, still not hung in the exhibition. So near yet so far. Each year I had to promise myself that next year I would make it.

Rarely by this time was I inspired with illustration work. It was all fairly routine and I found it difficult to feel particularly motivated. I was still looking for a new direction but, as yet, I wasn't sure which way to go.

FINDING A SUBJECT

In the mid 70's, in an attempt to have my work shown more widely, I set out to visit a few of the London galleries. I particularly remember what happened when I walked through the doors of the Omel Gallery in Albemarle Street. Sitting behind the desk was a large portly man who looked up at me and said "Hallo" in a friendly manner, only to become quite hostile when I explained that I was an artist. "I don't want to see artists" he said scornfully, "I want to see people who buy paintings!" My head shrunk into my shoulders and I was about to creep away when he looked up again and said, somewhat grudgingly, "O.K., let me see what you've got". I nervously showed him my portfolio and much to my relief he seemed to be reasonably impressed and then even suggested I bring along some of the originals.

A week or so later, I arrived with a selection of work including paintings of children, horses and buskers. I was fascinated by buskers at that time and there was a wonderful group called "The Happy Wanderers" who used to play in Oxford Street. I could watch them for hours on end and did numerous sketches of them while they played.

Over the following few months the Omel Gallery sold quite a few of my paintings. Then, one day, I confidently went in with a painting of the horses and carriages on Blackpool Front, another favourite subject of mine, but on this occasion they took one long hard look at the painting then turned round and gave me another big lesson about being an artist. They said, "The trouble with you, lad," (I've been called 'lad' quite a lot in my life), "the trouble with you is that you need to find a subject which is yours". They looked around and showed me various paintings - marine artwork, flower subjects, Paris cafe scenes etc., - which were very typical of a particular artist and they told me I needed to find my own special subject.

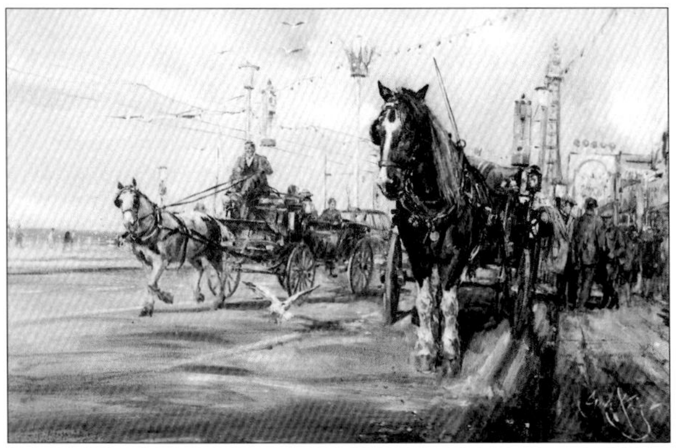

Blackpool Carriages.

They then gave me another important lesson. "Also", they said, "you've got to do a painting that looks as if it took you a week to do but actually only took you two days. Your paintings look as if they took two days but actually took you a week!". I knew they were right and I went off with my mind reeling, wondering where on earth I would go from here.

Generally, when I had things on my mind, I would throw myself into some heavy illustration work, and let myself brood on them for a while, hoping that something would turn up - I tend to be a bit of a fatalist in this respect. I'd had my show in Nucleus, I'd done my prints, I was concentrating more and more on my paintings, but I was far from knowing what the next move should be until, in September 1977, there was a knock at the door.

Standing on the doorstep was a round faced jovial looking chap who introduced himself as Paul Cooper from Michael Stewart Galleries saying he wanted to buy some of my work. I showed him a couple of oil paintings of old coaching scenes, which he bought and, typical of Paul Cooper, 48 hours later he was phoning me to say he wanted some more as he'd sold them both. I could hardly believe it. I painted a few more for him including a few hunting scenes as there was a boom in hunting paintings at the time. Although I had been to one or two hunts over the years I didn't really know one end of a pack of hounds from the other, let alone where the scent would be for the fox, so I thought the time had come to do some research. I got up early one morning, bought a copy of the "Horse & Hound", and checked out where and when the hunts would be taking place. This was in the pre-hunt-saboteurs era when hunting was an acceptable part of the English tradition and therefore quite peaceful. I found an appropriate vantage point with the rest of the flat cap brigade (I never actually succumbed to a flat cap although I did wear a pair of green wellies!) feeling cold and miserable as I waited, at 6 or 7 o'clock in the morning, trying to work out where the hounds would appear. When they eventually came into sight I enjoyed the sheer energy and enthusiasm of the chase and loved the red coats of the riders flashing by. It was this feeling of excitement that I tried to capture in my work.

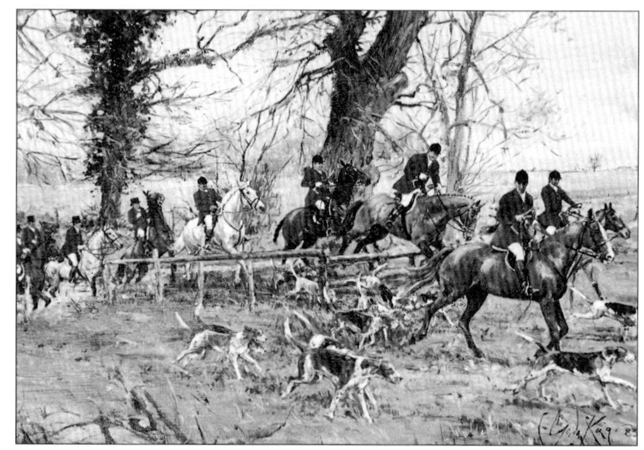

A Hunting Scene.

For some time I continued to wear both hats, as illustrator and painter. Although by now I had drastically reduced the illustration side of my work I remember one or two jobs that were particularly interesting. One was when I acted as the official artist for the local M25 Enquiry. Cameras were not allowed inside the courtroom so I sat in on many heated debates, enjoying the drama of the occasion, and my artist's impressions of the lawyers and principal witnesses were used to illustrate the press reports in the local papers each week. Another project I remember was of Mike Yarwood, the impressionist, who's popularity was at his peak at that time. I portrayed him surrounded by all the various characters he impersonated so well and it was a thoroughly enjoyable commercial job to do. Most of my work, however, was now channelled into producing large oil paintings, normally 36" x 24" or 36" x 28" canvasses, which were going out regularly to Michael Stewart Galleries.

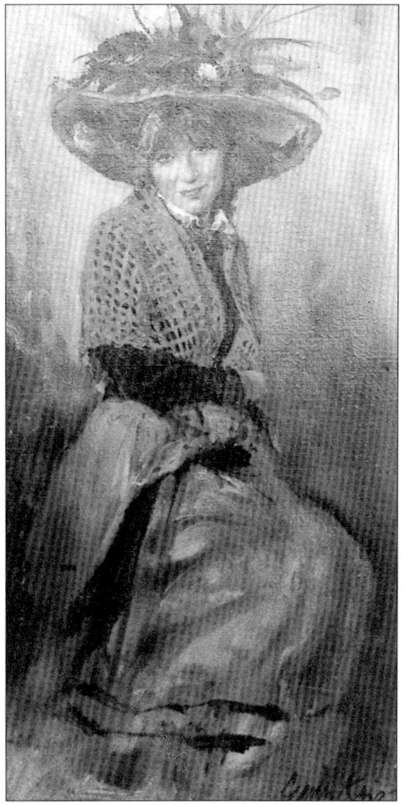

Louise posing (Oil).

One of the new subjects I started painting was the old London Theatreland. Standing outside the theatres, I would imagine them as they would have been in the heyday of Edwardian life with the horses and carriages outside and the elegant ladies in their ballgowns and evening dress. I loved the atmosphere and spent hours searching out different theatres and researching their history. Indirectly this was to prove to be the first stepping stone in my search for a subject which was mine.

The next step came when a gallery commissioned a painting through Paul Cooper of the flower sellers in Piccadilly. They had seen my theatre paintings which had included flower sellers as a part of the composition although I had not seen them as particularly significant. My daughter, Louise, who was 15 at the time, posed for me, so she became my first "flower seller". I hired some Edwardian costumes from Nathan's, the costumiers, with large hats and shawls, to try and make it as authentic as possible and did three paintings - one for the commission and two other versions for Michael Stewart who were going to show them on their stand at the NEC Gift Fair, the big trade show for prints and originals in Birmingham.

Almost as soon as the show opened, I had an excited phone call from Paul Cooper saying how successful the paintings of Louise had been and urging me to do some more like them. They had sold instantly and people were clamouring for more - the "Flower Girls" had been born.

From then on I was inundated with commissions through the trade to do more flower girls. They were going all over the place and, hard though I worked, I found it difficult to keep up with the demand. I recruited two more of Louise's friends as models, combined them with my horses and carriages, and thought to myself, this is it, I've really found something.

These large oils were fun to do but one of the things that sometimes niggled me was that I was creating characters from the past, rather than painting from the life that I knew in the present. In this respect I felt strongly that I was still being an illustrator, but they were popular and it was good to have such a boost to my career. The illustration work was being almost completely pushed to one side now. When I received phone calls from the advertising agencies in London asking me for work I started playing hard to get. Gone were the days when I'd be in London at 6 o'clock in the morning, taking on anything they cared to throw at me. I'd made my decision and was definitely going to concentrate on my own paintings from now on.

Early the following year I made my first visit to America. Ever since my days in the Army I had felt a certain affinity with the U.S. We were going to spend three weeks with our friends Chris & Yvonne who then lived in California and we toured the West Coast including Las Vegas and the Grand Canyon. It was a marvellous holiday. While we were there I visited some of the galleries in San Francisco. I had packed two or three small oils of the flower girls just to gauge the response and found myself overwhelmed by their reaction. The City Gallery were impressed enough to offer me what I thought was a tremendous price, and I remember sitting back thinking incredulously to myself, gosh I've made it in the U.S.!

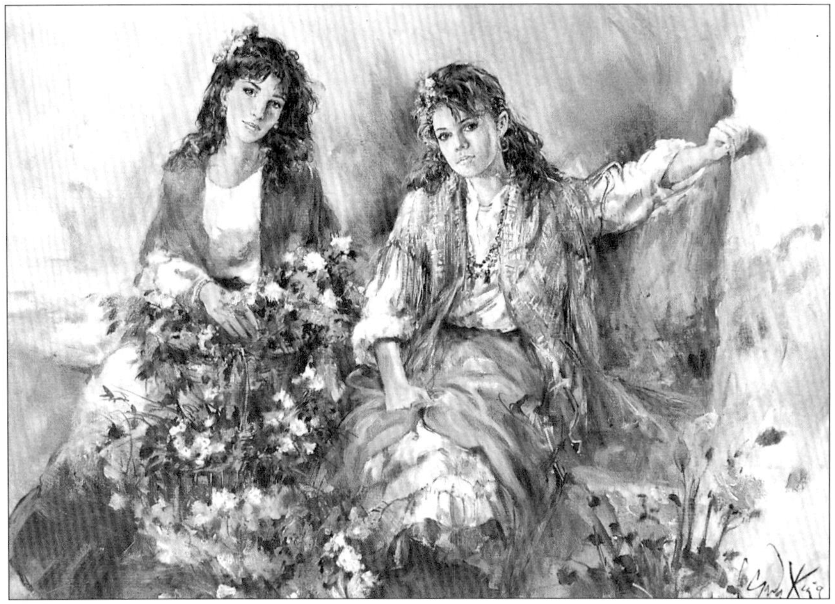
Flower Girls (Oil).

However, when I returned home it proved difficult to keep up this contact from such a long distance, especially with the demand from Michael Stewart and one or two other contacts such as the Christopher Cole Gallery who were taking my work by then but it was very satisfying to think that my paintings had a universal appeal. I suppose I should have realised this before from the number of these paintings which had been sold in Harrods Gallery, mostly to Americans and Canadians.

Although the flower girls were beginning to take over, I was still doing one or two fox-hunting paintings for the Michael Stewart clan who were very much into hunting, shooting and fishing and I had one last big fling with a hunting scene when I painted the Garth and South Berks Hunt. They commissioned a mass portrait of their members - whoever wanted to be in the painting had to be at a specially arranged meet. It was so gloomy that day that on my way down the M4 I had to use full headlights at 11 o'clock in the morning. When I arrived I was met by the Master of the Supporters who spent most of the day with me, showing me round and introducing me to the 46 members who turned up. In spite of the gloom I managed to do a few sketches and take some photographs. Afterwards, certain members of the hunt who'd missed that day insisted they be included so they sent photographs of themselves so that I could squeeze them in between the riders. A few weeks later I had produced a painting in which every rider, horse and hound was a portrait, even the crowd going over the stream. The Christopher Cole Gallery put on an exhibition to launch the print and also to put all the sketches on show. It was all very exciting but inside I still felt strongly that my new subject was going to be the girls.

Until now, all my work had been in oils but in the period from the late 70's to the early 80's I started experimenting with one or two watercolours and had been commissioned to do the occasional painting or portrait in watercolour. The first time had been through Alan Hart, who was then in charge of BBC Sport and about to be promoted to Controller of BBC 1. In recognition of what he had done for sport on television, the Minister for Sport, Dennis Howell, had arranged a collection for him as a farewell gesture and when asked what he would like, Alan opted for a portrait of his children. When they approached me, on the spur of the moment I suggested using watercolour which was agreed so it became the first portrait I'd ever done in this medium.

After this I thought I would try my hand at doing the flower girls in watercolour. In the 70's all the demand had been for oils. By the 80's, however, things were beginning to change and, ultimately, this became the decade of watercolour.

The flower girls seemed perfectly suited to the new medium and my technique. I found it totally natural. I remember going to see the Christopher Cole Gallery with a batch of watercolours of Louise and her friends in various poses. Two young couples were looking round the gallery at the time and when they saw these loose watercolours, unmounted and unframed, they both snapped one up. I had only popped in to show him the new kind of work I was now doing.

Back in my studio the watercolours started to take over quite rapidly. It was just sheer demand. I was buying very expensive handmade Green's pasteless watercolour board, 300lbs, beautiful to work on, and I was using Louise and her friends as models. Then, quite unexpectedly, I found myself taking the final step in the search for my very own subject.

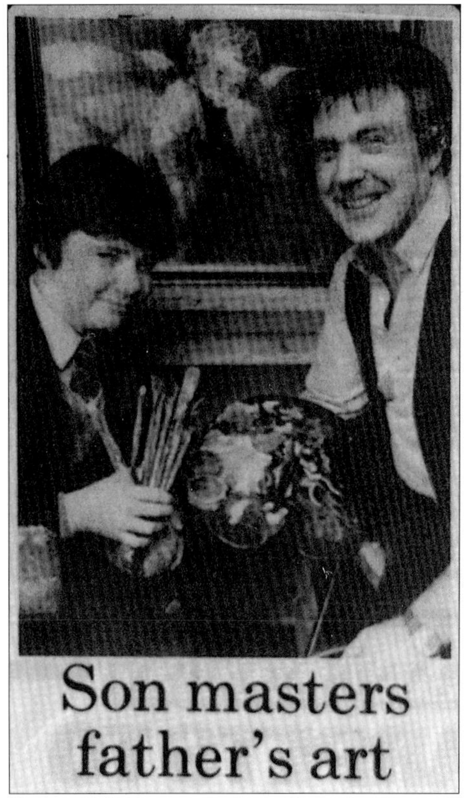

Press coverage of joint success.

My son, Richard, had a girlfriend, Nicky Horgan, who he met at Wycombe College where they were both studying for their 'A' Levels. Nicky was a slightly built girl with large eyes who found time between her studies to come and model for me. It is hard to define the quality she brought with her, but it was something very special, something that sparked off shape and movement. She posed happily in the garden amidst the assorted paraphernalia that I'd collected over the years - old wheels, flowerpots, hanging baskets, statues etc.

One Sunday morning she arrived to do some posing for me with a friend and as they walked in I looked at them and suddenly wondered what on earth I was dressing them up for. They looked so exciting and attractive the way they were. After the fashion of the 70's with the straight and structured Mary Quant look, the mini skirts had now gone and the girls were wearing the new flowing peasant-style skirts, putting bows in their hair and using flowers and jewellery as decoration. It was a pretty look that had suddenly taken over. You could walk round Covent Garden and see Flower Girls everywhere. This was how Nicky and her friend looked. At long last I had found my subject.

THE FLOWER GIRLS

The early 80's was a significant period in my career. Not only had I found my own special subject but I finally made it into the Royal Academy Summer Exhibition, had my first real one-man show and also saw my work being published successfully in print form. Additionally, my son Fraser, at the age of 12, was having his first taste of success by winning the Electricity Council painting competition for schools.

It was quite extraordinary how popular the girls became - girls with flowers, girls with cats, girls on steps, girls with clothes on, girls without - any permutation of background would do as long as it had a Gordon King girl in it. I thought I'd been pretty busy as an illustrator but that was nothing compared to this. Paintings were being whisked away almost before the paint was dry. All I could hear was "more .. more ..more".

A girl standing beside a flower stall in Berwick Street, London, was even the subject of my first painting to be hung in the Royal Academy's Summer Exhibition, a small oil painting called "Morning Market". The street markets in and around London had always been a fruitful source of inspiration and I had often travelled up early in the morning to wander around soaking up the atmosphere with the colourful stalls and fascinating characters, and it was one of these scenes which was finally successful.

For the last four years my paintings had been accepted but not hung and I was beginning to think I'd never succeed but at last, in 1982, there it was in black and white, that little card had arrived confirming that, this year, I had made the exhibition, together with my invitation to the Varnishing Day and the Private View.

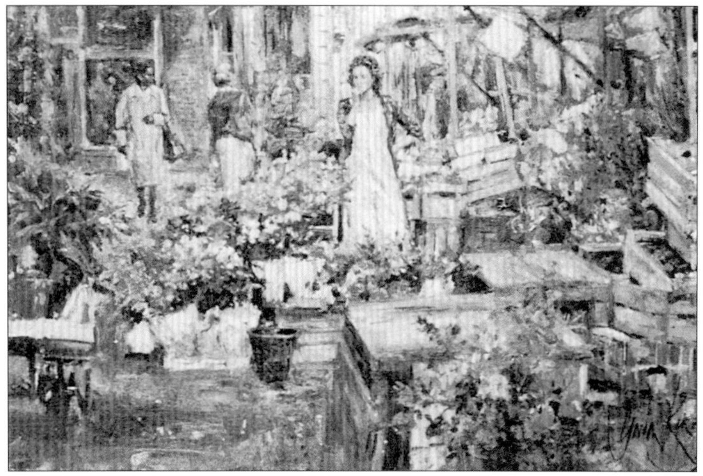

Morning Market (Oil).

Naturally, I was over the moon and even more so with the unexpected publicity it received when it was featured in a television programme on BBC2 in which certain celebrities were asked to choose their favourite piece of work from the exhibition. One of the celebrities was Angela Rippon, the television newsreader and presenter, who chose my painting, "Morning Market" as her favourite piece in the exhibition. Thank you Angela.

At the time the whole nation was nervously on the edge of its seat with the Falklands War going on but nothing could dent the elation I felt over the success of "Morning Market." The following day I had been invited to the F.A. Cup Final at Wembley as a guest of Alan Hart, now Controller of BBC1. Being an ardent football fan I was in seventh heaven in the company of people like Sir Alf Ramsay, of World Cup fame, Seb Coe, the athlete, and all the commentators.

The following year I was accepted again by the Royal Academy with one of my Henley river scenes. This was an ideal subject for me with lots of interesting looking people, attractive women against an interesting background of flowing water and the banks of the Thames. Most of these paintings were being sold through the Christopher Cole Gallery in Henley and it was here that I decided to have my first real one-man show.

I had recently returned from another trip to America visiting friends in California where I had again taken the opportunity to visit some of the art galleries in Laguna Beach and San Francisco who had enthusiastically bought some more of my paintings. Everything seemed to be going so well that on my return, after further discussions with Christopher Cole, we confidently set the date for my show for June 1984.

This gave me nearly a year to accumulate the necessary work which was to be predominantly on the Henley theme with large river scenes and sporting subjects, but would also, of course, include a few flower girls as well. For an artist, working towards an exhibition requires tremendous discipline and organisation. Unlike the normal routine, enough work has to be done and put to one side so that nearer the time when the final selection takes place there is sufficient to provide a well balanced show.

Being my first major exhibition and aiming to have between 30 and 40 pieces of work on show, I became totally and utterly absorbed in what I was doing and eventually, after months of high tension and hard work my big day finally arrived. Having been nationally advertised it was well attended and many of my friends came along to show their support and helped to make it a truly memorable day.

Unfortunately, whilst I had been so totally preoccupied with my work preparing for the exhibition, I had failed to see that my marriage was falling apart. The break up came as a great shock and for a while I just buried myself more than ever into my work while coming to terms with the inevitable changes that were about to take place.

One small highlight in this gloomy period was that for a third year running I had a painting in the Summer Exhibition. Another highlight was the success of my work as fine art prints, both unlimited and limited editions, which were destined to far surpass anything I could possibly have envisaged at the time.

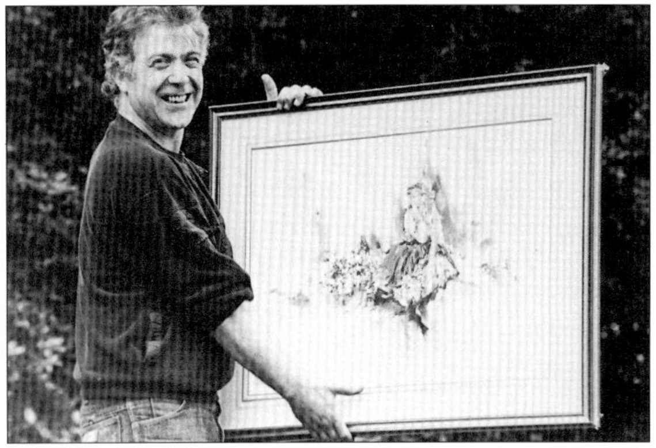
With 'My Fair Lady.'

For some time now, both Michael Stewart and Solomon & Whitehead had been considering publishing my work in print form. The first to do so was Michael Stewart who reproduced two of my flower girl paintings as the first pair of limited edition prints - "Suzie & Selina". They were done in watercolour, one modelled by Nicky Horgan and the other by Suzanne Nuttall, the sister of one of Fraser's friends.

Soon after this, Solomon & Whitehead produced their first unlimited print of my work. 'Squee' Solomon had been looking at my work for selection for some months but until now the right painting hadn't come along. However, with all my energy now being channelled into the flower girls it wasn't long before they found what they were looking for. Confirmation that I had been right to let my illustration work and the old hunting scenes take a back seat. My new subject felt so right somehow and Solomon & Whitehead must have thought so too as they bought three of these paintings from me, one of which they decided to reproduce as a print. "My Fair Lady" was again based on Nicky, and rapidly became a best seller becoming one of the Top 10 prints of that year. Solomon & Whitehead and Michael Stewart both followed up the initial successes with further prints and, suddenly, although my home life was in disarray, my work was more popular than ever. The prints went from strength to strength and the demand for my originals seemed to be insatiable.

On the home front my divorce came through and life was gradually settling down and getting back to normal - if normality can be living and working at home with three children. Louise was working in London, Richard was at University doing a Maths Degree, and Fraser was studying for his A levels. The house was always full of students and young people and sometimes it felt as if there was a permanent party going on. My solace was in my local tennis club in Chalfont St. Peter where I played regularly and had many friends who all gave me tremendous support and encouragement.

Nicky, who had been such an inspirational model, went away to college but Fraser did a great job recruiting his friends (and friends of friends) to come and model for me. He was at a mixed Grammar School in Chesham and somehow managed to persuade some really super girls to come along, all sorts, some of whom modelled on numerous occasions, others just a few, but every one of them bringing something unique for me to capture in my painting. It was so very simple. On the one hand I had my garden with all its assorted pots and statues amongst the flowering tubs, and on the other I had the girls dressing in their own attractive way. I just put them together. It was such a natural subject and the possibilities were endless.

The watercolours were completely dominating the oils now and there wasn't much I could do about it even if I wanted to. It just happened. Painting under glass was the new look and that suited watercolours far more than oils.

In view of this, in addition to the Royal Academy's Summer Exhibition, I began submitting paintings to the Royal Institute's Annual Exhibition of Watercolours, a prestigious show held at the Mall Galleries in London, and was fortunate enough to have my work shown there for a number of years.

After the success of the Henley show, I decided to concentrate on exhibitions from now on rather than selling so much of my work through a dealer. I had always accepted and appreciated the importance of galleries to the artist and had got to know quite a few who sold my paintings - Roland Miller of the Magee Gallery in Belfast, who used to come over and see me regularly, Diane Sissons in Yorkshire, the Nowells at The Unicorn Gallery in Wilmslow, John & Mavis Birch and Sue Simmonds of the Whitgift Gallery in Croydon, and many others who were all very supportive in those early days. So whereas most of my originals had so far been sold through Michael Stewart, I now started to deal more directly with other galleries.

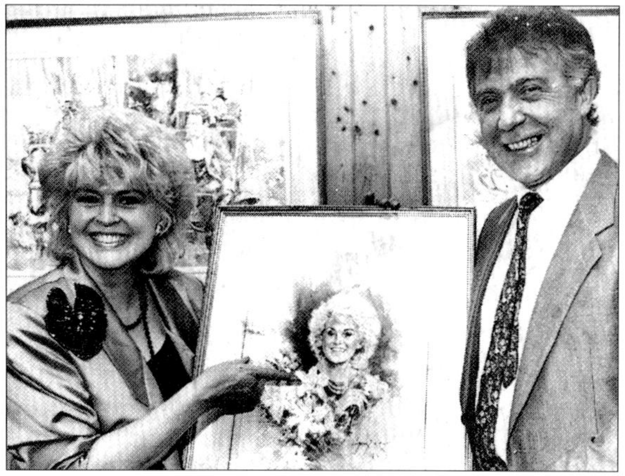

Presenting a portrait to Gloria Hunniford.

Doing exhibitions not only enabled me to travel around a bit more and meet some of the people who bought my paintings, it also sometimes provided a welcome change of subject. Now that the girls were threatening to overwhelm me, although it may have been my most popular subject, I was keen not to be totally typecast and to continue to paint other things as well.

Some exhibitions had very specific themes such as the one called "Cats", organised by the Halcyon Gallery in Birmingham. Later that year the subject turned to polo when I was involved in an exhibition of polo paintings held at the Hamilton Gallery in London. It provided an excellent excuse to spend a few enjoyable weekends at Smith's Lawn, Windsor, meeting some interesting people and watching the polo players in action - including Prince Charles.

Then, in 1987, I returned to the Henley theme again, one of my old favourites with the Regatta and the River Thames, in a one-man show with the Century Gallery at their newly opened gallery in Datchet near Windsor.

Shortly afterwards, Roland Miller of the Magee Gallery in Belfast suggested having a one-man show of my work in Ireland. We had talked about this for a long time and as it was 20 years since he had staged the very last one-man show of Sir William Russell Flint, who had sadly died a year later, Roland thought it would be a fitting tribute for me, as another figurative watercolour artist, to follow on 20 years after. We finally set the date for May, 1988, and in our discussions he suggested that we might ask Gloria Hunniford, the television and radio presenter, if there was any chance that she could open the show. In due course it was arranged for me to meet Gloria over afternoon tea at The Ritz and I was delighted when she kindly agreed to come to Belfast and do just that.

Prior to the show I had spent a few days in Ireland specially to find subjects with a local flavour. One of these, called "Steady Boy", picturing a young lady and her dog in the Ulster countryside, was selected to be a limited edition print done especially for the show. This was the first venture of this kind that I'd done with the Gallery and proved very popular. I also had my first experience of live radio when I was interviewed about the exhibition by Wendy Austin on BBC Ulster's Morning Show.

Needless to say, Gloria, who has always been very popular with the Belfast people, encouraged a large crowd to come along, and the show, which opened in the middle of a heatwave, was a great success. I had painted a portrait of Gloria which was presented to her at the show and we have remained good friends ever since.

THE HALCYON YEARS

By the late 80's things were going really well again. On the work front my paintings seemed to be going from strength to strength and on a personal level I had formed a strong relationship with one of my friends from the tennis club who proved to be a tremendous support in all aspects of my work.

The gallery which had really caught my imagination during the previous few years was the Halcyon Gallery in Birmingham run by Paul Green, an enthusiastic entrepreneur with apparently boundless energy and exciting plans for the future. A few years earlier at the "Cats" show I had been impressed by the standard of presentation and the sheer excitement they seemed to be able to generate. I now had the opportunity to take part in more of their exhibitions as they were planning to extend their exhibition base to London and subsequently joined forces with Selfridges of Oxford Street to put on a number of varied events.

The first of these was a mixed show including artists such as David Shepherd and Gerald Coulson. It is particularly etched on my memory because a few hours before the preview, I had a frantic phone call from Paul Green. They had been expecting David Shepherd to come and say a few words on behalf of the artists but at the last minute he couldn't make it - would I mind standing in for him? Never one to refuse a challenge, I agreed.

Driving up to London that evening with Mary, my new partner, I nervously mulled over what I would say and thought of one or two anecdotes which I hoped would be amusing, mainly to do with the advantages I felt I had over a wild life artist along the lines of my models being more controllable, certainly not growling at me and never running away!

In the event my short speech was well received with warm applause and laughter and my temporarily raised profile was instrumental in attracting the special attention of some of the guests that night, leading to two unexpected invitations.

The first was from the Chairman of Young Variety, a branch of the Variety Club of Great Britain, to a forthcoming event at Pinewood Studios, which ultimately led to another event at the Dorchester Hotel in London where one of my paintings was auctioned for the charity.

The second invitation was to a hospitality day at Henley from a large jovial man called Clive Thomas who we had first met in the Selfridges lift earlier that evening. His company, Prestige Promotions, specialised in corporate hospitality, organising a number of promotions and charitable functions. We took him up on his offer and had a wonderful day at Henley and were to become good friends in the future.

The Halcyon Gallery subsequently put on another show with Selfridges called "Masters of the Female Form" featuring work by a number of figurative artists including Erte, Heindel and Annigoni. In taking part I had to confess to feeling somewhat humbled at the prospect of being a Master of anything, let alone the female form!

Whereas the previous Selfridges show had provided me with my first platform for public speaking, this one found me on national BBC Radio Two talking to an audience of 6 million! Since my exhibition in Belfast I had kept in touch with Gloria Hunniford and in the run up to the Masters show I was invited to be on her afternoon show to talk about the exhibition. It was a daunting prospect but fortunately she nursed me along quite gently while I told myself to stay calm and try to sound as if I did this sort of thing every day of the week. I was surprised how many people phoned me afterwards to say they'd heard the interview and all of them seemed to remember the bit about being in more bedrooms in the country than anyone else - my paintings that is, not me! Gloria was kind enough to come along to the preview of the show at Selfridges and has subsequently become quite a collector of my work.

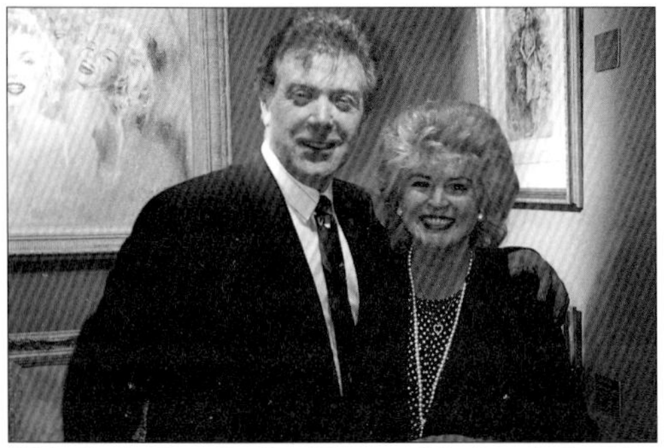

With Gloria Hunniford at 'Masters of the Female Form.'

It was during this period in the run up to the Masters Show that I became involved with Washington Green, the new publishing arm of the Halcyon Group, under the direction of Glyn Washington. During the previous couple of years I had done five limited edition prints in conjunction with Paul Cooper Galleries. It now seemed appropriate to let Washington Green take over the limited edition side of my prints, whilst Solomon & Whitehead continued with the unlimited prints. The first print of mine to be produced by the new company was "Camille" which I had done specially for the Masters Show.

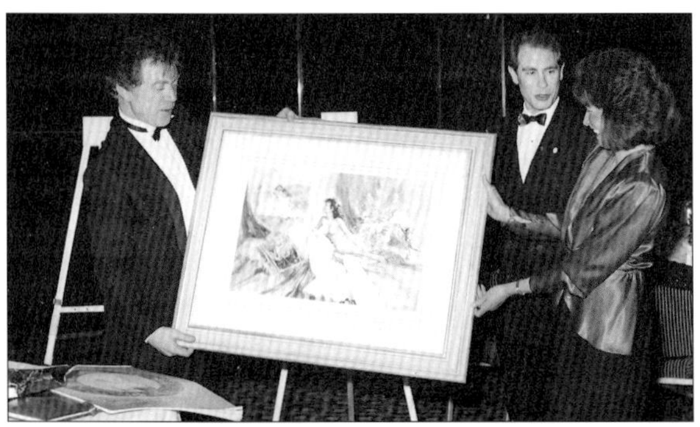

'Camille' print being presented by HRH Prince Edward.

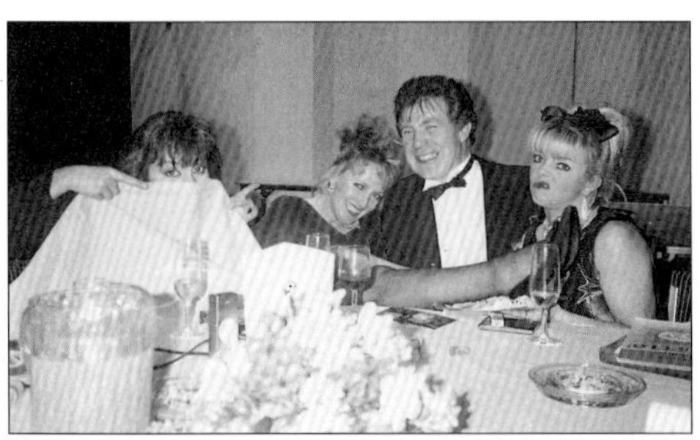

Fun with the cast of "'Allo 'Allo."

It was one of these prints of "Camille", together with the original working sketch, which I donated to Clive Thomas's next charitable function in conjunction with the 'Allo 'Allo team whose show was on at the Palladium at the time. After the performance we went with the cast to a grand dinner at the Hilton Hotel with Prince Edward and I was honoured to be one of those presented to him. Later in the evening "Camille" was one of the items included in the charity auction to raise funds for the Duke of Edinburgh Award.

Another major piece of work I completed for the Masters Show was a large oil painting of Marilyn Monroe. I adored her. Many years earlier I had cycled to Pinewood Studios just to get a glimpse of her when she was making a film there with Sir Laurence Olivier, but it was actually my son, Fraser, who inspired me to use her as a subject. He was doing a foundation course before going to Art School and one of the paintings he did was of Marilyn. It was so good and I remember thinking how much I'd like to paint her too. Selfridges exhibition, "Masters of the Female Form" had to be the perfect venue for such a painting so I did a large oil, a montage of different poses around a life-size head. I really did it for myself, out of sheer self-indulgence, but clearly it struck the right note with many others as well because it proved to be very popular, selling instantly on the preview night with requests for more. I subsequently did a set of four "Images of Marilyn", all in oils.

After the success of the shows in Selfridges, I had further discussions with the Halcyon Gallery and we eventually laid the foundations for me to have a one-man show in Birmingham in 1990. I was determined to have a really interesting and varied collection of paintings for the show and while I was building up material Mary and I managed to fit in a number of working trips both at home and abroad. Foreign travel has nearly always been a source of inspiration for the artist and certainly these journeys all provided a rich variety of subject matter and original ideas.

The first trip was to Morocco, thinking we would get some winter sunshine while we were there - not realising that even in Morocco it could be unexpectedly cold and extremely wet! However just to experience the excitement of Marrakesh, the whirling Dervishes and the beautiful Berber dancers made up for the weather and inspired several paintings, as did a visit to Corfu later that year where a visit to a Monastery high above the sea in Paleokastritsa was the inspiration for a subsequent print called "Afternoon Shadows". Some time after this we visited Barbados with its wonderful beaches and colourful people. The local girls were so friendly and made delightful models as they braided each others hair on the beach.

One trip, early in 1990, proved to be more inspirational than I could ever have dreamed of. Venice. It was instantly inspiring as so many artists have found before me and really did turn out to be what I was looking for. I had so many pictures going round in my mind that I didn't know where to start. Our visit to Venice was purely fortuitous - at one of Clive Thomas's charitable functions in aid of the Royal Marsden Hospital Appeal, we had been asked to put our names on a £10 note and put them into a barrel. There were several super prizes but we were attracted by the sound of the first prize - a Weekend in Venice sponsored by Britannia Airways and Magic of Italy. Before the draw was made we were already envying the prospective lucky winner and then it happened - Moira Stewart, the BBC Newsreader, pulled out the £10 note with Mary's name on it. Two months later we checked in at the Rialto Hotel right by the Rialto Bridge overlooking the Grand Canal.

Apart from the traditional scenes of St Mark's Square and the gondolas on the Grand Canal, I loved walking around the backstreets and exploring the many small shops which were crammed with elaborate costumes and beautiful masks. It all conjured up extravagant and colourful images of Carnival Time with glamorous young ladies preparing to go to the masked ball. I just knew I was going to enjoy painting anything to do with Venice.

Back in the real world, however, the tension and build up to the show in Birmingham was quite tremendous and I was living on nervous energy most of the time. Washington Green continued to publish further limited edition prints during this period. "The Rose and The Letter" were the first I had done in an oval shape and were released as a pair, the models being my daughter, Louise, and Sarah O'Connor, a friend of Fraser's. Then a couple of young ladies I met in Barbados, Charlotte and Emily Chatton, came to model for me.

The result was "The Enchanted Pool", but I have to confess to having used a considerable degree of artistic licence for this one - the pool is in fact the small swimming pool in my back garden so the waterfall and waterlillies were very much figments of my imagination but the white cat was real, having just strayed in from next door, and the parasol belonged to Mary's grandmother!

As the exhibition date grew closer, after the initial selection had been made of paintings for the catalogue, we were still undecided about which print to release for the show. With every exhibition the aim is to have one really special painting that can be used as the lead painting for the show - on the invitations, the catalogues and to be released as a print at the show itself. There were several paintings that would have been suitable but I wasn't totally satisfied that I'd got the right one until events took their own particular course.

I always use professional models to pose for my nude studies and on this occasion a new model arrived on the doorstep with her bag of clothes. She had brought some interesting things including one particularly attractive dress in a shiny metallic material which caught my eye. After a brief chat I took her into my studio to show her some of the recent paintings I'd done and the sort of thing I was thinking of doing that day. She looked at one of the nudes and said, "I think there's a problem here - I don't do topless". I looked at her in some confusion and she explained again that she did nude modelling - but not topless!

For once in my life I was actually lost for words. I queried what she meant and she reassured me that she had never had any complaints before and asked, "Haven't you seen my brochure?". Still feeling somewhat bemused I insisted that of course I had seen it and I thought the photographs of her were quite appealing which was why I'd booked her and, what's more, I had a contract for nude modelling from the model agency concerned."Yes", she insisted, "I do nude modelling - I do backs and sides...and I hold them". I looked aghast and pleaded that this was going to severely restrict my pose! Unmoved she assured me that what she did was classified as nude modelling but she definitely wouldn't do 'topless'.

At this point, feeling somewhat flustered, I decided to cut my losses. A quick call to the agency promised me a discount so I said we'd forget the nude modelling, and if she put that metallic dress on I would paint her in that. I posed her up holding one of the beautiful handmade masks I had brought back from Venice and, in spite of our inauspicious beginning, I knew I had something. Ultimately I did a series of paintings on the Venetian Masquerade theme using this model and one of them turned out to be "The Night of the Masquerade" which was subsequently used in all the publicity for the Show and became a best-selling print. These things happen sometimes. You can never guarantee that you'll produce a winning print but, once again, fate had played its hand .... and I had learned a lot about modelling!

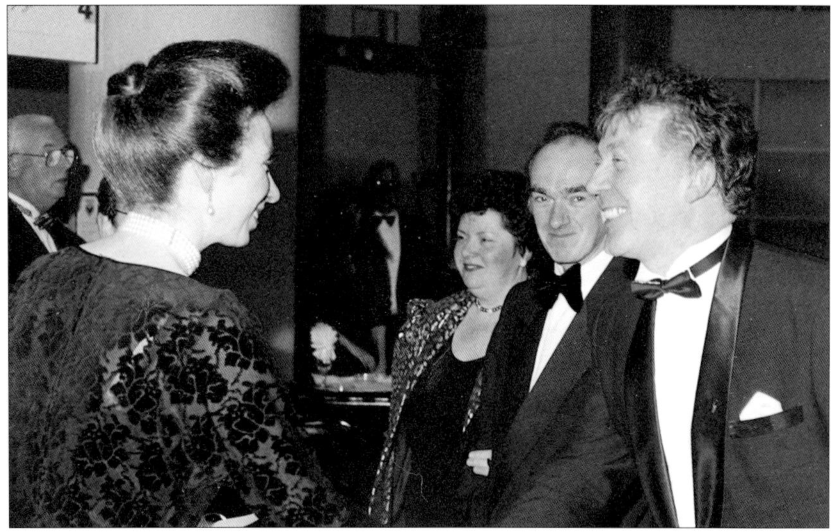
Being presented to HRH Princess Royal.

On the evening of the preview the exhibition was covered by Central TV who sent along a cameraman and a journalist to do a short feature. I'd done another painting of Marilyn Monroe, but this time in watercolour, called "Screen Goddess", and this became the focus of attention for the television cameraman. There's no doubt that there's something about Marilyn that captures the imagination and demands attention. This time the composition was a very simple head with an abstract background and somehow she looked much softer and more vulnerable in watercolour. So many people loved it that it was clearly destined to be published as the next limited edition print and I remember putting on the television in my hotel room the day after the interview only to be confronted with an image of myself at the exhibition with the Marilyn painting. It just happened to be on at that precise moment.

At the preview I met people I'd been to school with, people I'd worked with, and people who had been buying my originals and prints for many years. I was inundated with requests to sign the backs of paintings, prints and brochures. All very overwhelming. I enjoyed meeting so many people, some of whom have subsequently become good friends.

One couple I met that day, Bob and Carol Barrie, turned out to be particularly enthusiastic collectors of my work. It was Carol, stalwart fundraiser for The Save The Children Fund, who invited me to one of their charity dinners where I donated one of my drawings for auction and during the evening was introduced to The Princess Royal. Little did I guess that our paths would cross on two or three more occasions during the next couple of years as I found myself involved in a very personal way with The Save The Children Fund.

THE SAVE THE CHILDREN FUND PROJECT

The Save The Children Fund ran a special appeal called "Children in Cities" in Birmingham in 1992. Carol Barrie, being one of the organisers on the Committee, wondered whether I might be interested in helping in some way.

I certainly was and we spent many hours talking through various ideas until we finally decided that I would do a number of paintings which could be reproduced as Christmas cards. Furthermore, in conjunction with the Halcyon Gallery, it was agreed to combine this project with my next exhibition which would coincide with the final Gala Dinner in April 1993.

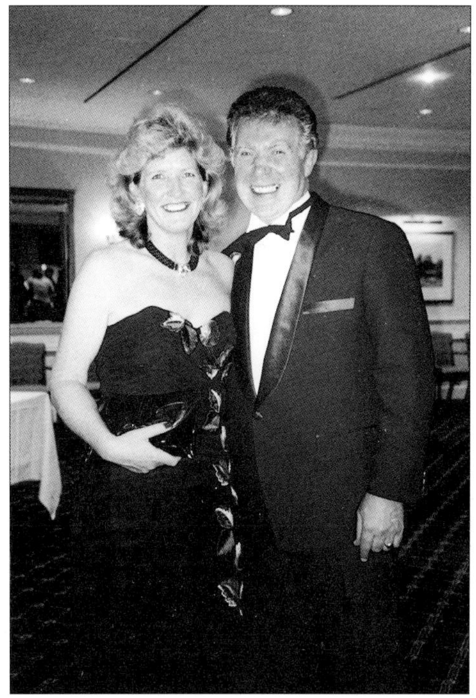
At the Gala Ball with Mary.

I already had several ideas in the back of my mind that had been around for a while but the ball really started rolling when a young lady called Deborah Hawley came to model for me and happened to mention that her parents had recently fostered a young girl. When I heard about the number of different homes she had had and all the difficulties she had experienced she sounded just the kind of child I'd like to paint for the Children in Cities project. Her name was Yvonne and she was 9 years old, originally from the North of England. Deborah brought her to my studio and she posed for me sitting on my front doorstep. I put a milk bottle beside her with a sprig of holly in it to give it a Christmas flavour - just very simple.

With the help of a number of other children I eventually had twelve paintings which were mounted and launched at a special preview with The Princess Royal, held at the Peat Marwick offices in Birmingham.

In addition to the cards we decided to do a special Limited Edition print for the Appeal. I had been mulling over ideas people had suggested of children playing, children doing this, children doing that, but I wanted to link it in specifically with the Save the Children Fund idea of all the children in the world and the picture which kept recurring in my mind was of a young girl surrounded by dolls from all over the world. A friend of mine whose daughter, Jade, was just about the right age invited me to meet her. She was perfect. She searched out every doll she could find and put on her favourite dress before posing for me, and that was how the painting "Small World" was born.

My travels were again to feature quite heavily in my work over this period and my first new destination was the Far East - visiting Hong Kong, Phuket and Bangkok. Although everywhere was in a total state of flux with high tension in the Middle East after Saddam Hussein's invasion of Kuwait, I had already booked the trip and in February, 1991, Mary and I flew out right in the middle of the Gulf War. It was a strange feeling with deserted airports and rigid security.

Nonetheless it was an exciting time and I remember being absolutely mesmerised by some of the Thai girls who worked in the hotel on the island of Phuket. One of them in particular was quite stunning so I very politely asked for permission to take some photographs of her in the surrounding gardens.

Unfortunately she said she couldn't take time off then but one of her colleagues enthusiastically volunteered to take her place - I felt obliged to take a few photos of her out of courtesy, even though she didn't possess quite the same qualities as her friend! I arranged to meet the first girl later that day but when I went to collect her there were five of them there all giggling with excitement and desperately wanting to join us, calling out "Me, me, me...". Not having the heart to turn any of them down I ended up taking all of them around the gardens, photographing them by the lilyponds and in the summerhouse.

Early in 1992 my destination was Africa. I'd admired the work of so many wild life artists and had actually done a couple of paintings myself for the Save the Elephant project. However, I was really quite keen to see the real thing and our trip to Kenya, to the Mombasa beach, with the burning heat of Africa was quite fascinating. Seeing Mount Kilimanjaro on our Safari trip was probably the highlight for me. The snowcapped mountain rising above the clouds with elephants all around us inspired a painting pretty well instantly. Although I have no aspirations of becoming a wild-life artist it was fun to do something completely different.

Other less distant ports of call during that period were the Isle of Wight and St. Tropez as guests of Rothmans International, which provided yet another change of subject - sailing. It was Cowes Week on the Isle of Wight and Rothmans were putting their maxi yacht through its paces for the Whitbread Round the World race. Going on the yacht was such an interesting and exciting experience for me and I later did a painting of the yacht in full sail with all the crew working on board. Other paintings were inspired by the music at the Admirals Cup Ball that night - The Glen Miller Swing Band and a Caribbean Steel Band were added to the list of musical subjects I've painted.

Later that year I was invited by Rothmans to do a portrait of Lawrie Smith, the skipper of the Rothmans Yacht. I didn't need much persuading, especially as they were now in St. Tropez and this was where I had to go to meet him!

One young lady who played quite a part in the build up for my show was Anna Baxter. I met her through Terry Carey at the Artist's Gallery in Bournemouth and she turned out to be a real fan whose great ambition in life was to be in one of my paintings.

Anna was 15 years old, fairly tall, with large eyes and long black hair. What's more she was very pretty and turned out to be a natural and more than willing model. I did several paintings of her for the show and since then she has appeared in lots of my work posing for me on the beaches around the south coast, in her garden and in and around my studio. She's been a great asset - after all who else could I get to model for me wearing a flimsy dress and standing knee deep in the cold sea without a word of complaint!

Rudolf Nureyev was another unexpected source of inspiration as the exhibition came closer. He had sadly died a few months earlier and I had been quite emotionally moved watching a television tribute to him. Again I had various pictures in my mind of the great dancer and one afternoon on a dark gloomy day, I did a painting of him, more as a tribute to him than anything else, feeling quite emotional as I worked, sad that a man of such talent was no longer with us. Glyn Washington happened to notice it on one of his visits and was immediately enthusiastic, saying he'd like to print it.

The night before the Preview of my 1993 exhibition I was invited to The Save the Children Fund dinner at the Conference Centre in Birmingham to mark the successful end of the Children in Cities Appeal. Three of the original Christmas card paintings were auctioned during the evening and I was privileged to meet The Princess Royal again.

Some of the Christmas cards had been simply framed to make attractive little pictures and several of these were among the prizes on a very extensive Tombola stand. One of the amusing things I remember that night was that The Princess Royal won one of the framed cards so I was delighted that she at least had a copy of one of my paintings. The bad news, however, (so rumour had it), was that her new husband, Commander Laurance, won a pair of ladies tights!

The exhibition itself represented $2^1/_2$ years of intensive work. The painting

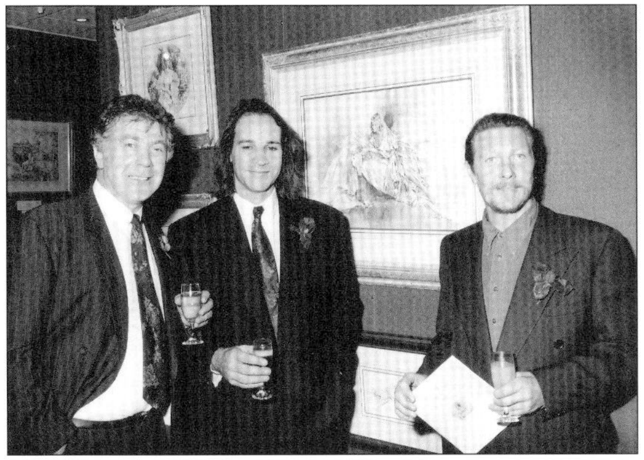

With Paul Green and Glyn Washington at the NEC.

we decided to use as the lead painting for the show was "Isabella" which had been launched as a limited edition print at the NEC Trade Fair in February.

"Nureyev - The Legend" was also released as a limited edition print for the show together with "Small World" which accompanied the entire collection done for Save the Children Fund. There were also a number of paintings from my travels to Hong Kong, Phuket and Africa, as well as a few more from Venice.

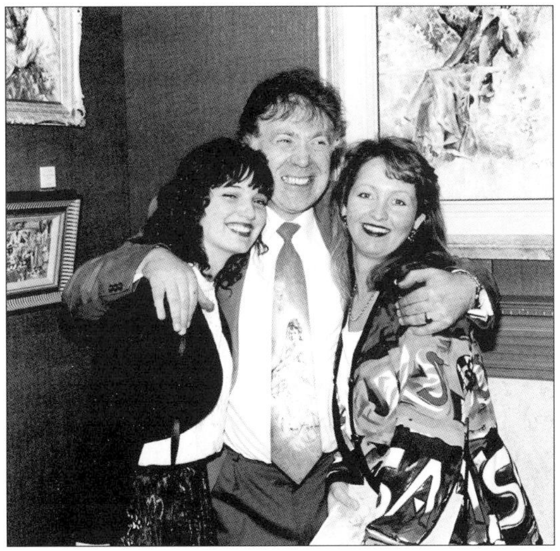

The Isabella tie - with Anna and Elaine.

One unexpected success at the Preview was the tie I wore that day - I had bought myself a new jacket for the show but couldn't find a tie I liked anywhere, so two days before the show I decided to paint one. I found a very old wide tie and painted onto it a miniature version of "Isabella" which everyone seemed to like - I certainly received a number of offers for it!

All in all it was a very successful and enjoyable period with the charity dinner and then the show. As with anything that has virtually taken over your life for a while, it's always difficult to come down to earth afterwards. In a way, it's as if you've put so much into it you've given birth and then, suddenly, it's all over.

THE ROAD AHEAD

Since the two Birmingham shows I've travelled the country from Scotland to the South Coast which has enabled me to meet even more of the people 'out there' who like my work. I've also had the opportunity to get to know other professional artists and it's always interesting to find out how they work and to understand something of their own individual perspective on their art.

Prior to a charity exhibition at Beverley Minster which we were both involved in, I had the opportunity of spending some time with Terence Cuneo, one of the artists I've admired since my school-days. It was very stimulating to meet someone of his experience who still has such enthusiasm and gets so much out of his painting.

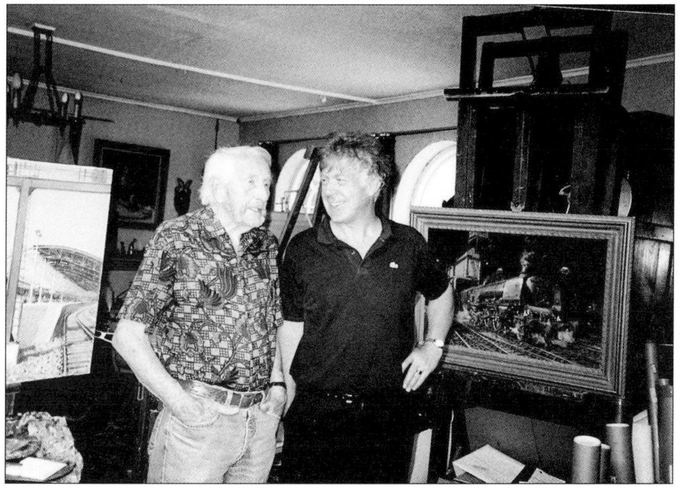

With Terence Cuneo in his studio.

One exhibition was particularly significant in that it took me full circle back to the Fife coast. The Picture Gallery in Kirkcaldy put on a show of my prints and originals and I was pleased to have the excuse to go with Mary back to the place of my childhood. My sister, Jean, also came up and we had a wonderfully nostalgic time visiting Kinghorn again - our old house, our school and even the rocks on the beach seemed just the same.

Down on the south coast, Terry Carey of the Artist's Gallery organised a couple of interesting social functions at the nearby Miramar Hotel to coincide with exhibitions of my prints and paintings. The first was a dinner after which I talked about my life and work. The second was an invitation to "spend a day with Gordon King" watching me paint. Being Anna's home territory I invited her to be my model for the day.

During this period I also had the opportunity to branch out into a slightly new direction. For some time now I had been talking to Daler Rowney, the artists' materials manufacturer, who had suggested that I might like to join their Road Show team. This entails the artist being on stage with his easel, demonstrating his art, being wired up for sound and filmed as he works with the picture being projected onto a large screen in close-up so that everyone in the audience can see every brushstroke clearly.

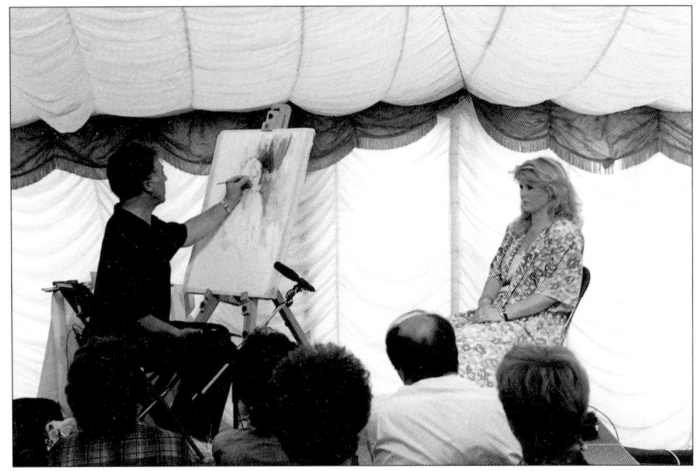

Daler-Rowney Road Show.

Initially, I wasn't really sure whether this was something I wanted to do. Over the years I had given a few informal talks and demonstrations to local groups and Art Societies just as a bit of fun but the Road Shows were really going to put me in the spotlight and be a lot more demanding. Daler Rowney took me along to Norwich to see the artist, Alwyn Crawshaw, at work. It was interesting to watch his performance, which is what it was - a true performance involving lots of communication with the audience who were all enthusiastic budding artists.

Eventually I decided that I would enjoy the challenge and before long I was scheduled to do my own Road Shows in Liverpool, Cardiff and London. Certainly it was different from anything I had done before - a different audience, a different environment and a different experience. I appreciated the dedication and enthusiasm of the people I met and found this new form of communication extremely stimulating. It was quite demanding compared to working in the relative seclusion of a studio where if something doesn't work out first time there is the comfort that it can be thrown into the bin and no one will know! But up on stage, with the model maintaining her pose, the challenge is to produce a painting which is at least reasonably good, in a fraction of the time it would normally take, whilst talking to the audience at the same time and trying to be entertaining.

It was when I was telling a friend of mine about these Road Shows that my next charity project began to take shape. John Mather had long been involved with the Chiltern Cheshire Home in Gerrards Cross, close to where I live. I had often thought about trying to organise a "Paint-In" as a means of getting as many people as possible, all ages and abilities, to come and have a go at painting. When I approached Daler Rowney they were enthusiastic about such a novel idea and agreed to sponsor the event, providing all the art materials for the day and donating prizes for the best paintings.

The first "Paint-In" was held at the Chiltern Cheshire Home in Gerrards Cross on a beautiful day in June 1993. Several celebrities including Rolf Harris, Val Doonican and Roy Castle kindly donated paintings for the auction and lots of people came along. Some sat in the gardens, some in the large hall, some in wheelchairs, all enjoying the painting experience. In the afternoon a young lady volunteered to model for me, so I did a painting of her which was sold in the auction later that day.

A year later I was delighted to be invited to open the Chiltern Cheshire Home's Annual Open Day. During the afternoon, Roy Castle, who had been a friend and a supporter of the Home for many years, came along for a brief visit. He

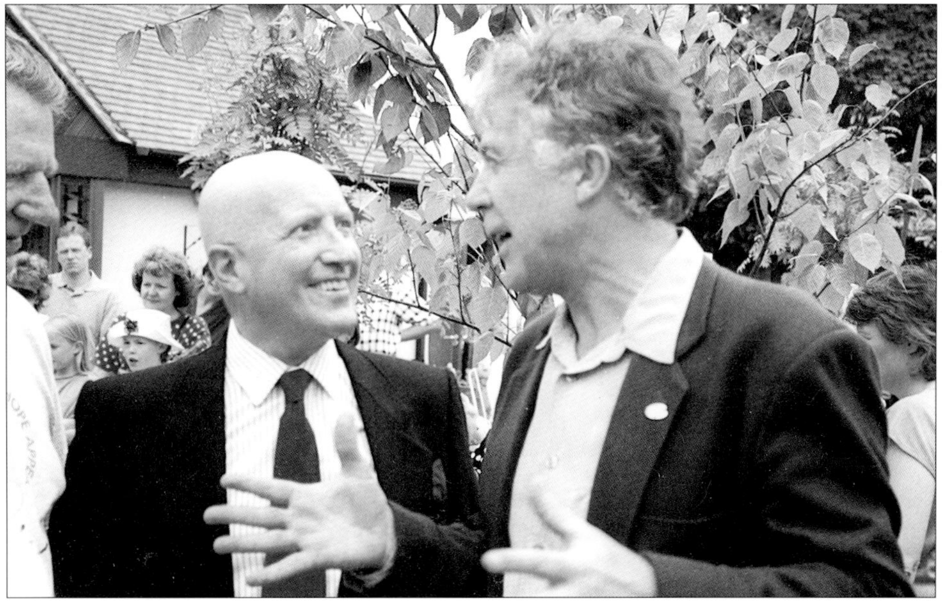

With Roy Castle.

was bravely fighting for his life at the time but still seemed more concerned for others than for himself. He even took a trumpet from the band and played a couple of impromptu numbers with them which delighted the crowd.

Plans are currently under way for the next "Paint-In" venture. In conjunction with the Chiltern Cheshire Home, an Artists' Day is to be held in May 1995 in the glorious setting of Chenies Manor in Buckinghamshire providing an opportunity for artists everywhere to come and paint for the day.

One of my great pleasures now is watching my son, Fraser, having progressed from Art School through to painting as a full-time artist. We had our first joint show recently. Father & Son. We were delighted when Roland Miller in Belfast suggested this because it had been on our minds for some time. We flew over during the summer months to collect material and had the show in November 1993. Fraser was very silent and apprehensive. It was a big one for him. I was trying to take a back seat. In the end, when the show started, I had no option but to take a back seat. Everybody was all over Fraser. It was a sell-out and I felt really proud of him. We sat in the Hotel that night, just the two of us, me with a large Scotch, Fraser with a good Irish Guinness, not saying an awful lot but knowing that we couldn't have asked for a better result. Since then Fraser has gone on to participate in other shows and is going from strength to strength.

In April, 1994, my eldest son, Richard, and his girlfriend, Jane, were married. It was a wonderful occasion and provided an opportunity for the whole family to get together again. I did a painting of the two of them which was used on all the wedding stationery and subsequently presented to Jane's mother. As this book goes to press, I am delighted to say we are celebrating the arrival of my first grand-daughter, Darcy Jane King.

With the launch of this book and more exhibitions around the country, the future certainly looks exciting and I'm looking forward to the next chapter.

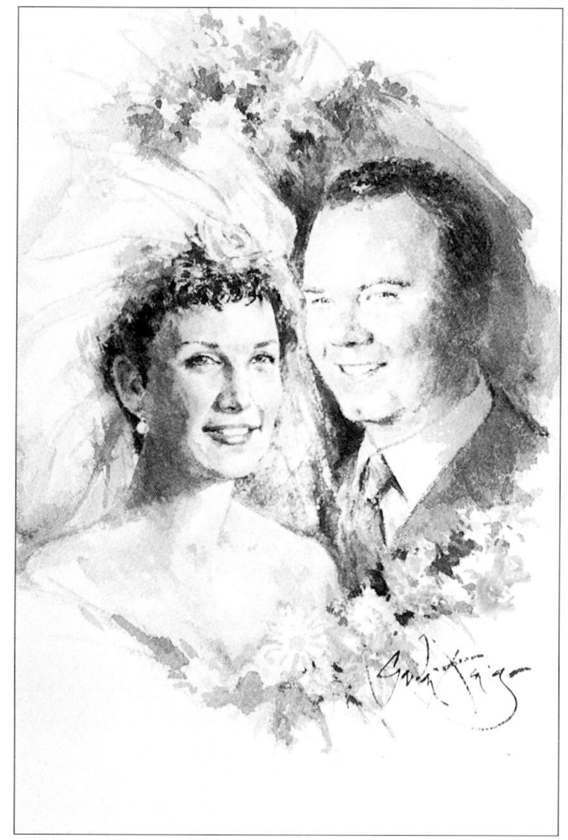

Richard and Jane.

Gallery 1

This has been a classic subject for many artists over the years. I have particularly admired the wonderful work of artists such as Whistler, Tissot and, more recently, Sir William Russell Flint.

During my career, the girls developed as a subject in their own right when I realised that the models who were posing for me dressed up as Victorian flower sellers could bring so much more to a painting by simply being themselves.

In encouraging them to express their own personality in the way they looked, the way they dressed and the way they moved, I was able to let the girls themselves provide the inspiration rather than trying to make them fit into a preconceived idea.

With the colour and composition evoked by the simple surroundings of my garden together with a prop or two, I found that between us we were able to create something which was both original and unique.

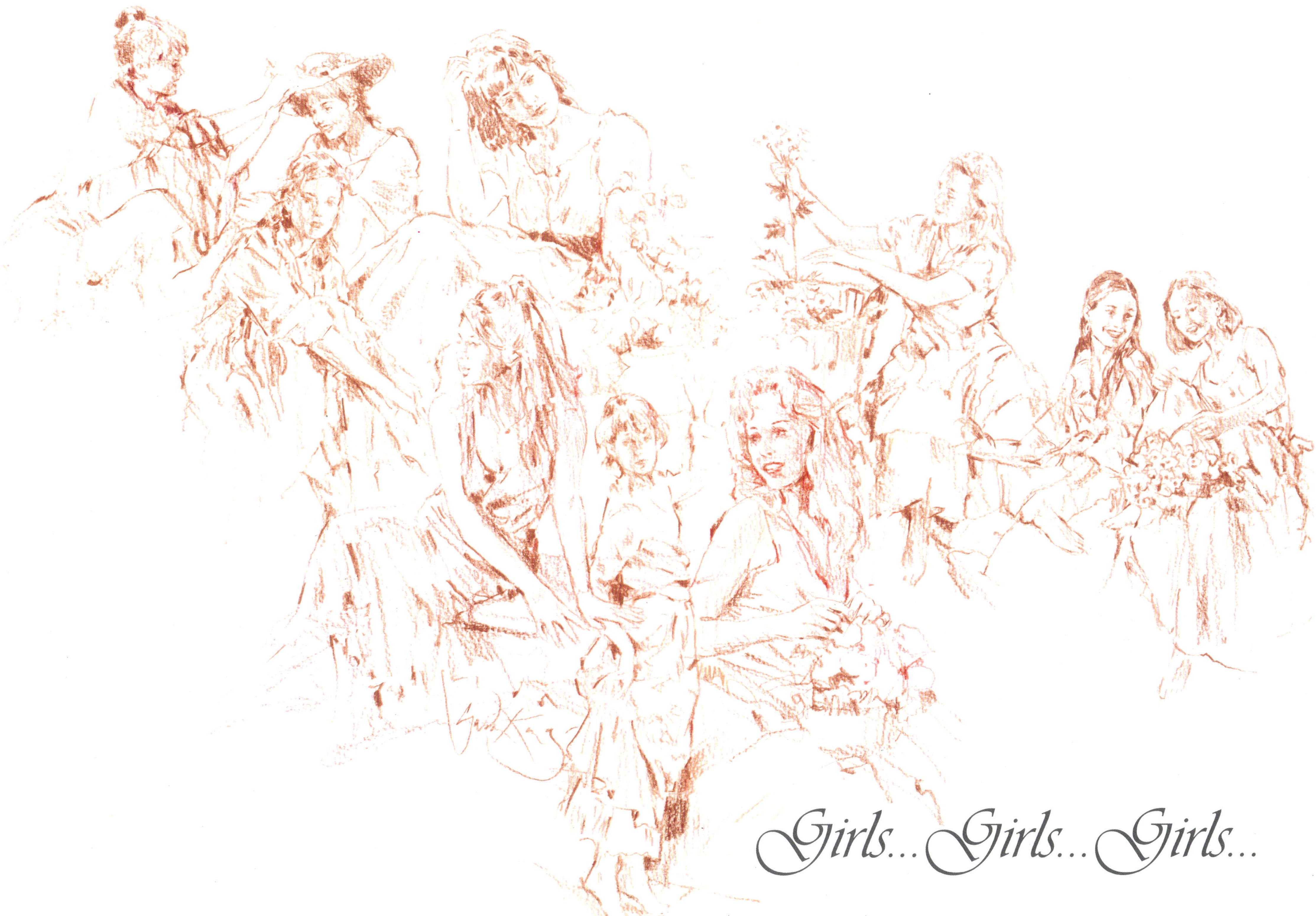

Girls…Girls…Girls…

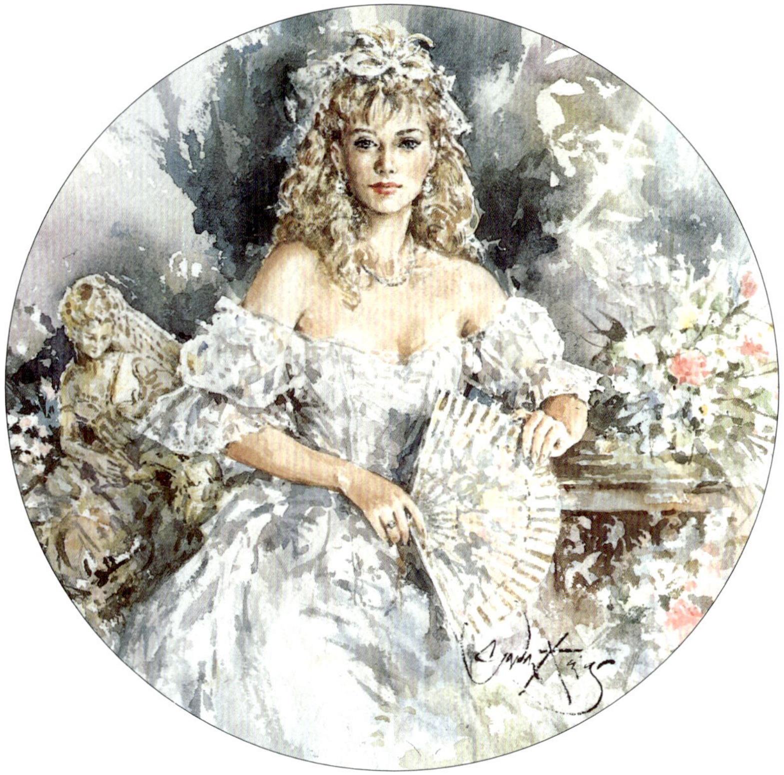

THE FAN

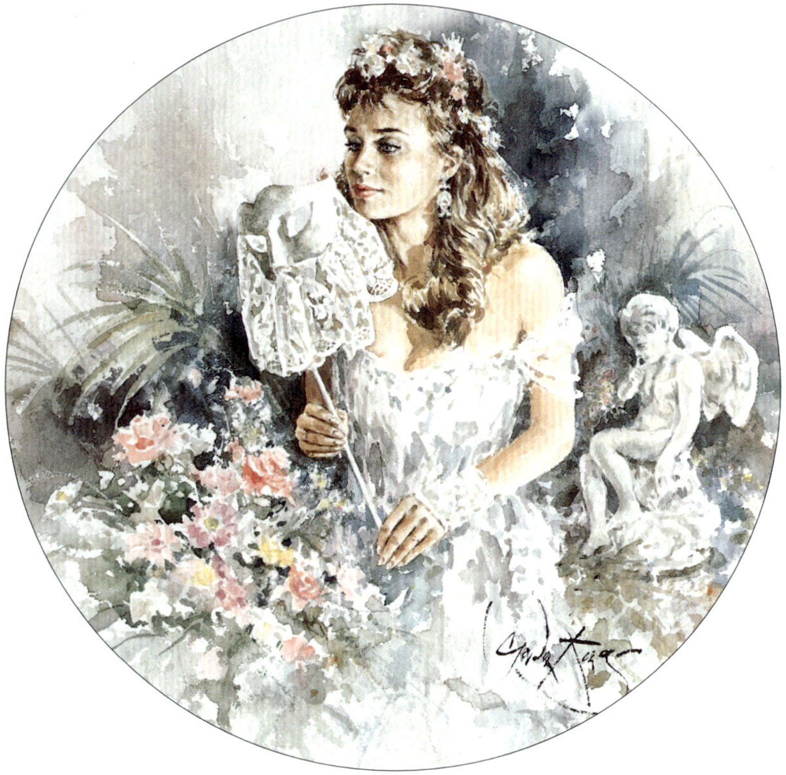

THE MASK

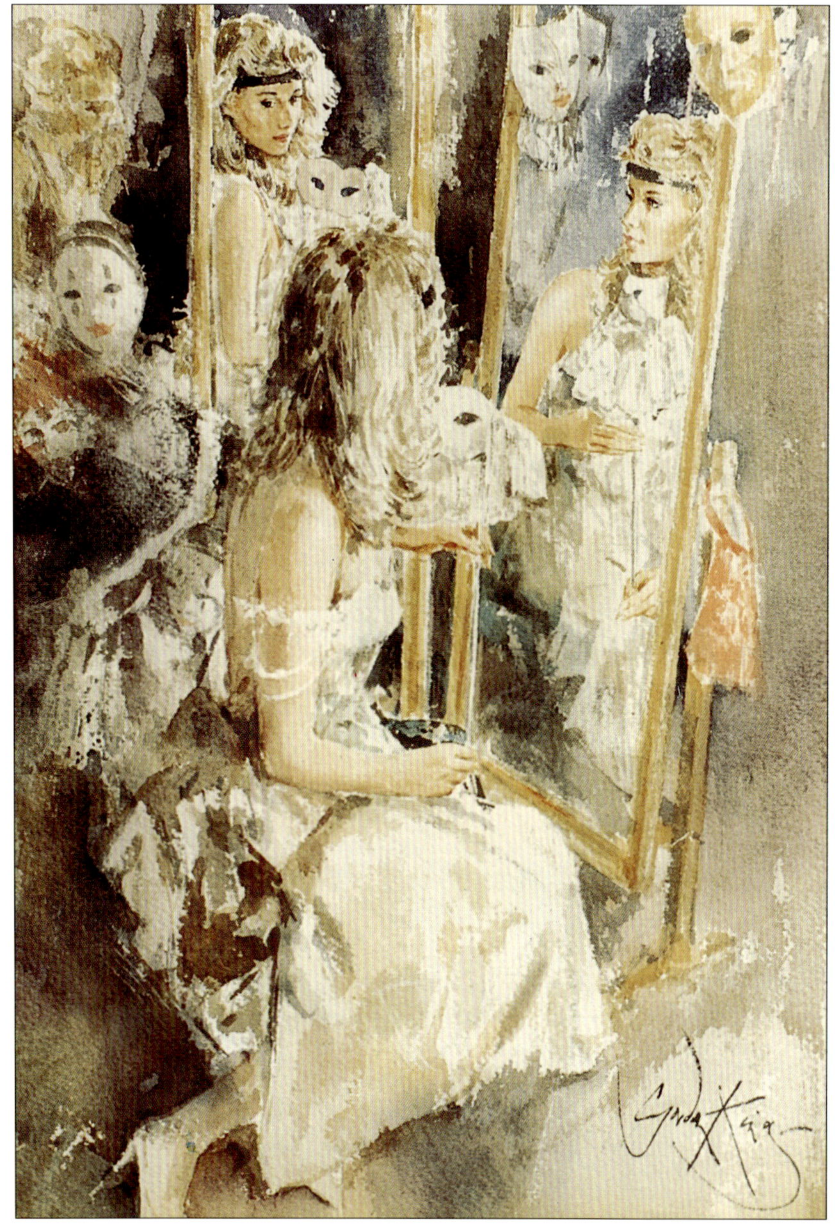

REFLECTIONS OF THE MASQUERADE

These paintings were inspired by the glamour and excitement of the carnival season in Venice. I loved the many backstreet shops crammed with extravagant costumes and delightful masks which conjured up images of young ladies preparing to go to the Masked Ball.

Opposite: NIGHT OF THE MASQUERADE

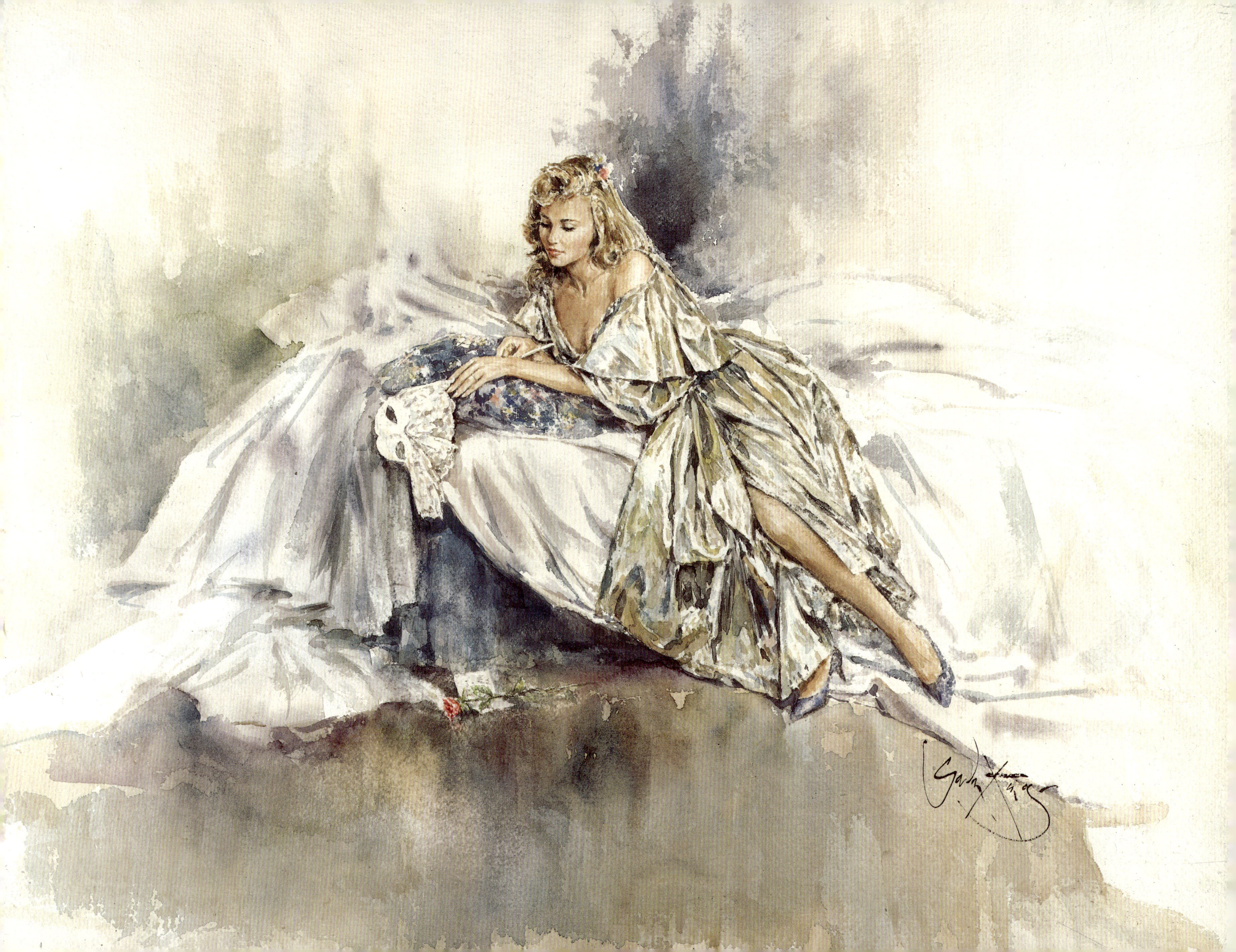

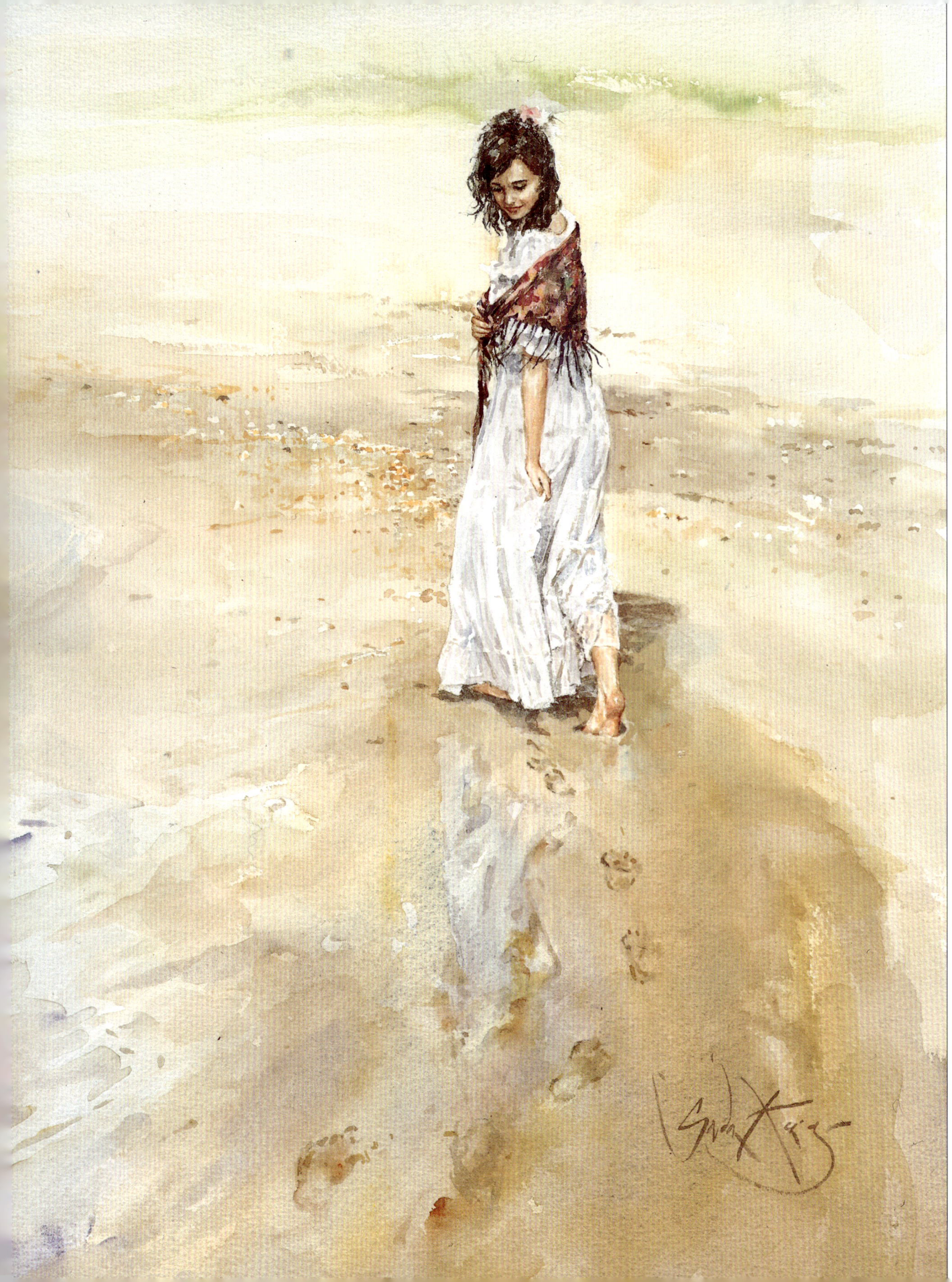

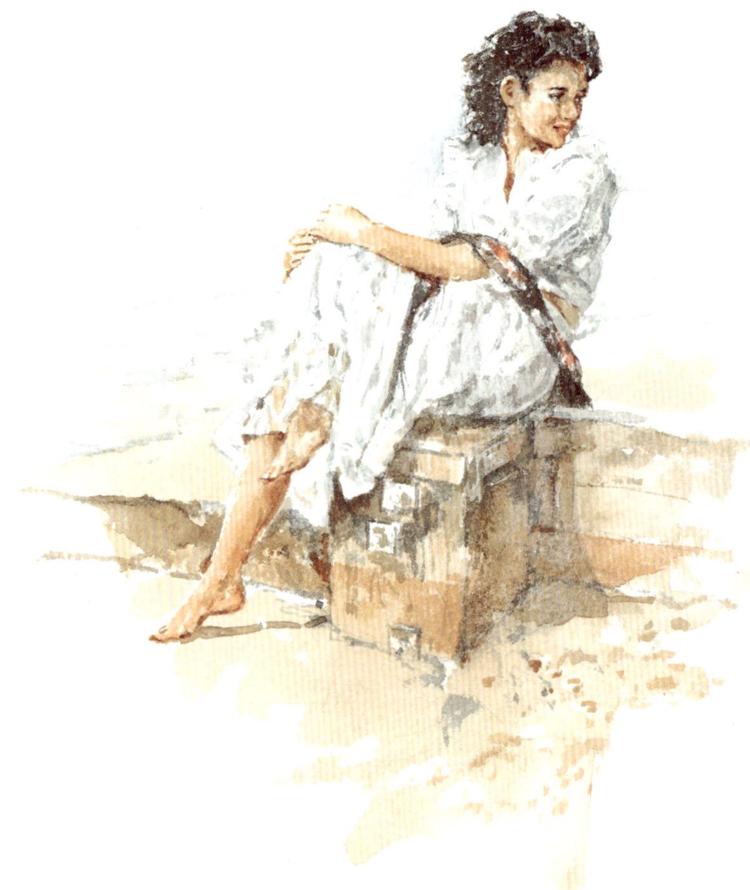

Imagine a vast stretch of sand washed smooth by the tide, leaving it pure and untouched. You can almost feel the wet sand under your feet leaving a trail of footprints for just a moment or two before being washed away again by a restless sea.

The swans in 'The Swan Girl' were at Mudeford on the south coast, looking round inquisitively as the girl walked through their midst.

Opposite: THE SWAN GIRL

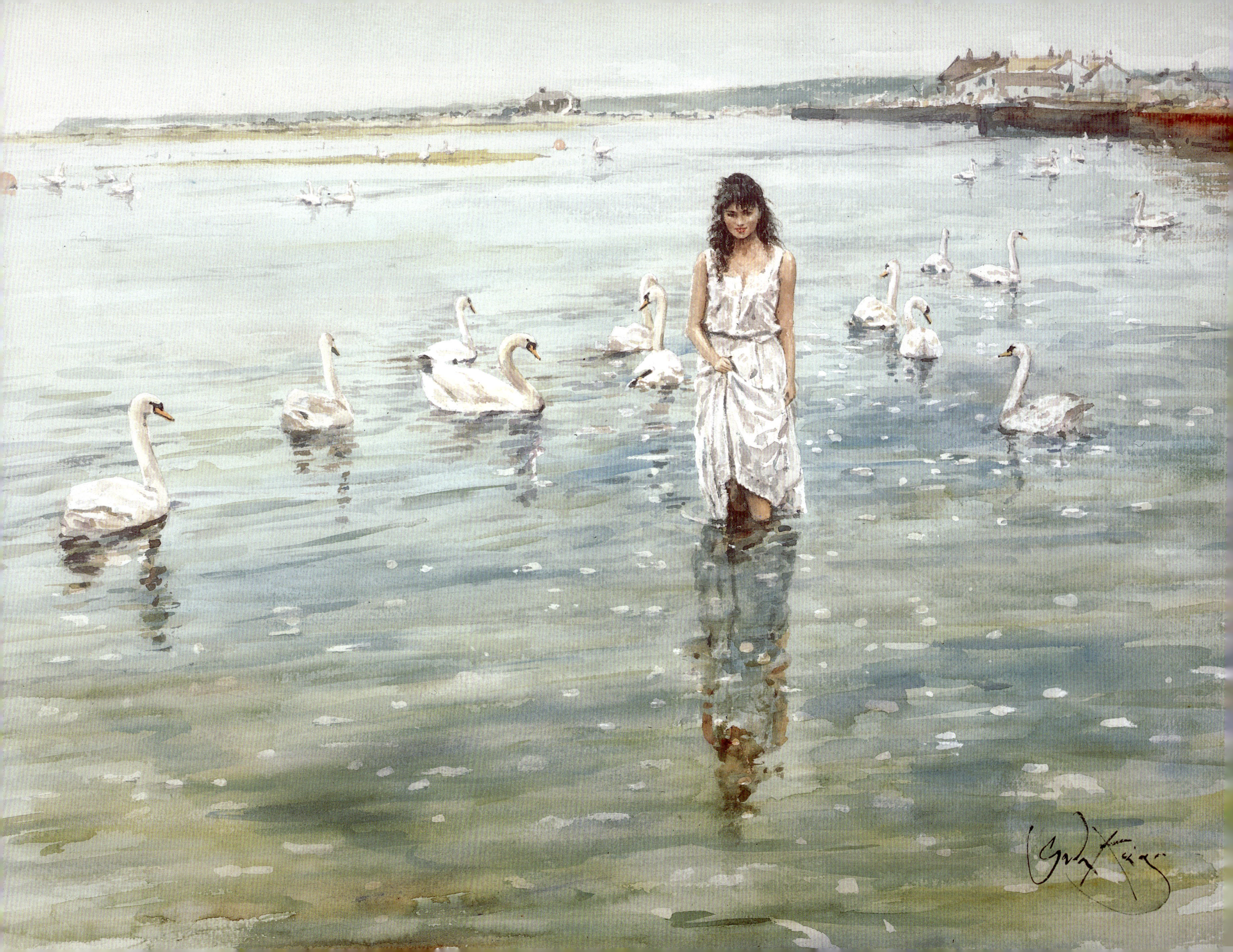

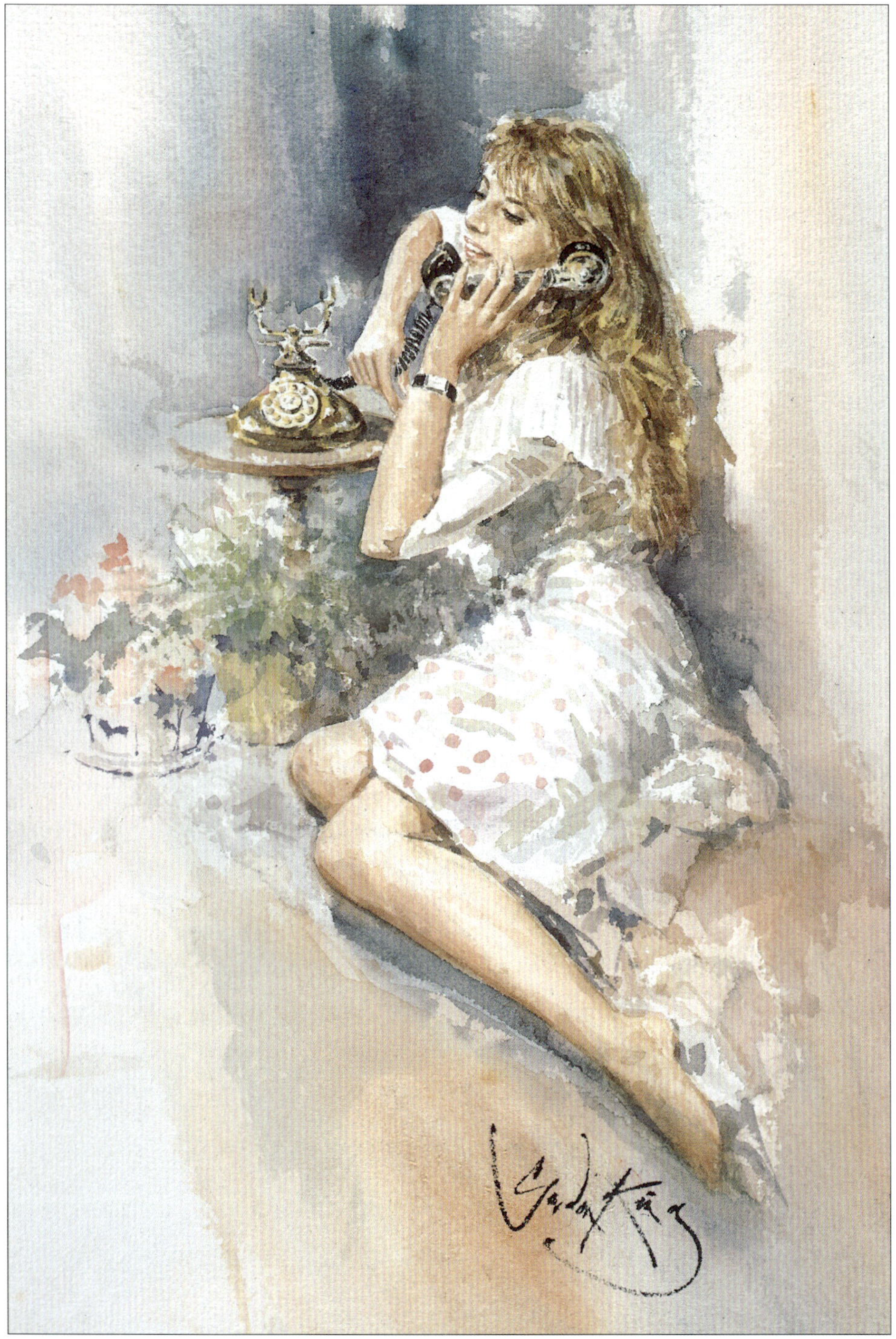

I JUST CALLED...

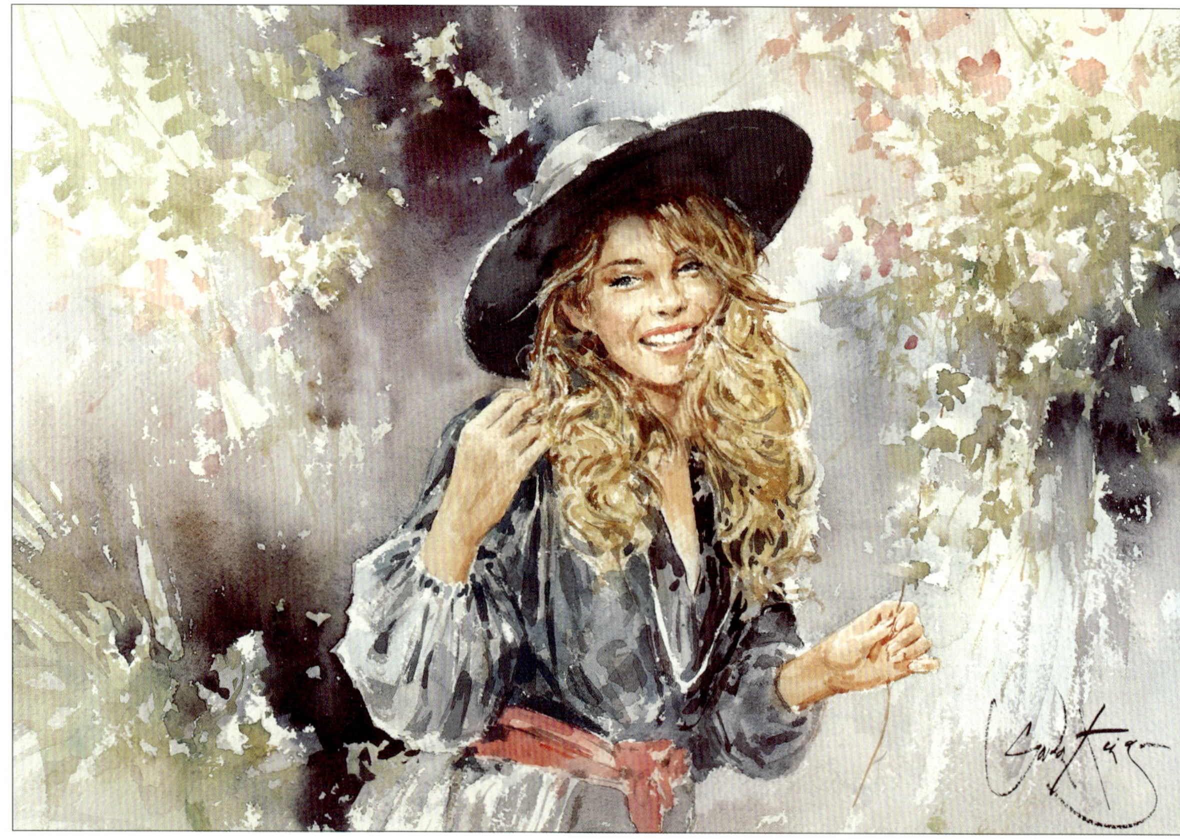

HAPPINESS

There is something extremely infectious about Emily's smile radiating a feeling of happiness all about her.

'I Just Called..' was inspired by a certain song which I always found very romantic.

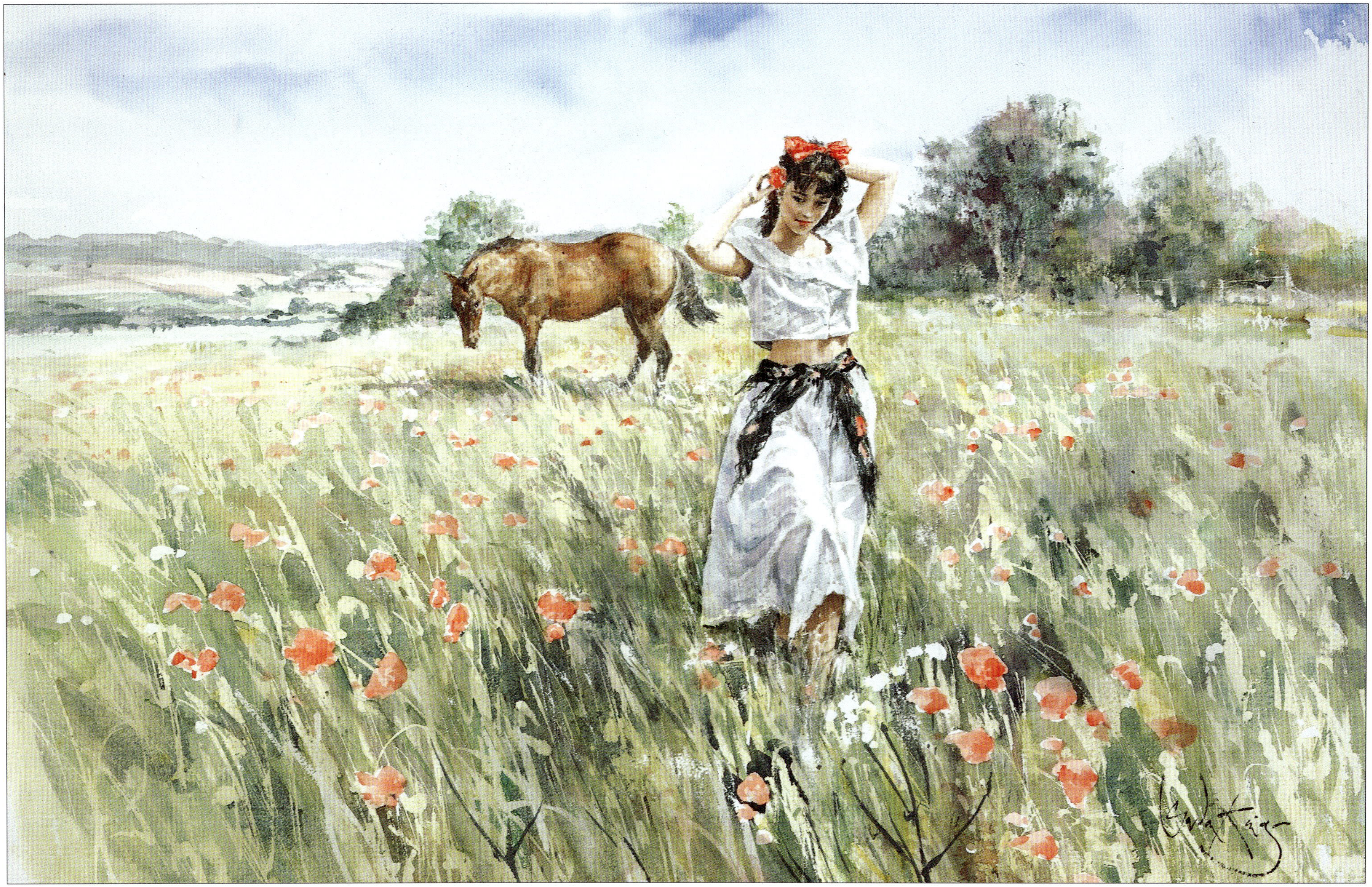

DAYS OF SUMMER

A hot summer's day in the middle of the countryside. As the poppies burst into flower the long grass comes alive with bright red splashes of colour as far as the eye can see. Almost approvingly the horse looks back as the girl takes a handful of poppies to put in her hair as she walks away.

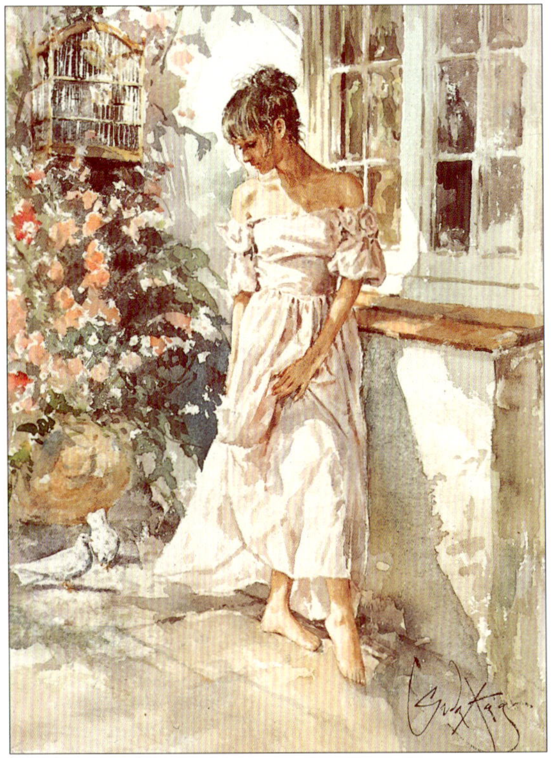

PEACE

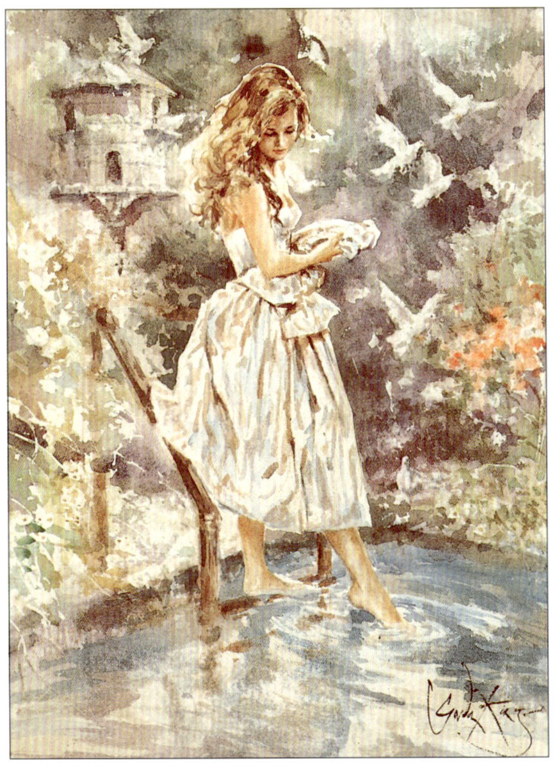

HARMONY

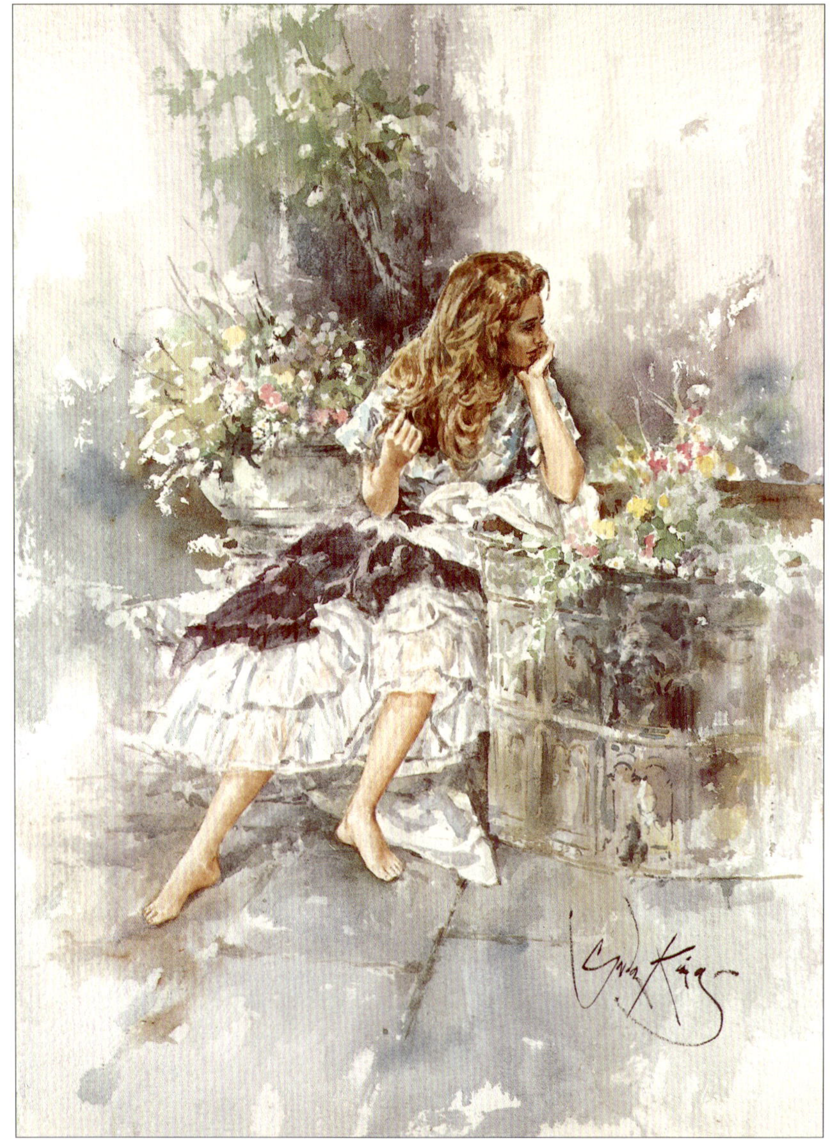

LOST IN THOUGHT

These paintings were all set in my garden in Buckinghamshire and have all been successfully reproduced in print form. 'My Fair Lady' was my first print with Solomon & Whitehead, painted in 1983, featuring Nicky as a typical flower girl, the look that became so popular.

Opposite: MY FAIR LADY
By kind permission of Solomon & Whitehead (Guild Prints) Limited

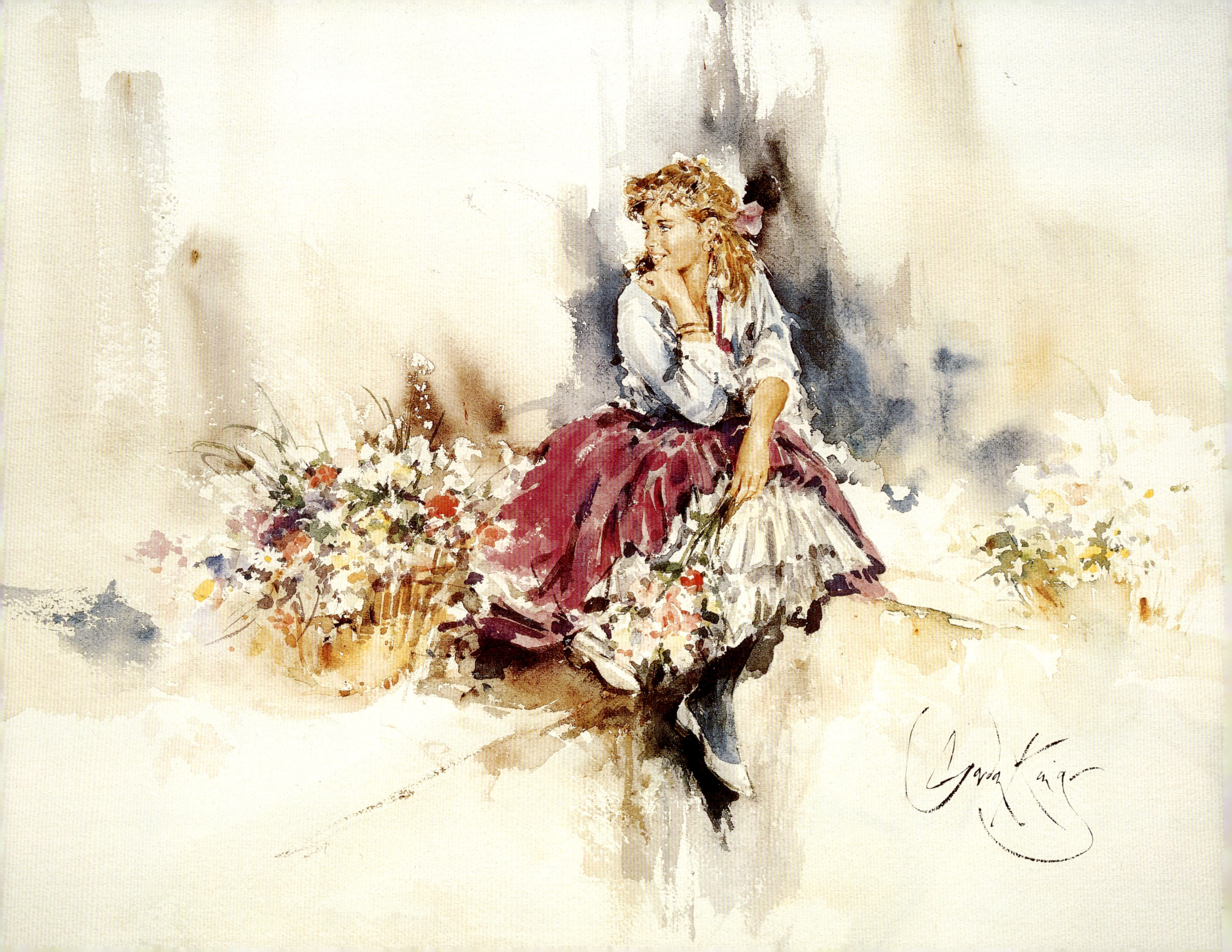

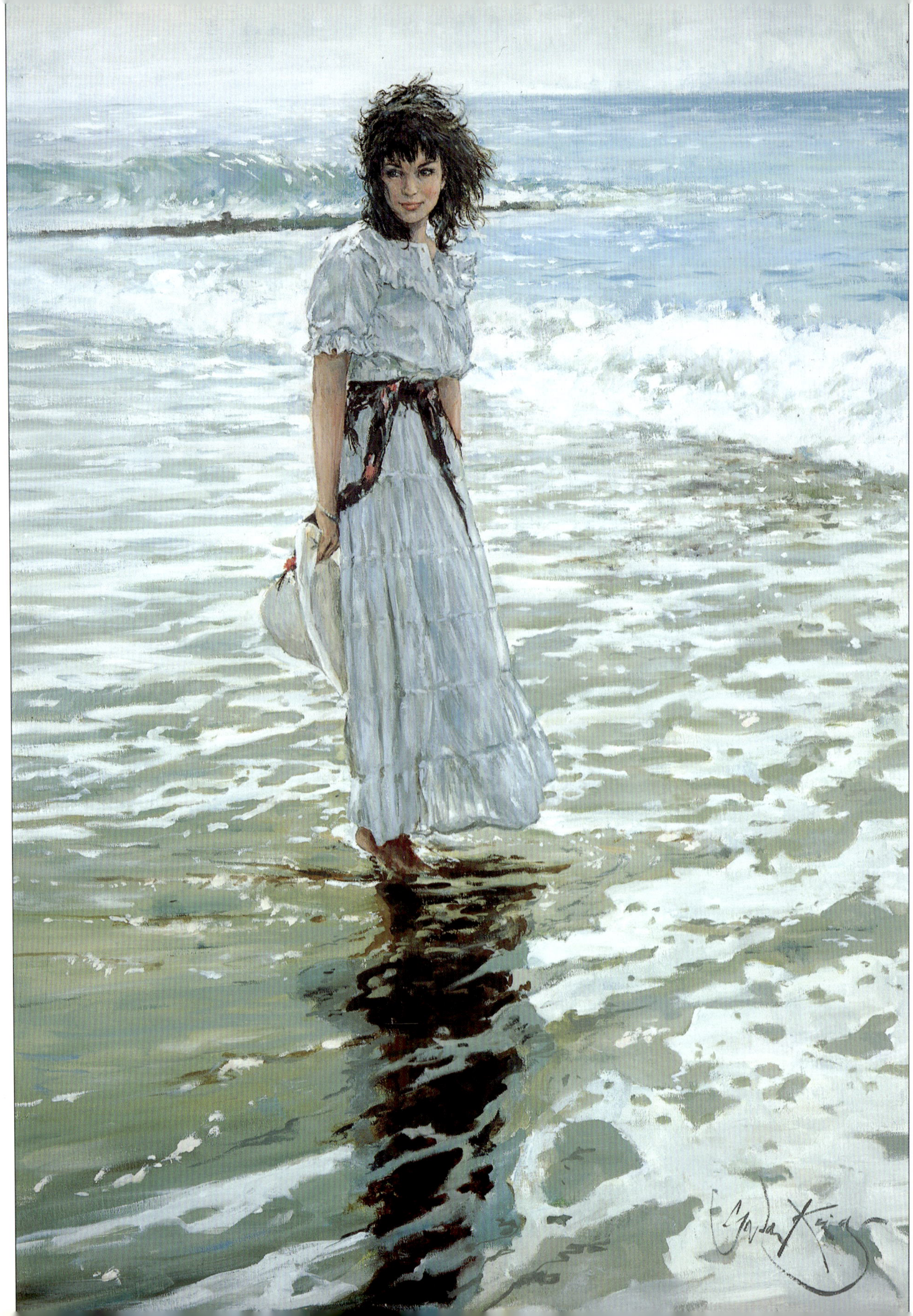

SPARKLING WATERS (OIL)

These two oil paintings were painted in the same period. I wanted to produce a strong vibrant look with lots of atmosphere. In 'Sparkling Waters' I enjoyed the challenge of portraying the movement of the surf with the sparkling light over the sea. The girl appears to be quite transfixed by the water around her. In 'Carmel', however, the girl is strolling confidently along the shore feeling the breeze gently blowing in from the sea.

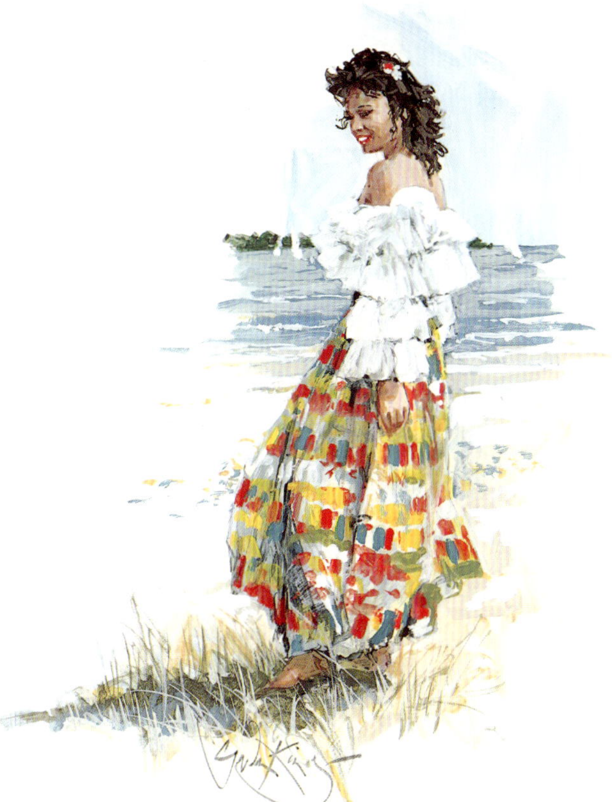

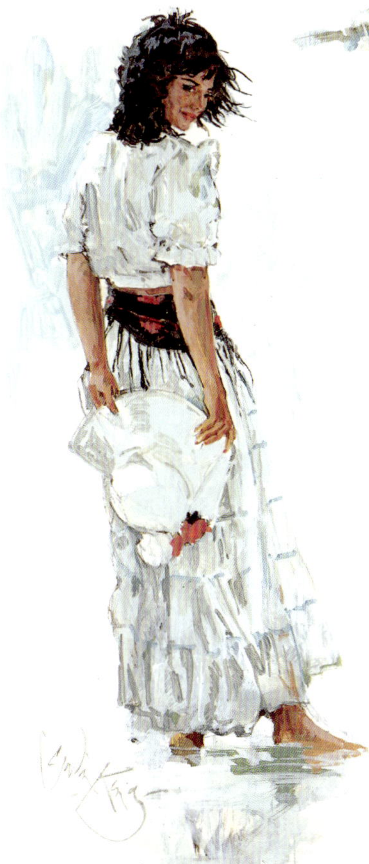

CARMEL (OIL)

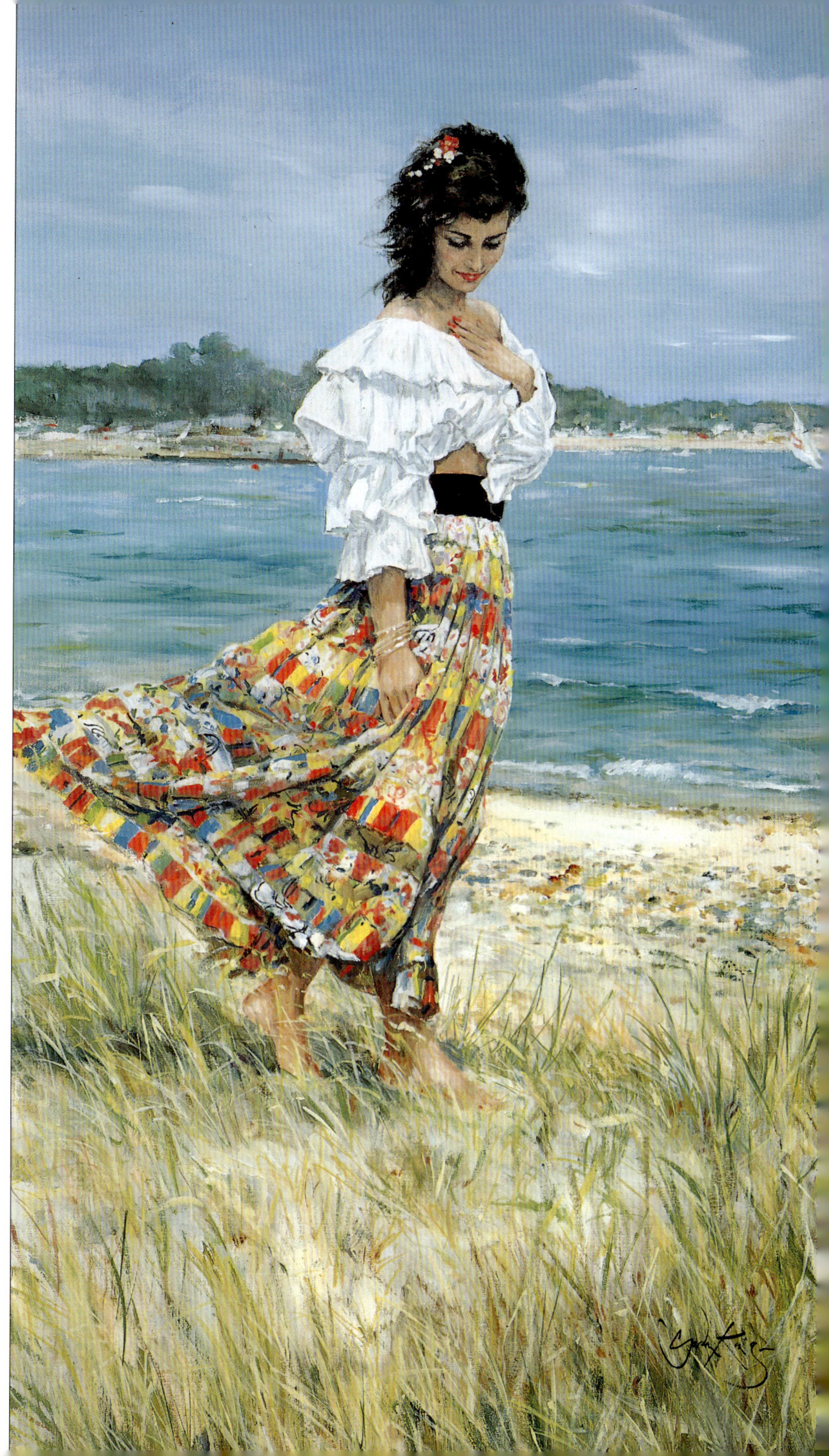

Gallery 2

I've been painting and drawing nude models ever since my first life drawing class at the age of 15. It was an important learning curve and a discipline that has stood me in good stead.

The nude study is another classic subject for the artist, forming the essential foundation for any figurative work. Traditionally, it has been used for the practice and perfection of drawing techniques but it is also recognised as a work of art in its own right.

Most of my models for nude studies have been professionals and I've tended to use the subject to create a form of beauty and mood, going for an elegant pose and soft colour with a hint of mystique.

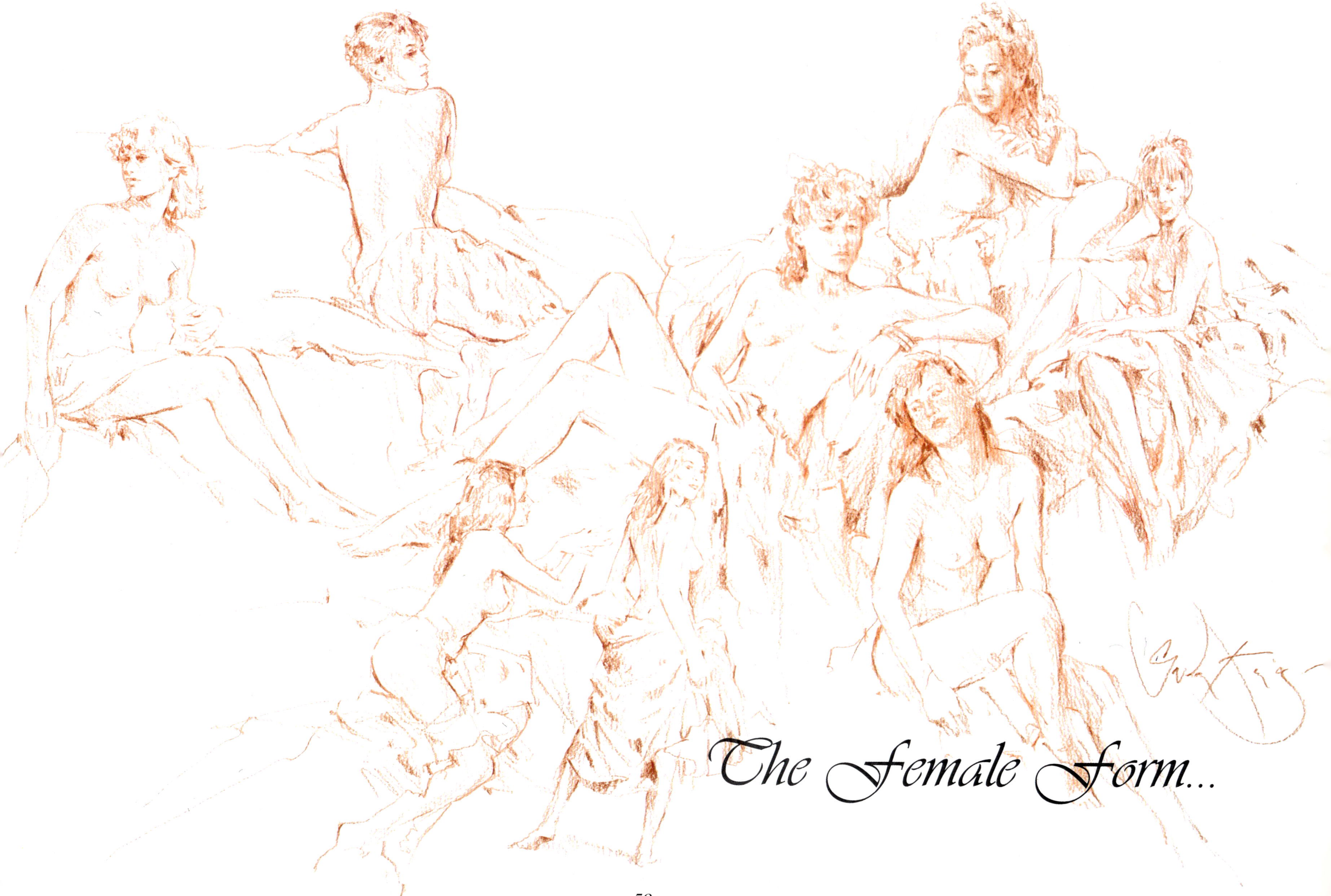

The Female Form...

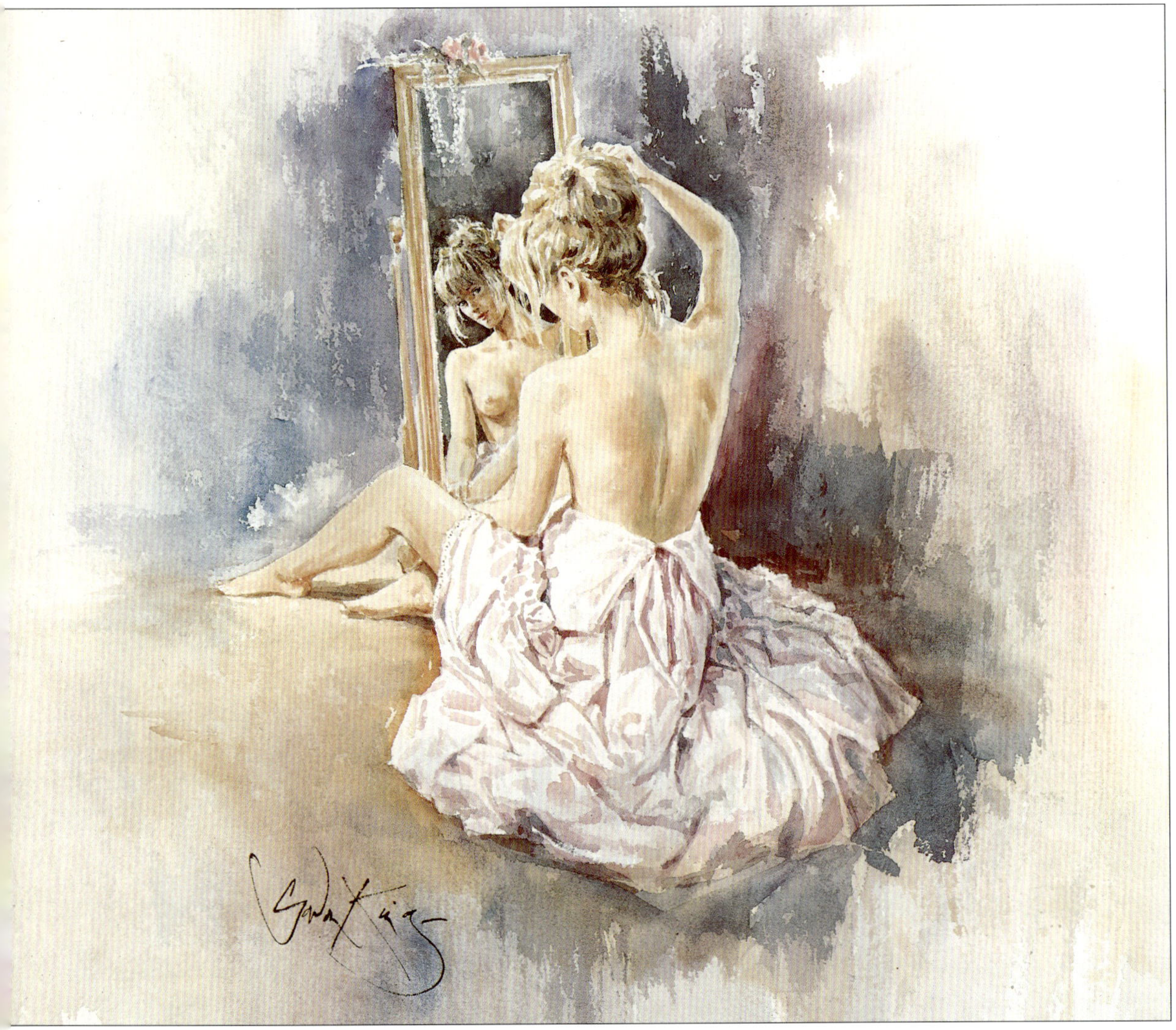

MIRROR IMAGE

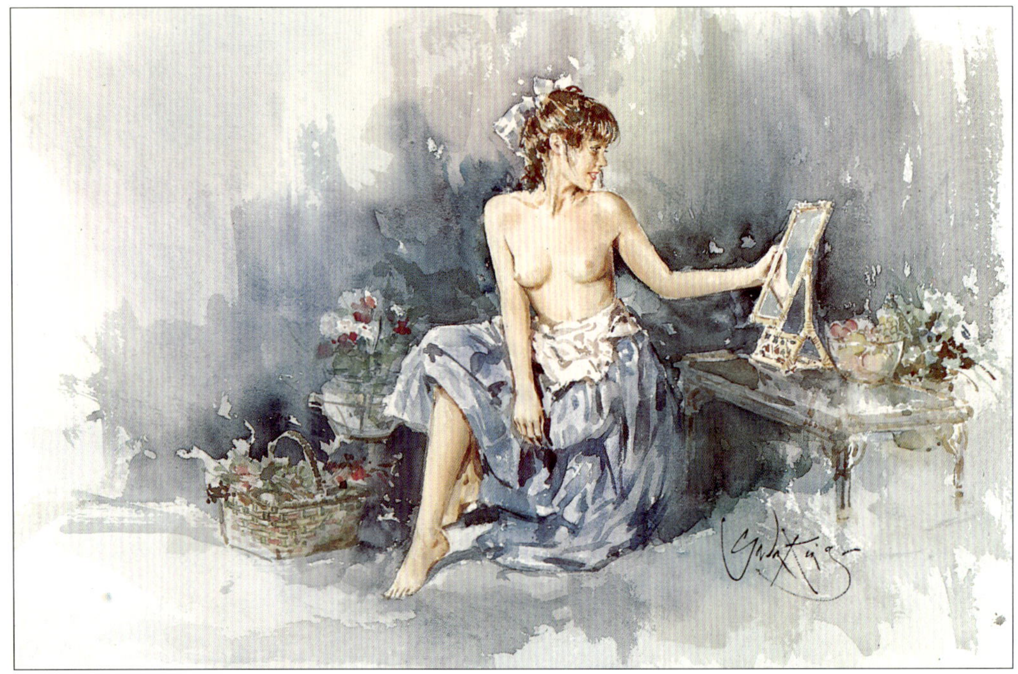

THE LITTLE MIRROR

Painting the female form has always been an exciting subject for me. Flesh tones, especially in watercolour, are always a challenge and the image of a girl looking into the mirror and the particular shape of her dress would have been very much visualised in my mind before the model even arrived. With Isabella I tried to capture a feeling of grace, poise and beauty together with the air of mystery that seemed to surround her.

Opposite: ISABELLA

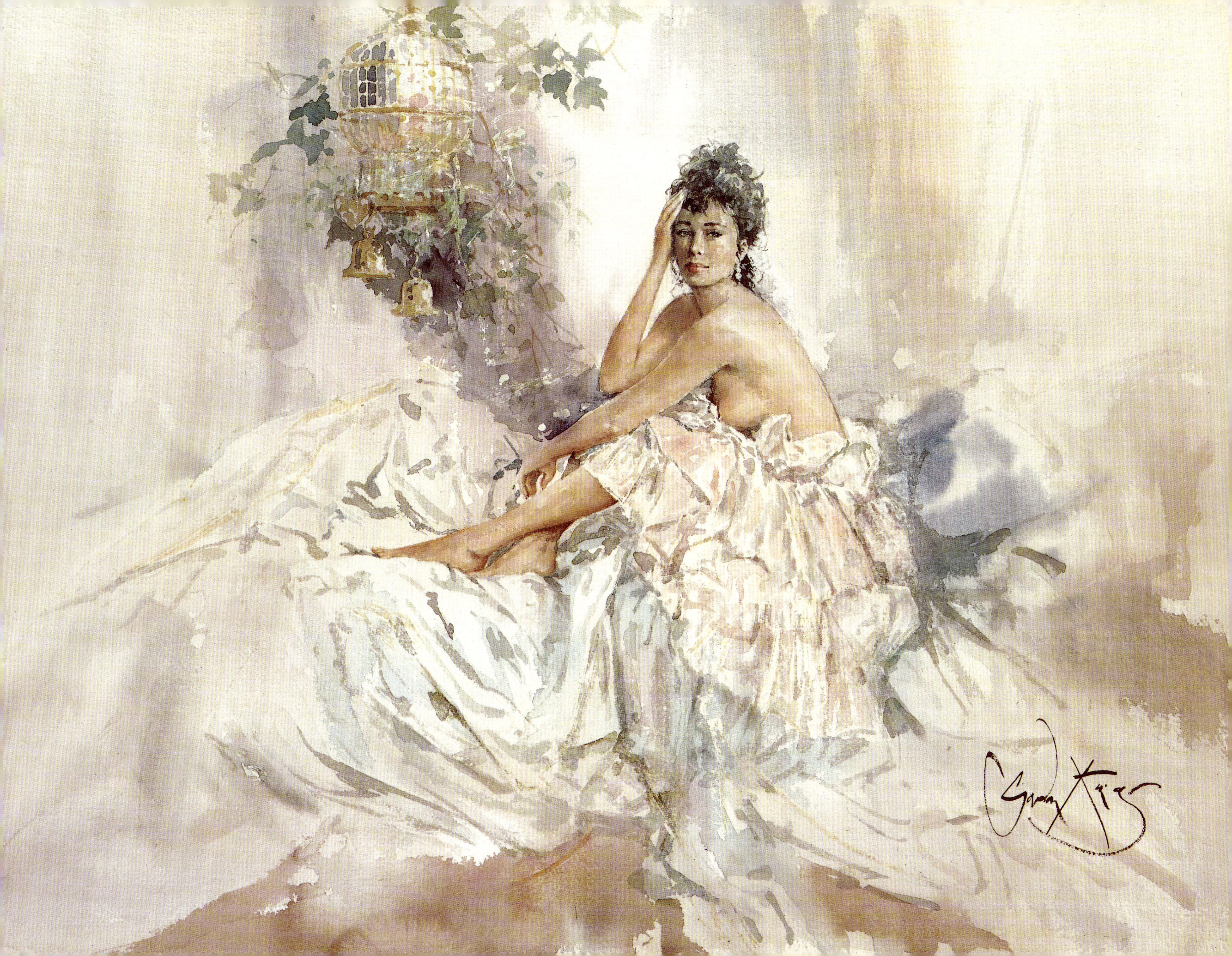

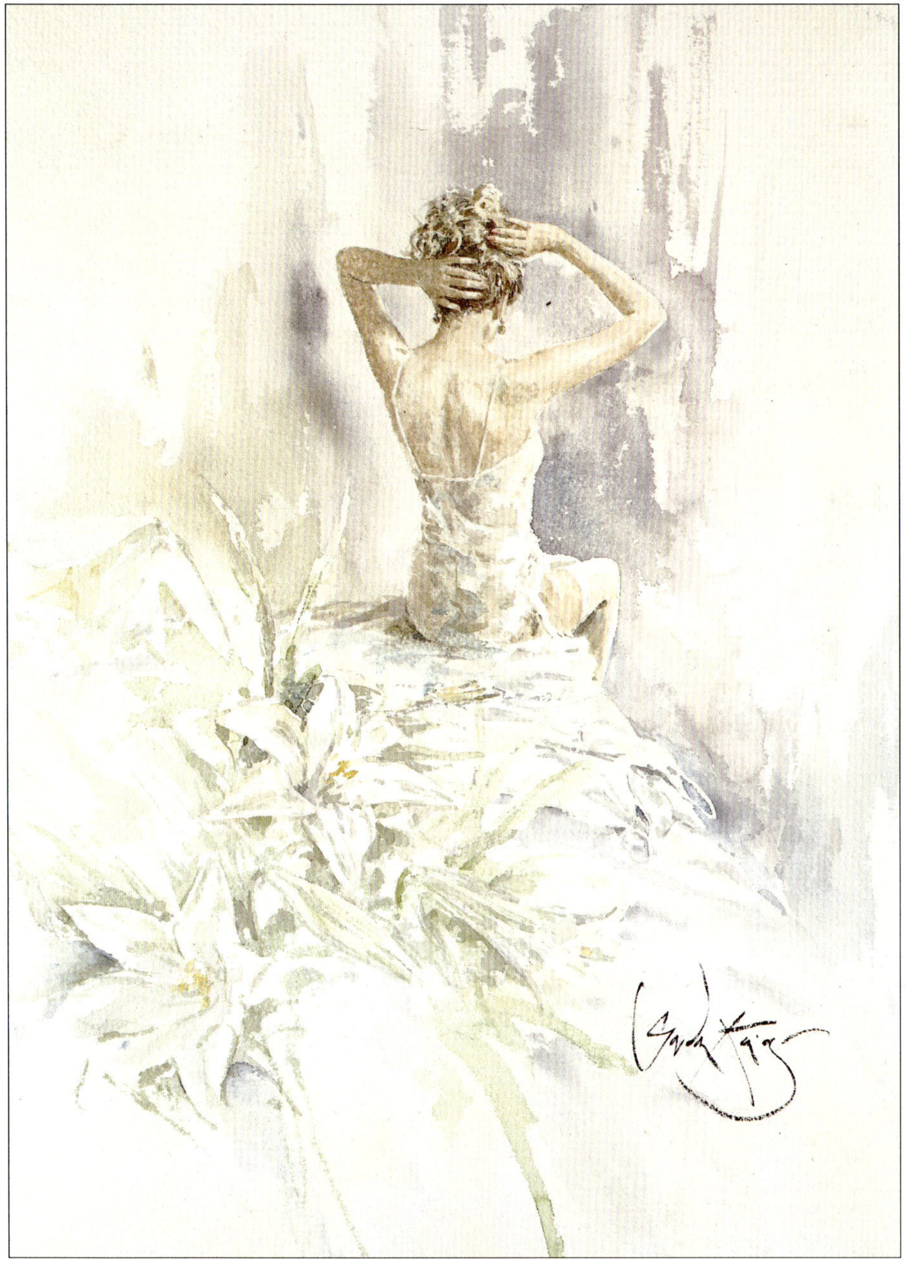

A SENSE OF STYLE

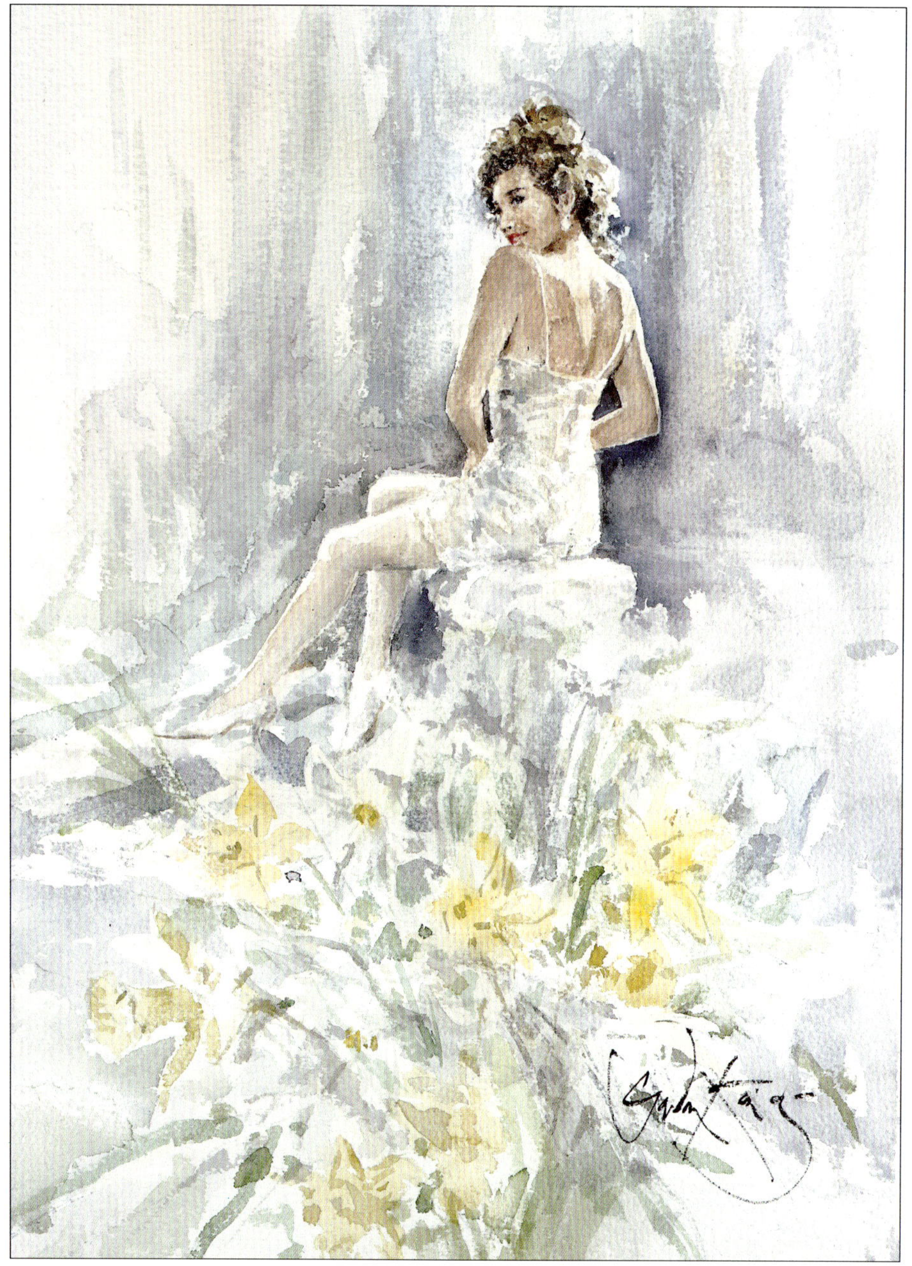

A SENSE OF ELEGANCE

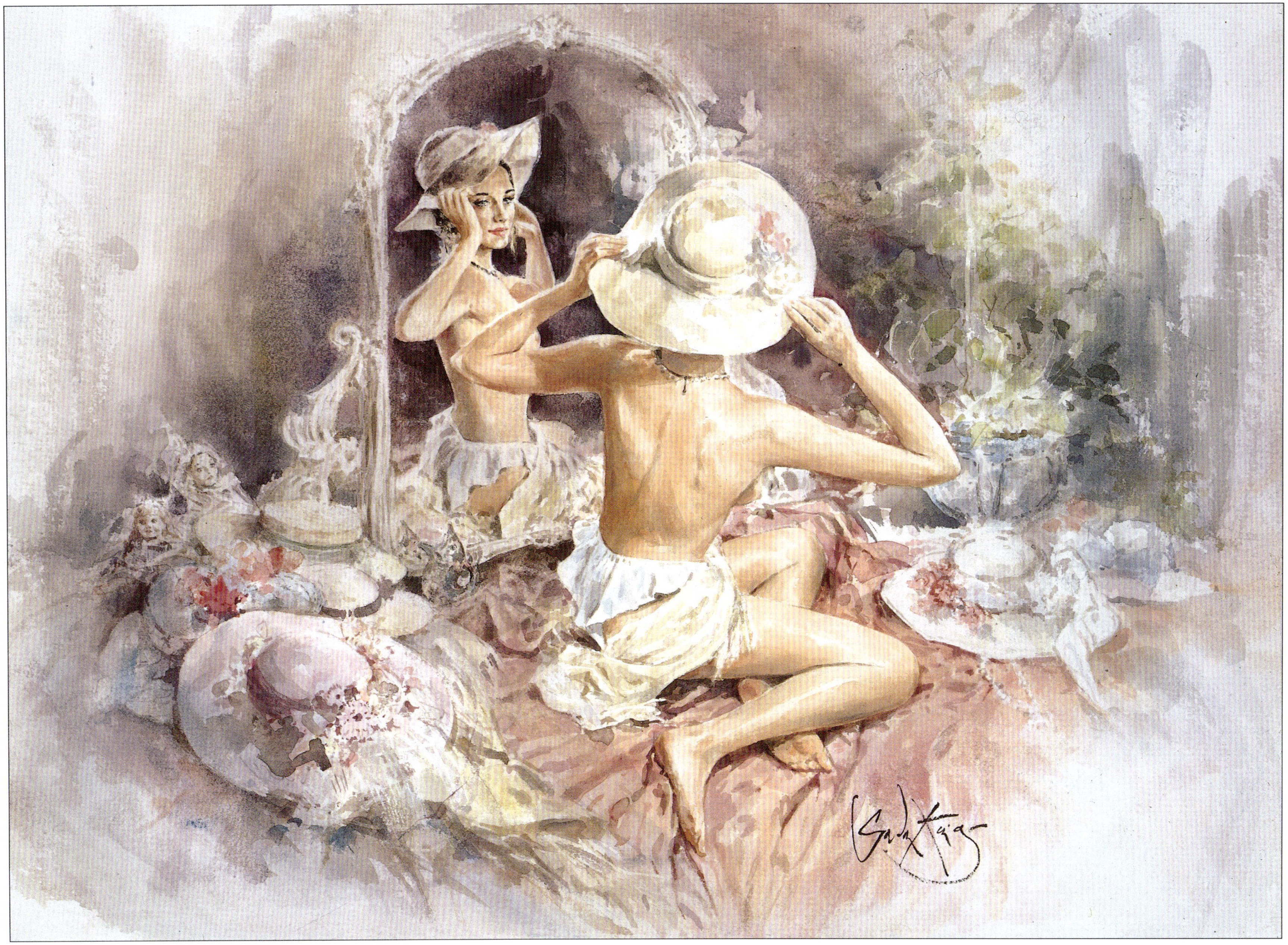

THE PERFECT HAT

I have a collection of old hats in the studio which come in useful for occasions like this.

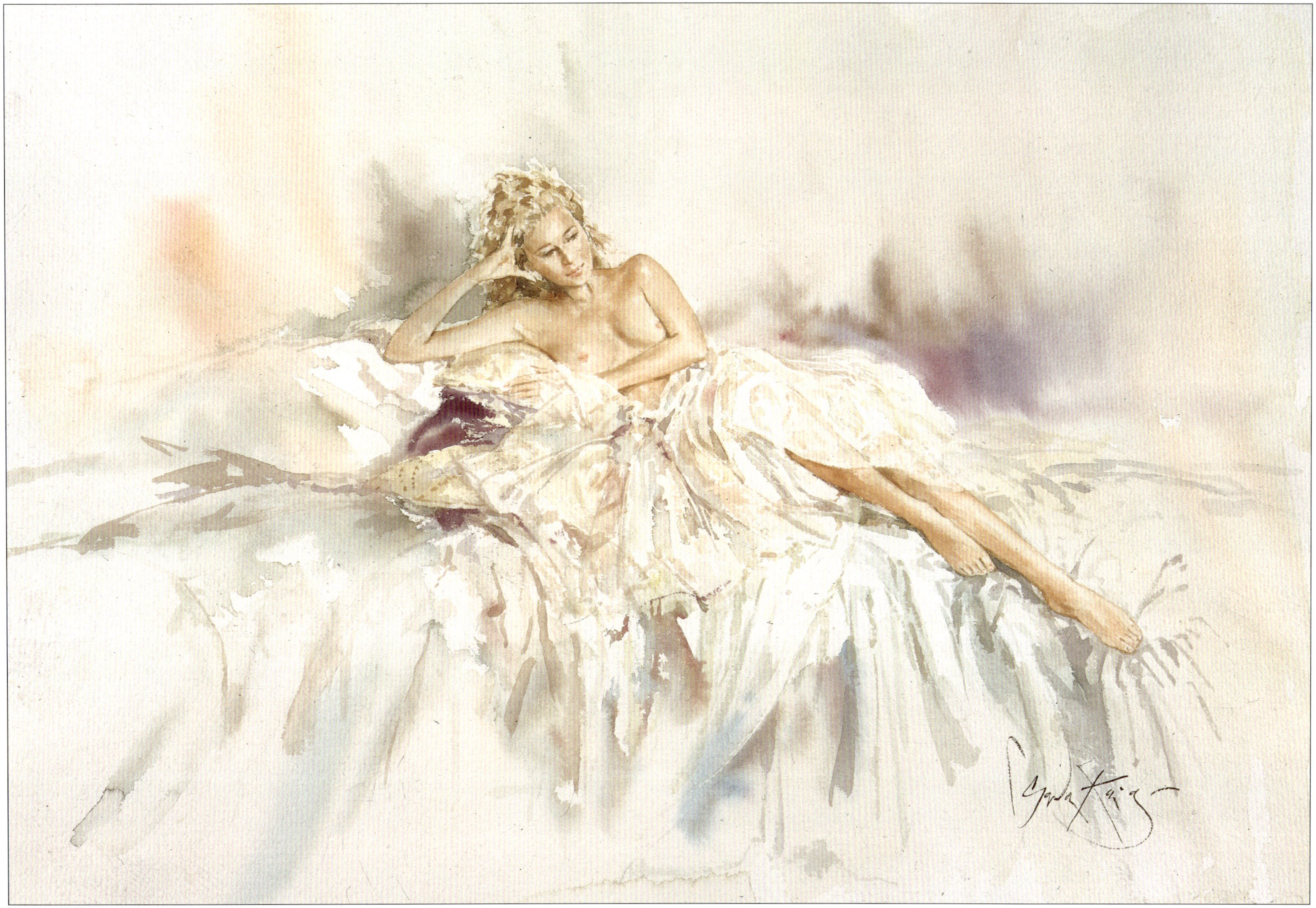

SERENA

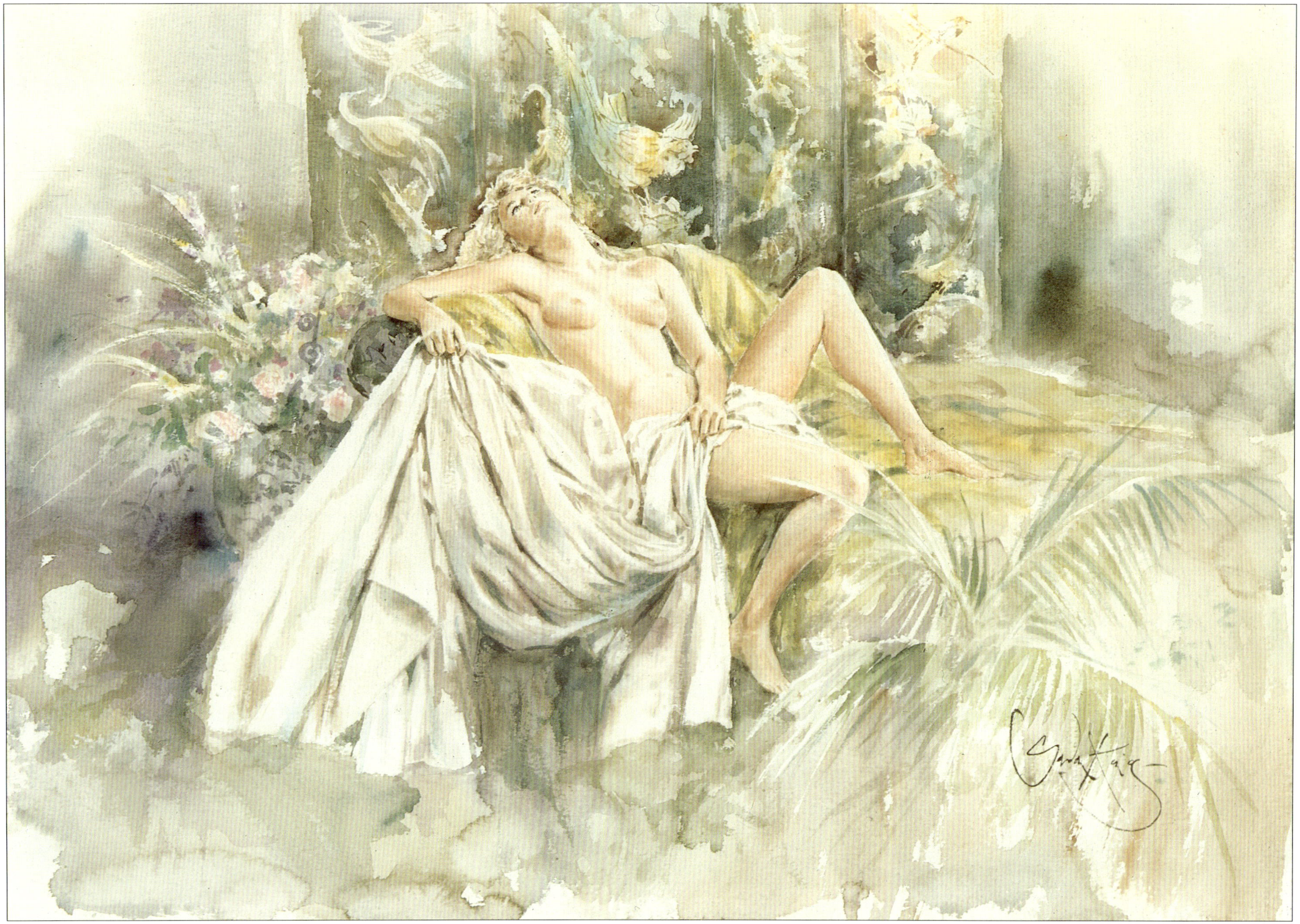

THE SCREEN

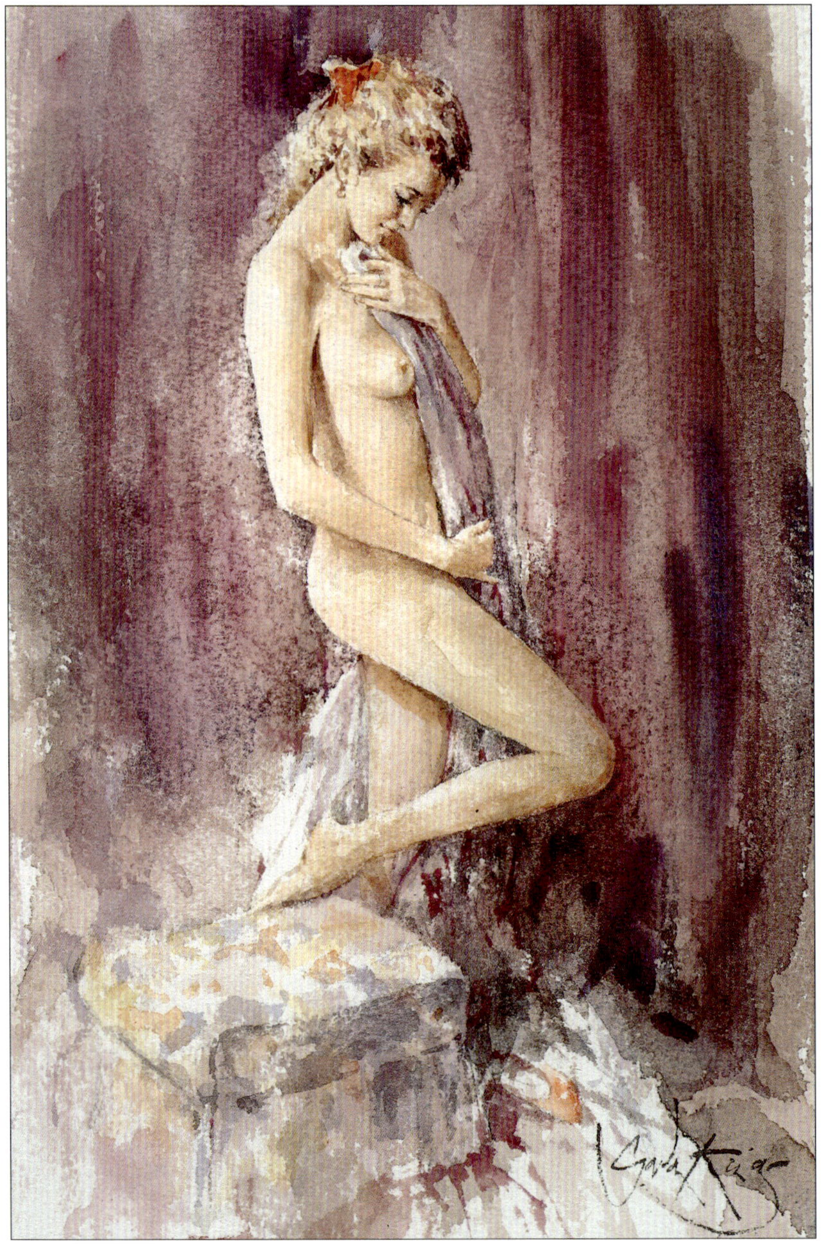

THE BLUE DRAPE

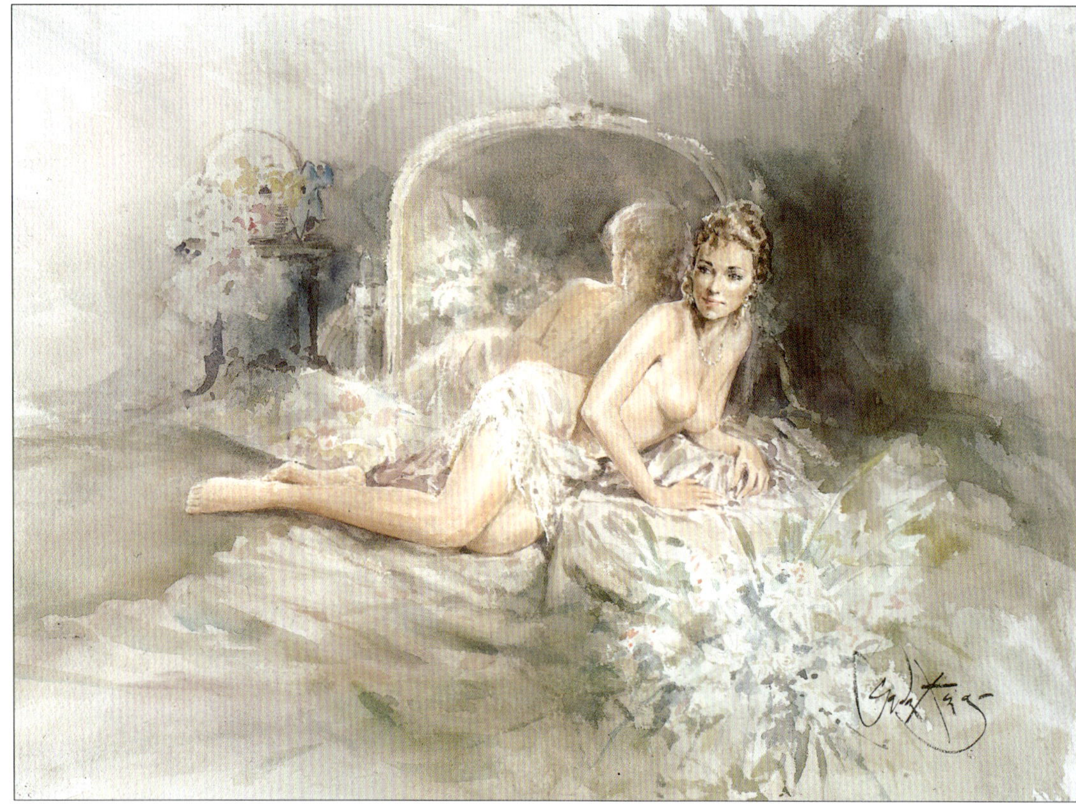

IMAGE OF FLEURETTE

PANDORA

I love the name 'Pandora' and this model gave me that special pose and drape providing the kind of image I'm always looking for.

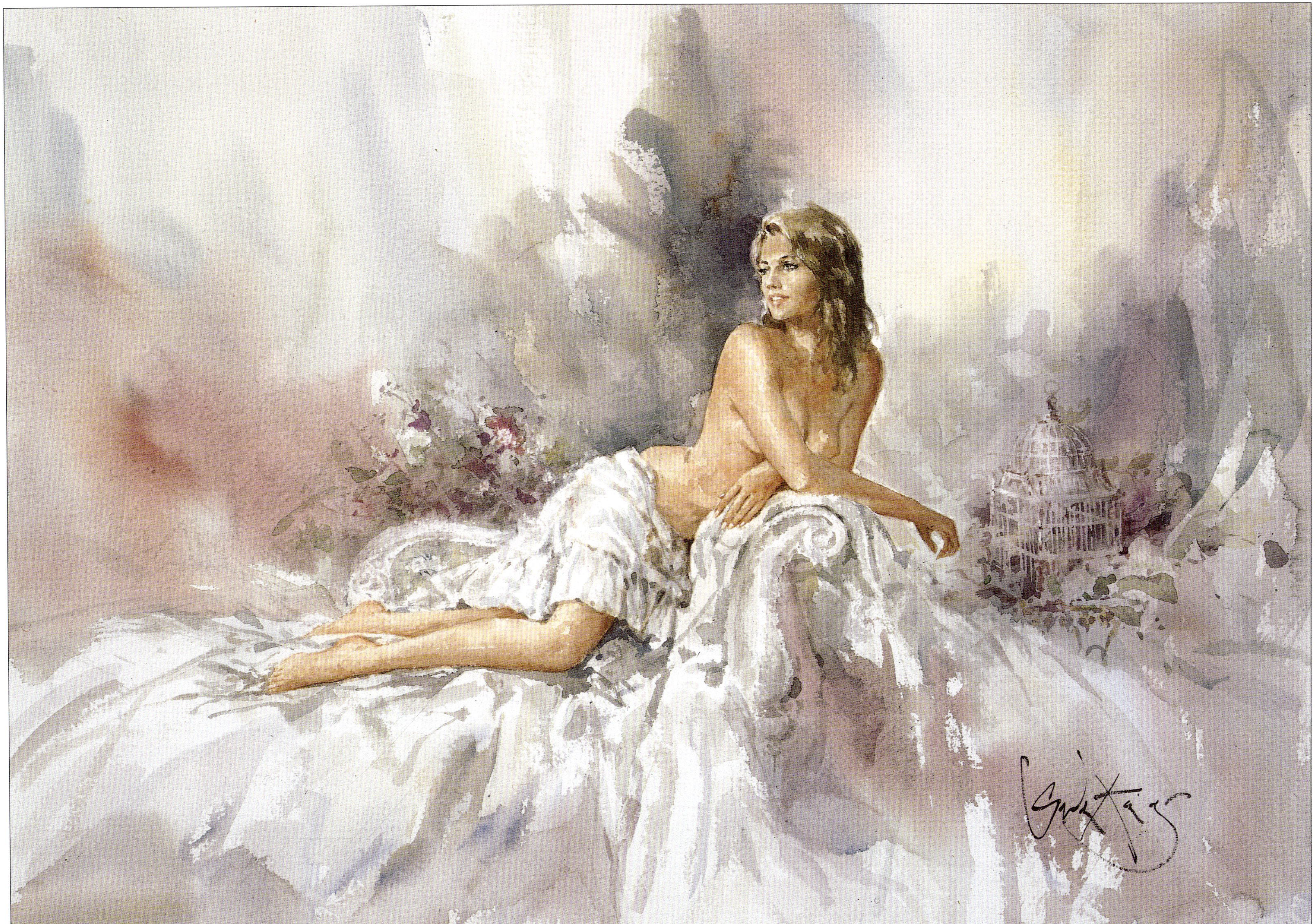

PANDORA

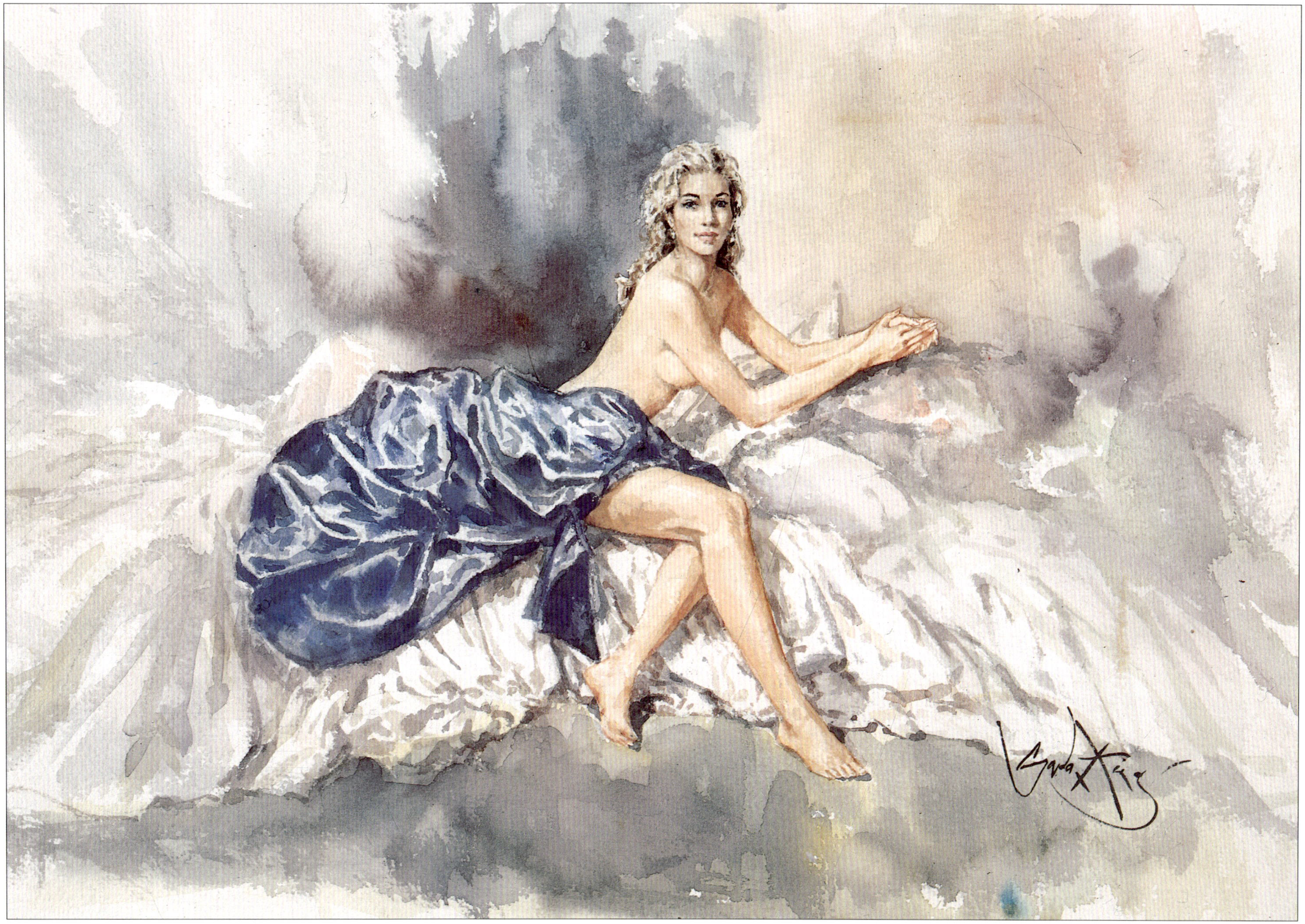

STUDY IN BLUE

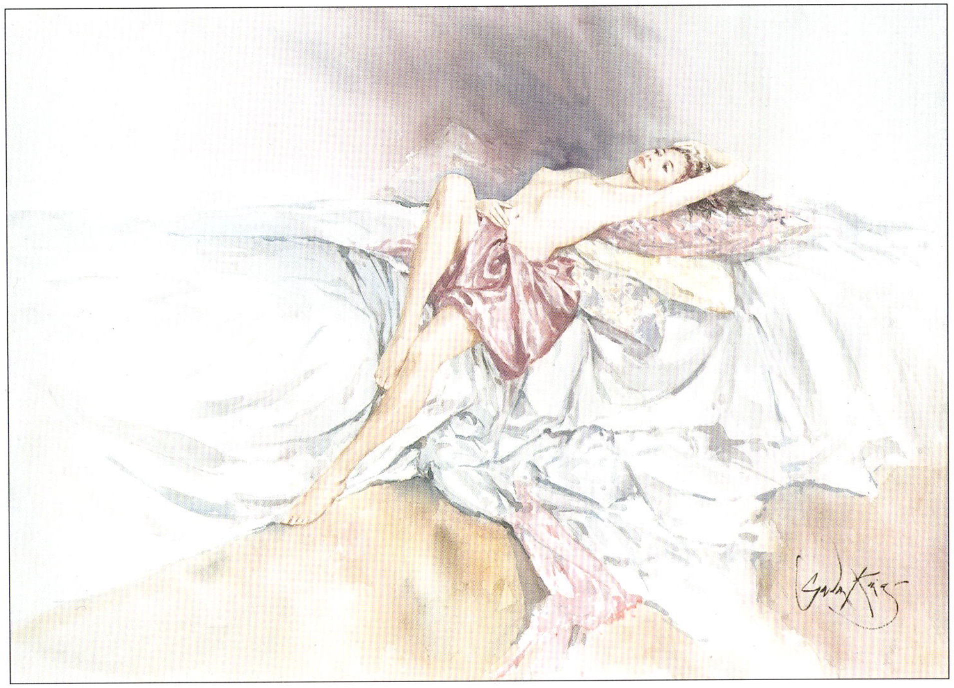

THE PURPLE DRAPE

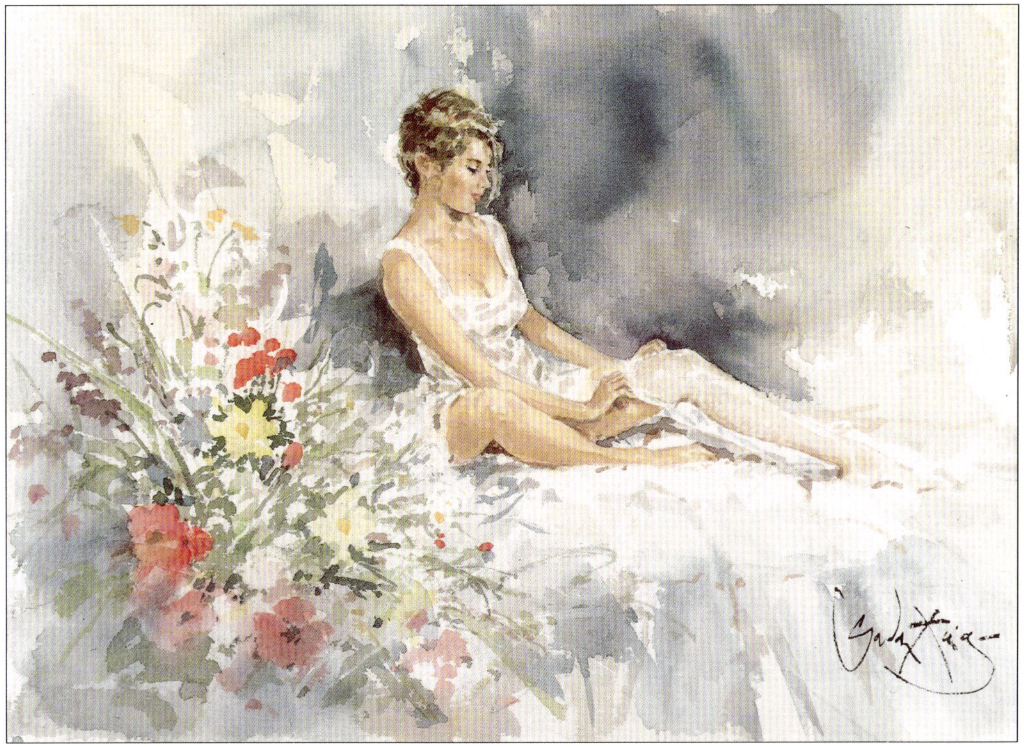

THE WHITE STOCKING

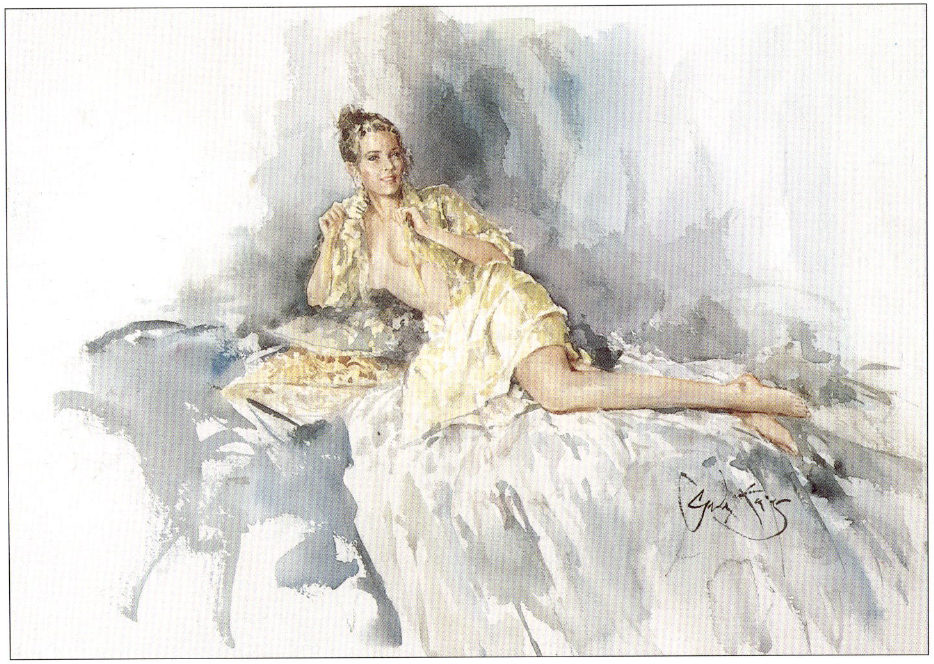

STUDY IN GOLD

Painting fine fabrics and materials, especially silk with its rich colour and sheen, gives a certain challenge to a watercolourist, with the highlights being so important.

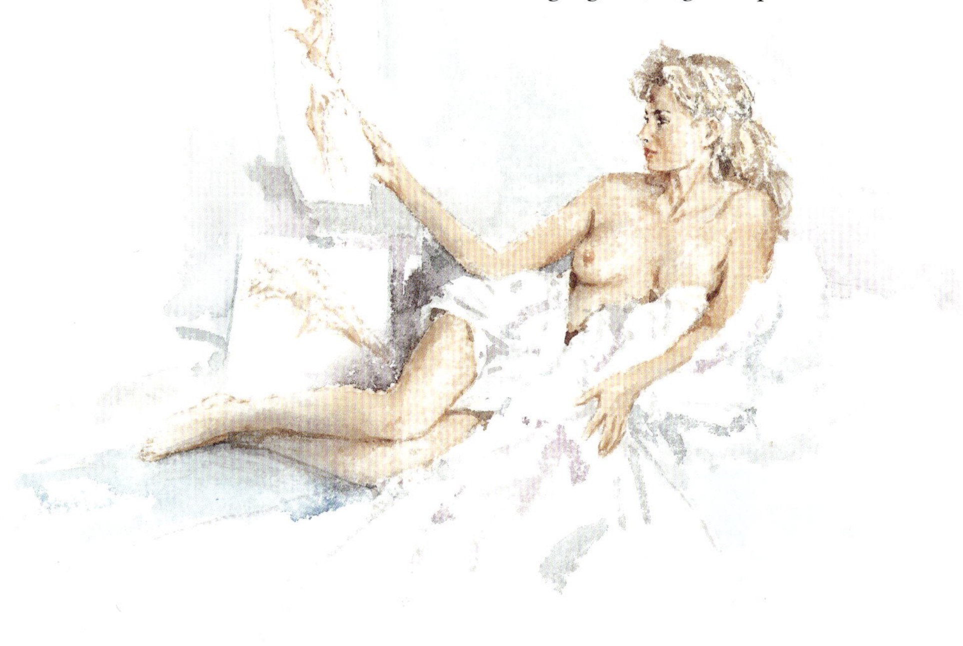

Gallery 3

Actors say "never work with children or animals - they'll steal the show" but as a subject for an artist this is, of course, an advantage. Consequently, they have always had tremendous appeal as shown by a historical perspective from the renaissance paintings with cherubs flying all over the place, to the more narrative compositions of the nineteenth century.

When I use children as a subject it's that elusive quality of innocence combined with their carefree spirit and natural exuberance which I try to capture. With animals the emphasis tends to be more on the relationship that develops between them and the people around them, whether it be a man and his dog, a girl with her cat, etc.

Horses have been a favourite subject of mine since I was young and, again, it's that harmony of movement both in harness and under saddle that makes it so exciting.

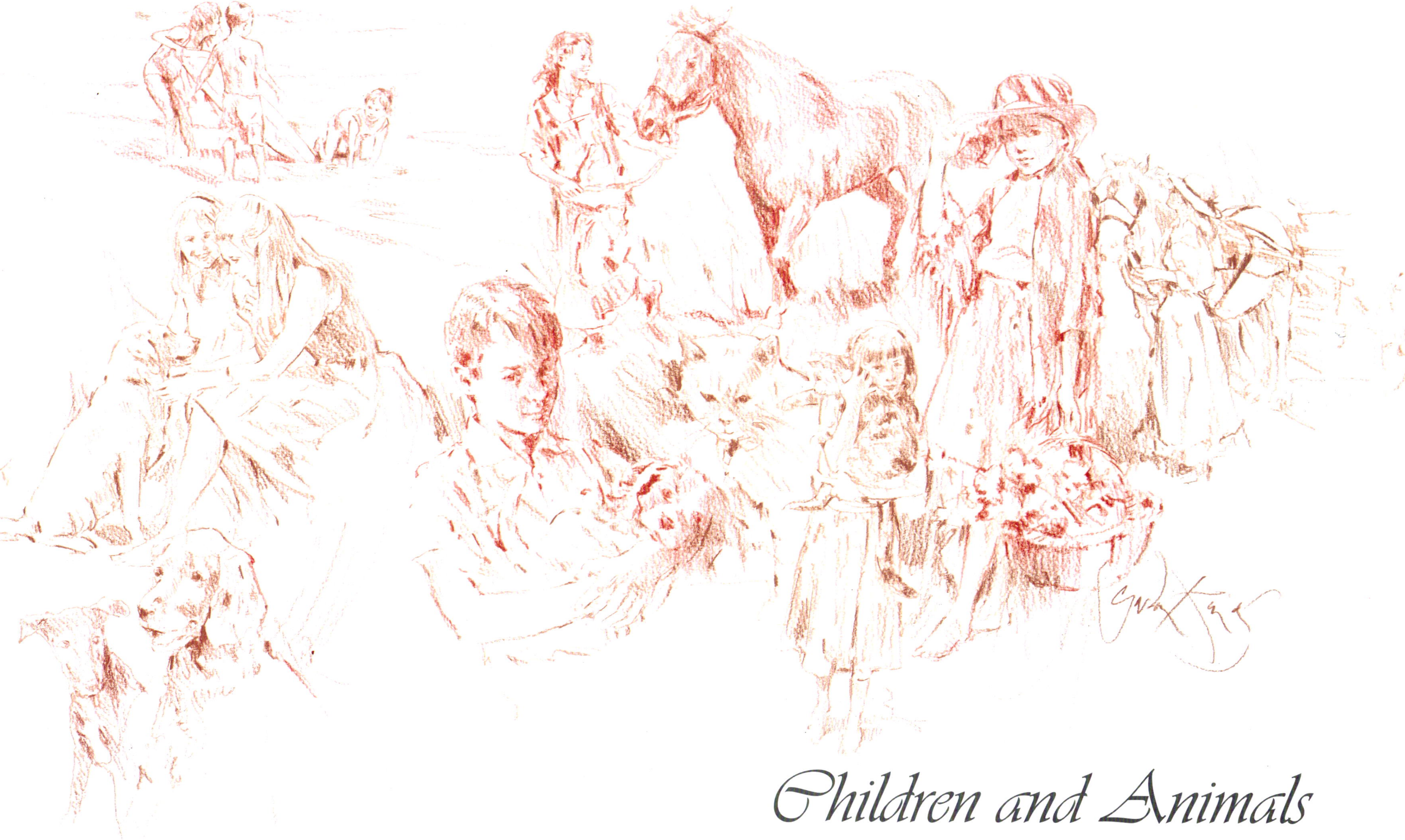

Children and Animals
The Scene Stealers...

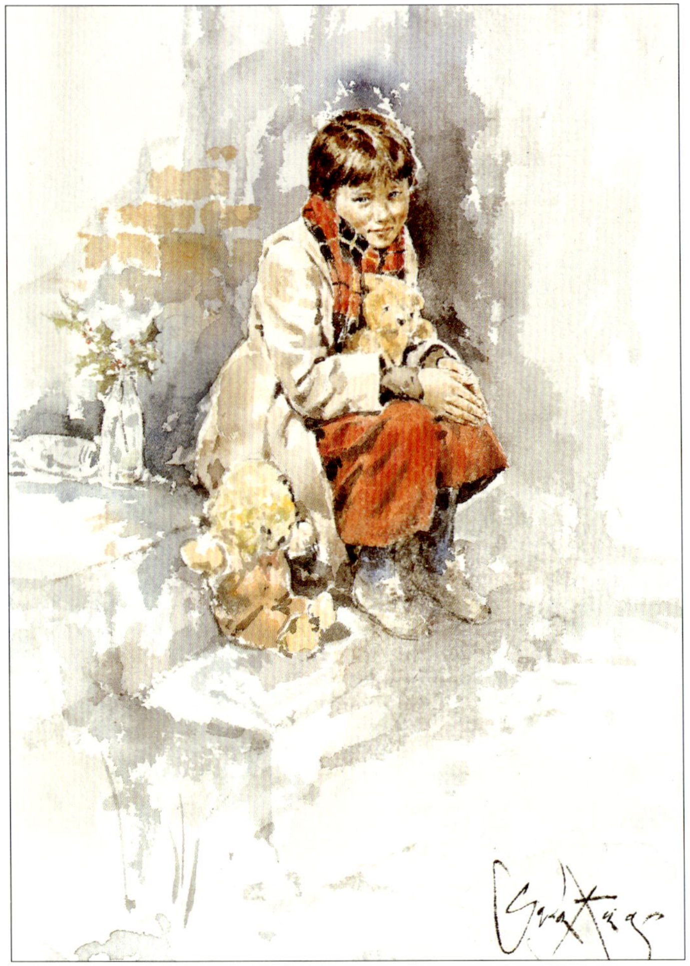

WISTFUL THOUGHTS

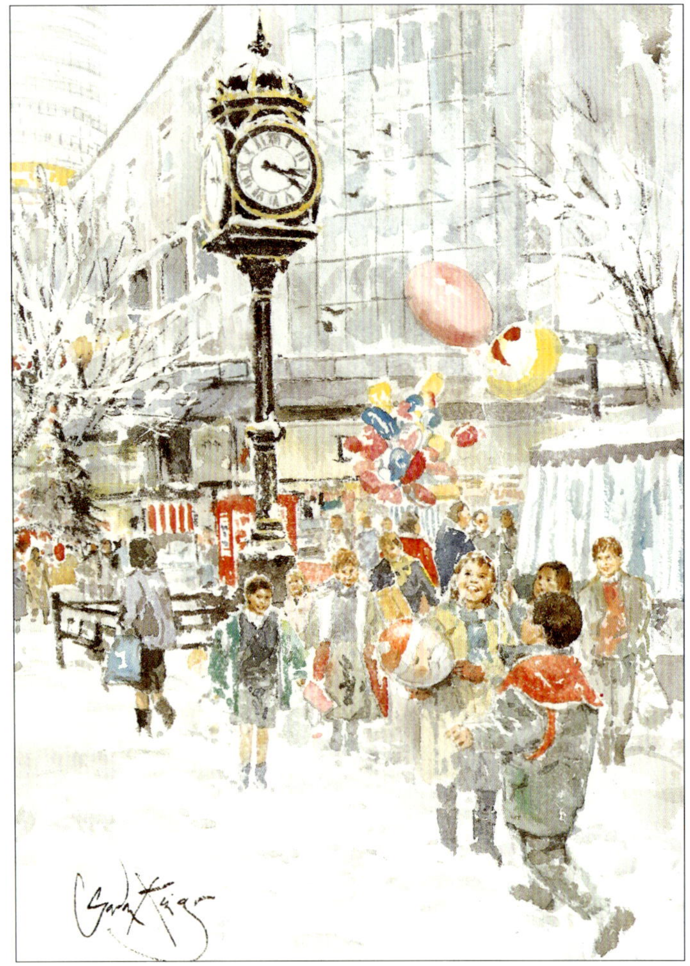

TIME FOR CHRISTMAS

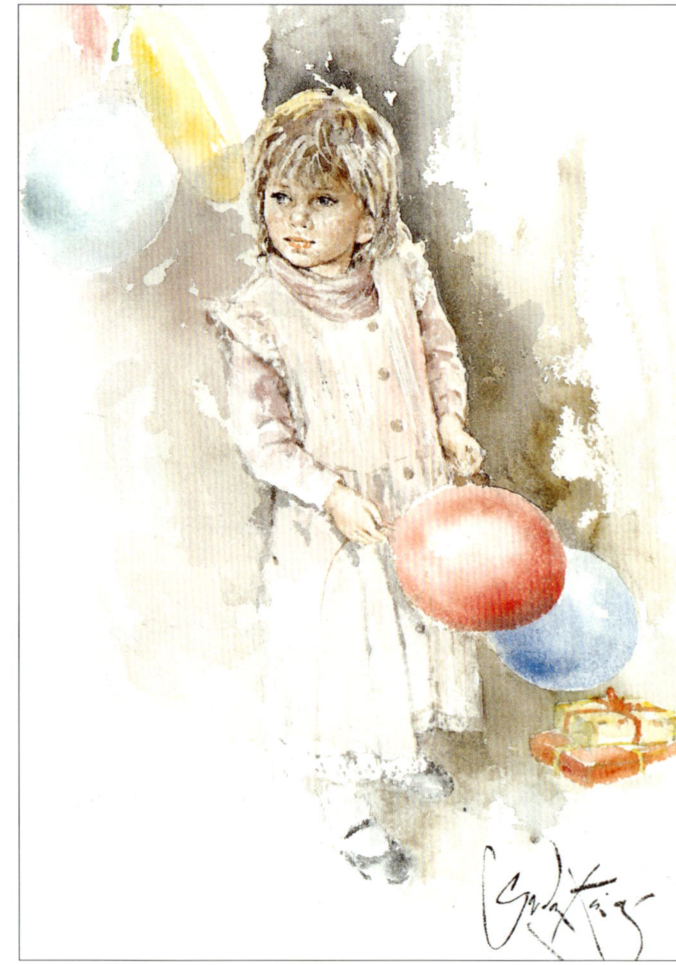

PARTY DREAMS

These three paintings are taken from a series of twelve which were done for reproduction as Christmas Cards to raise funds for the 'Children in Cities' charity project, part of the Save the Children Fund.

In 'Wistful Thoughts' young Yvonne sat on my front doorstep posing for me with her teddies and a simple sprig of holly in the milk bottle beside her. Then I spotted a delightful little girl at a nursery school Christmas party. She was appropriately called Holly and became a natural subject for 'Party Dreams'. In 'Time for Christmas' I painted these school children by the clock in Birmingham centre as they made their way home in the snow after breaking up for Christmas.

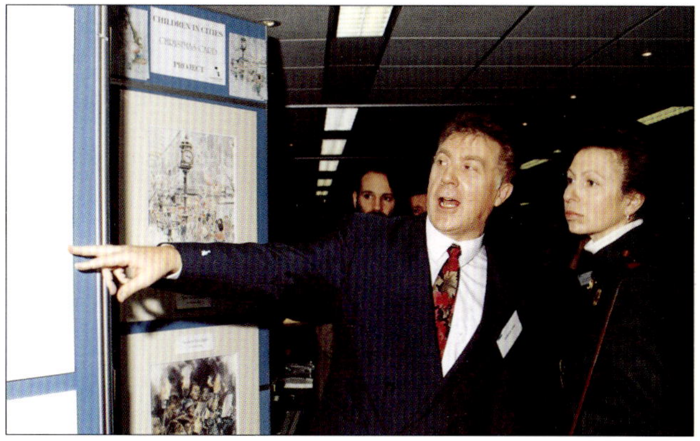

This was published as a special signed
and numbered charity limited edition
for 'Children in Cities.'
The idea of a young girl surrounded by
dolls of the world was something that
had been going around in my mind for
some time and it seemed perfect for
this particular project.

Children
in Cities 92
Save the Children

SMALL WORLD

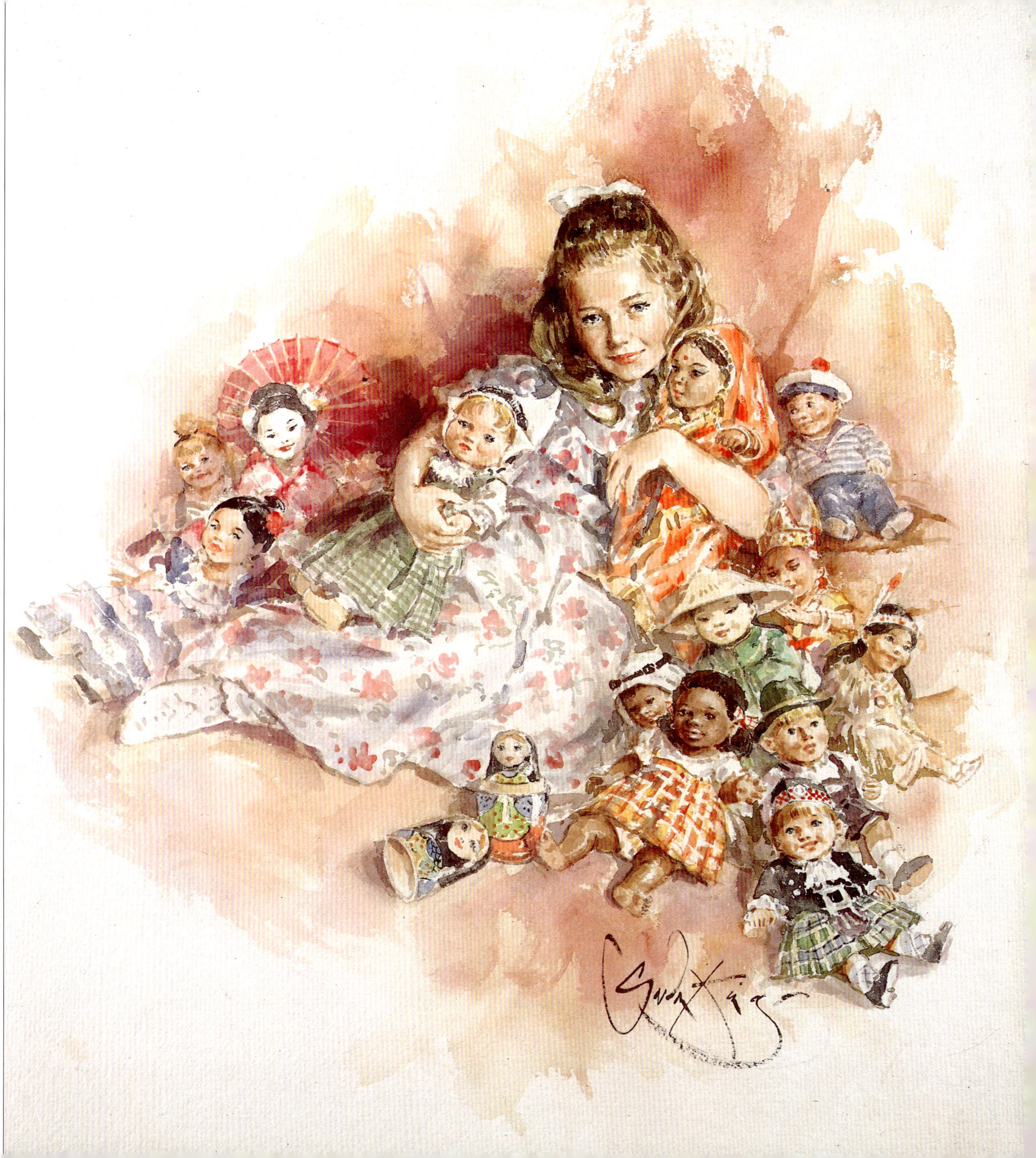

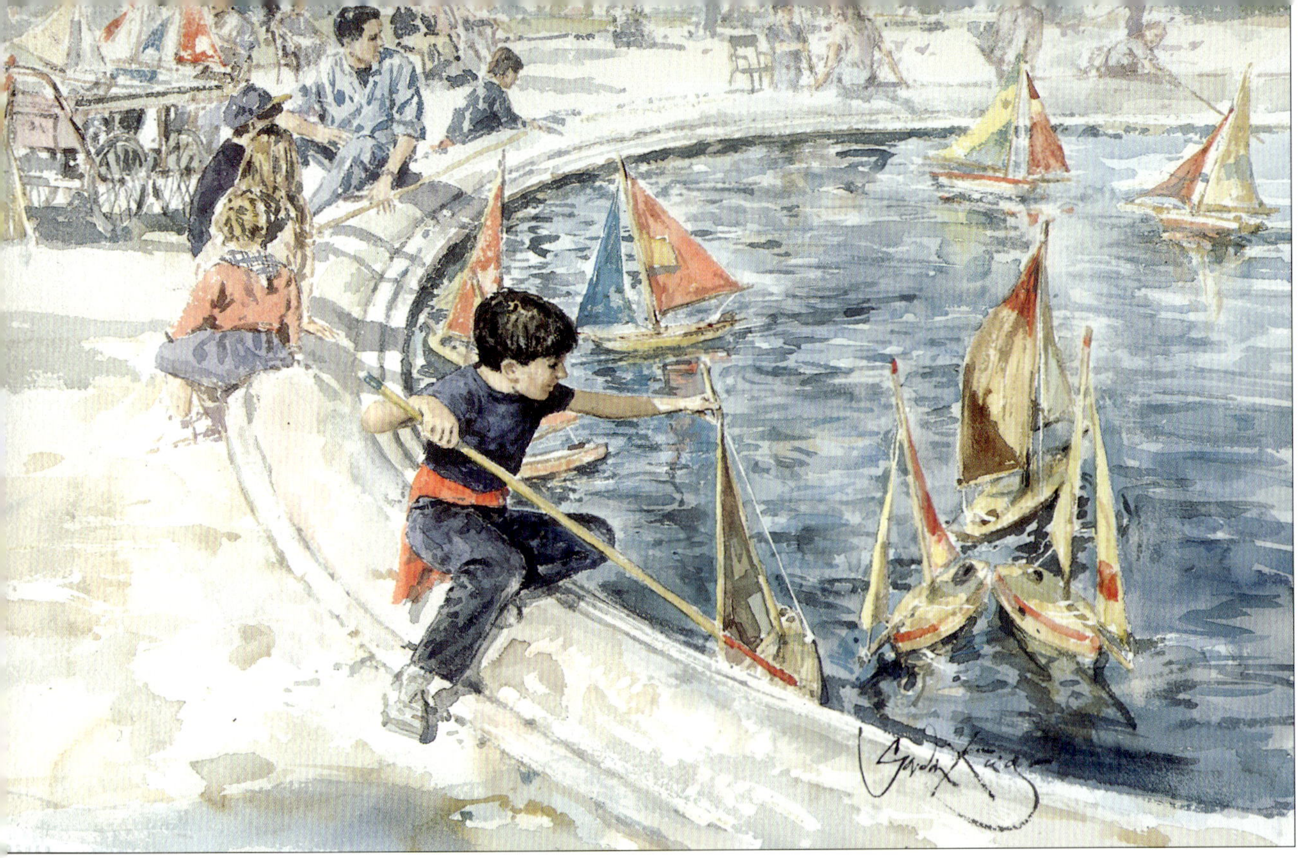

THE BOAT BOY

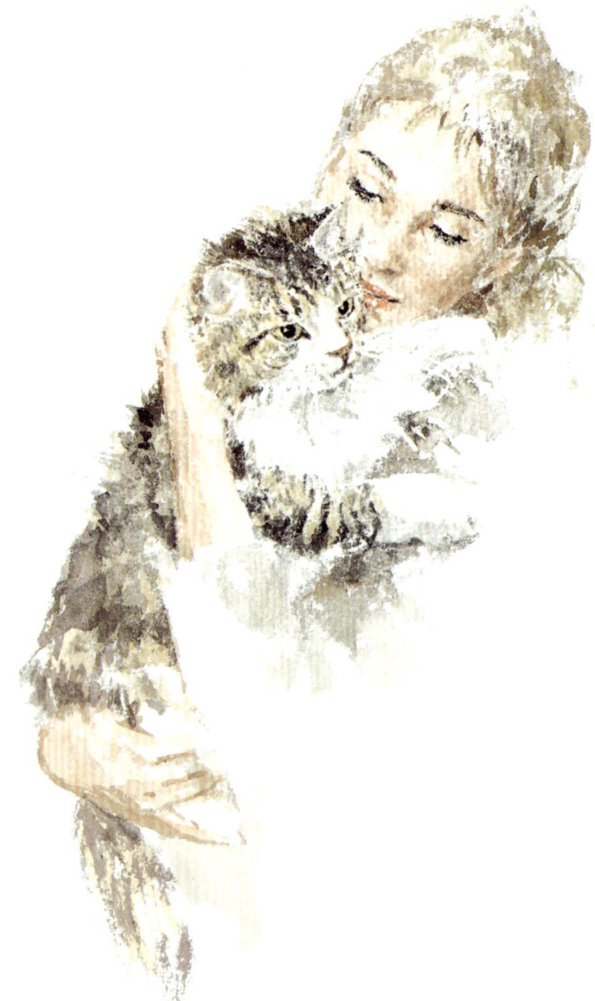

SWINGING SMILES

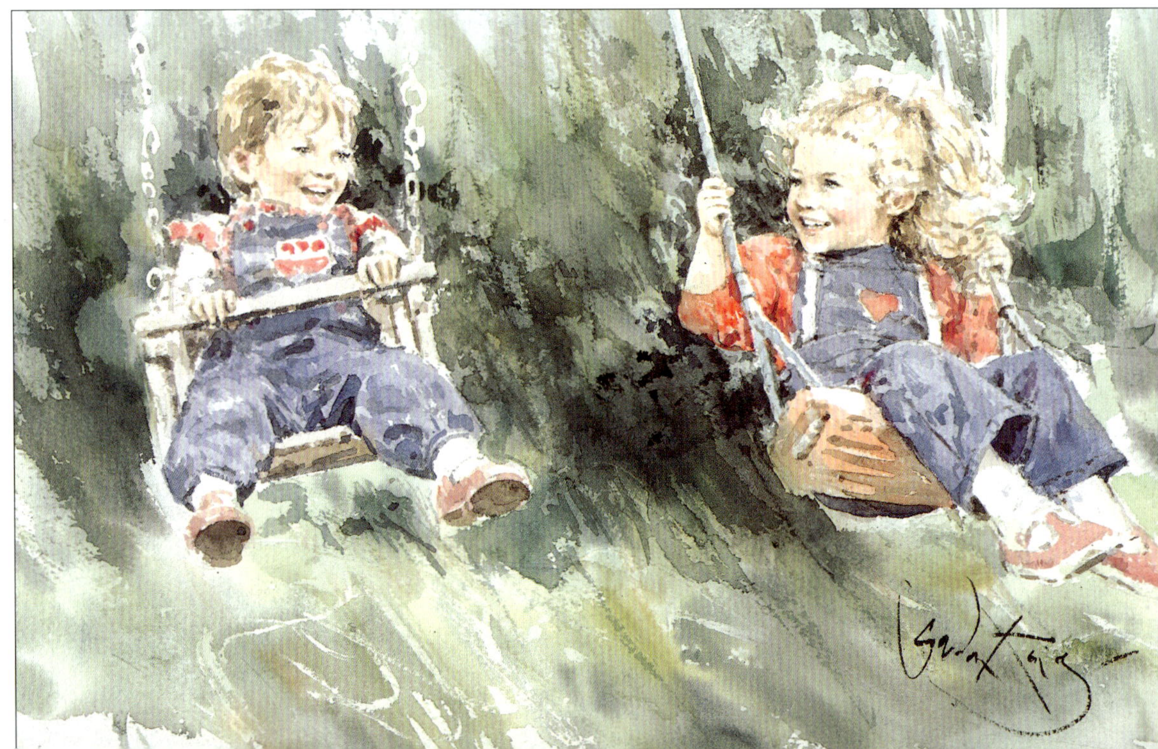

These delightfully old-fashioned boats added a rather timeless quality to this scene in the Jardin des Tuileries in Paris.

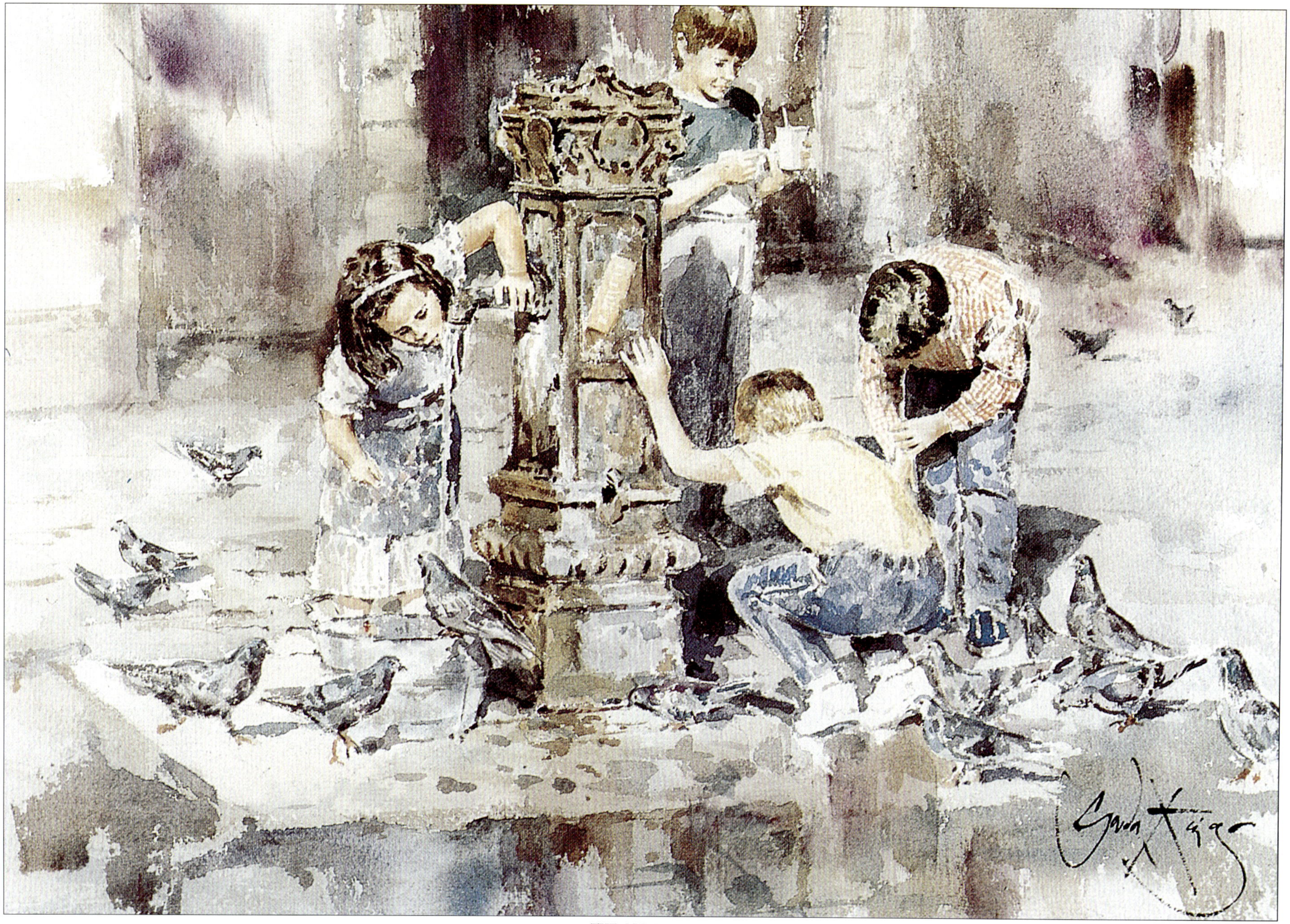

THE OLD PUMP

I found these children having a welcome drink amongst the pigeons close to St. Mark's Square in Venice
– a subject I just had to paint.

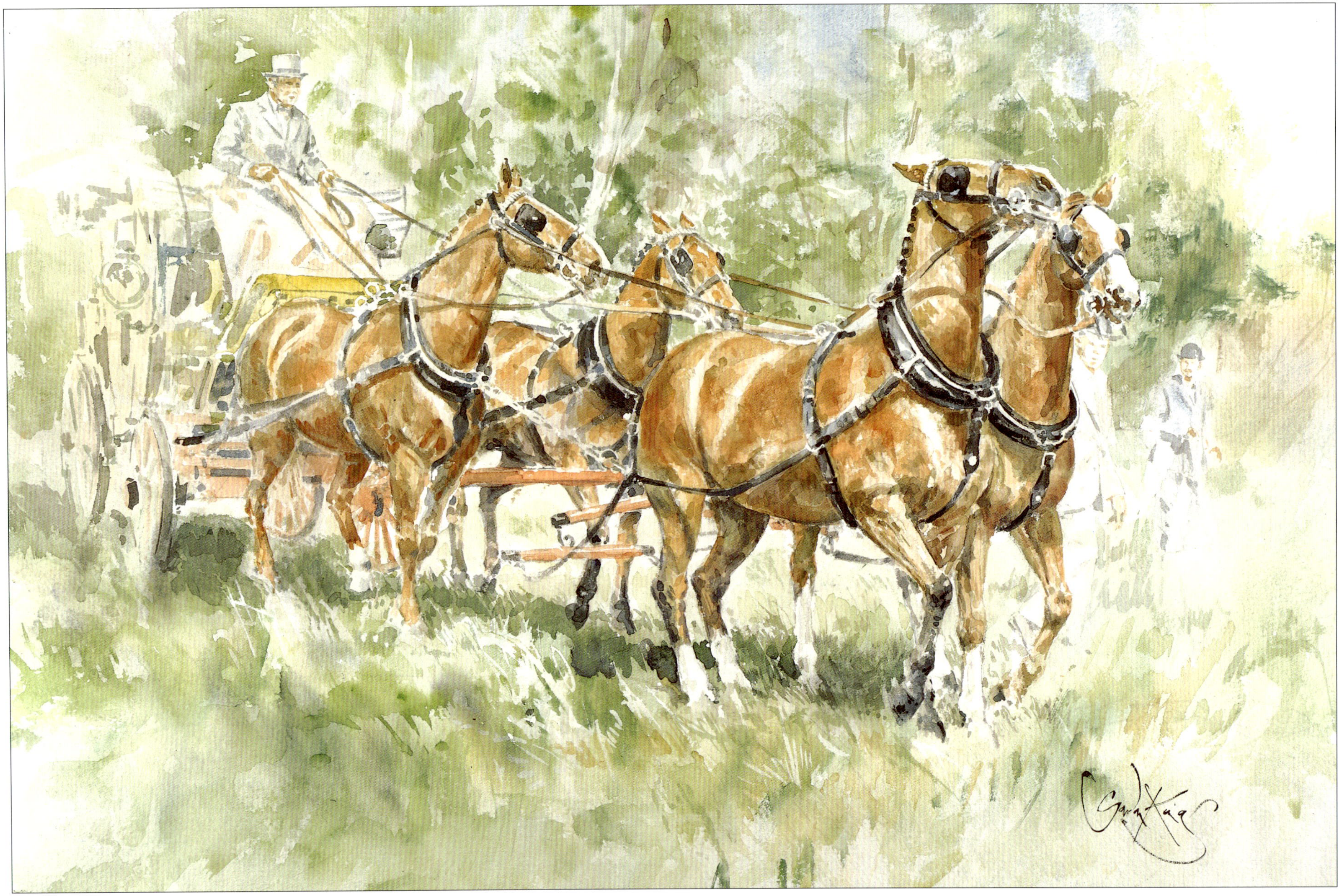

FOUR IN HAND

I've always been fascinated by horses in harness and the degree of control exerted by the driver. It's a dying skill which I'm glad to see still thriving in the sport.

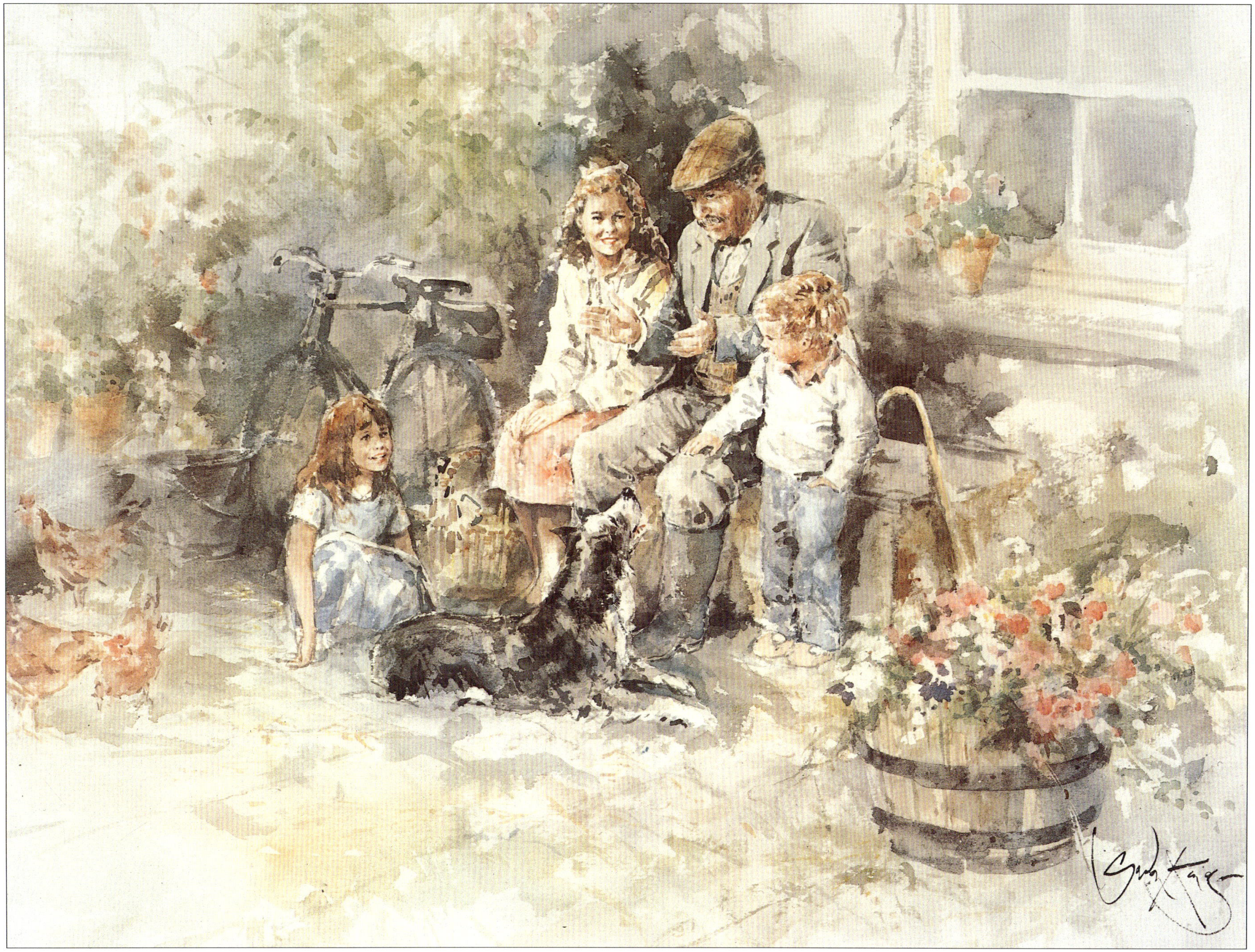

GRANDFATHER'S TALES

This was specially done for my Belfast exhibition and reproduced as a Limited Edition print to coincide with the launch of the show.

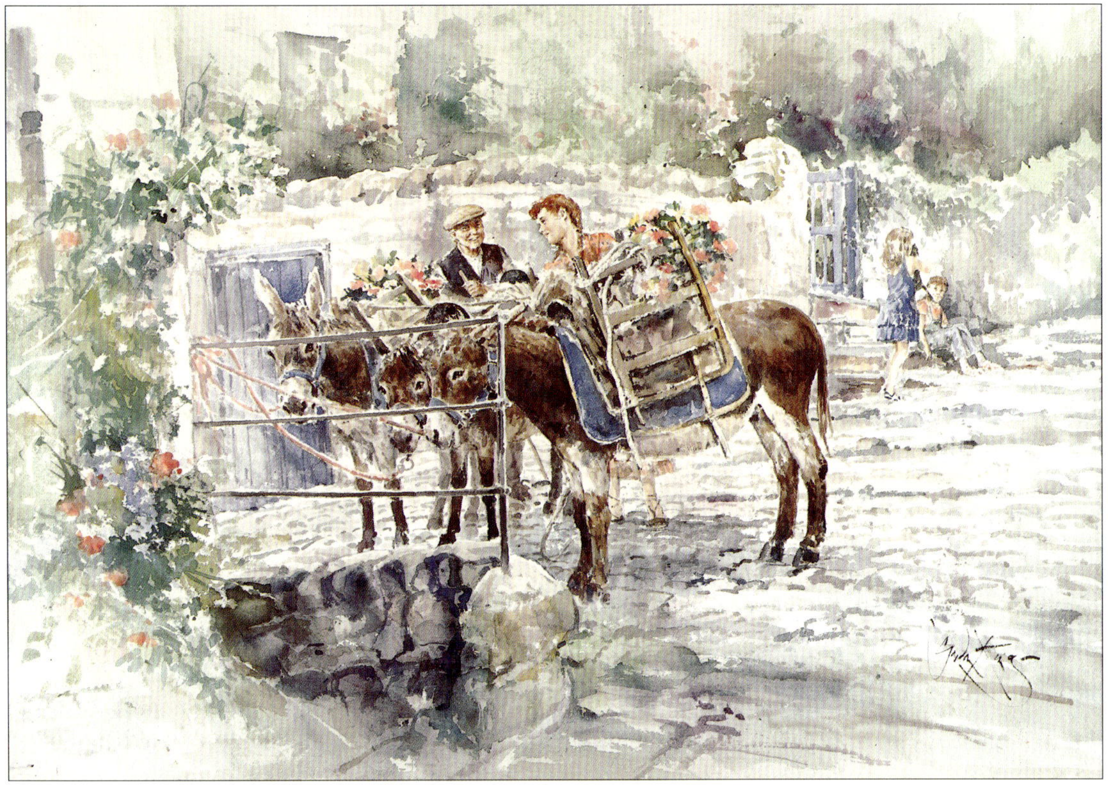

CLOVELLY DONKEYS

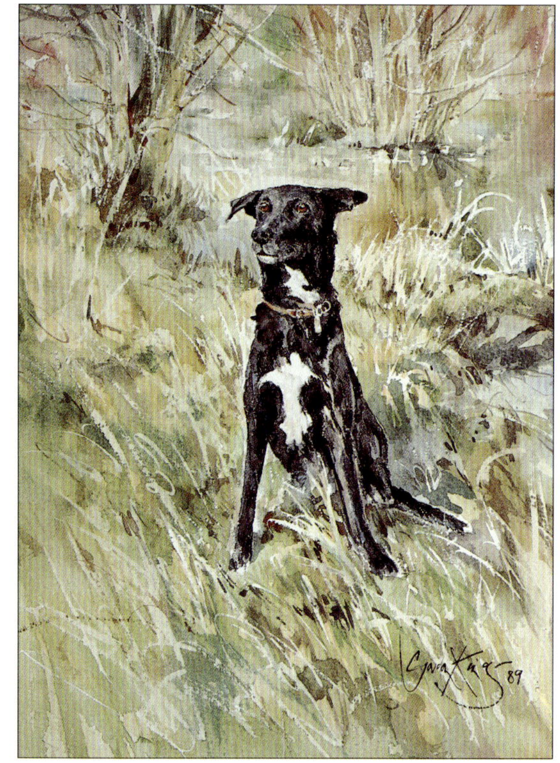

FLASH

The donkeys are the main form of transport up and down the steep cobbles of Clovelly and these three seemed to peer expectantly at me whilst they were being loaded.

Flash was the first dog I really got to know who used to rush up to me on arrival at the Tennis Club. Nothing can beat that kind of wonderful welcome.

In 'Shades of Red' Deborah and her lovely red setter posed for me in her garden.

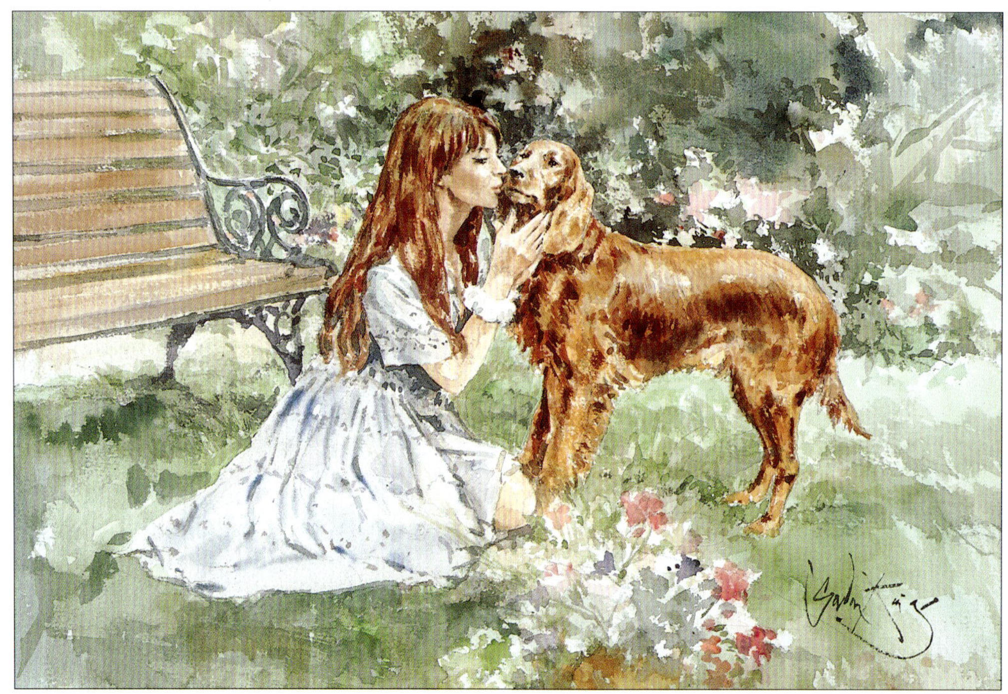

SHADES OF RED

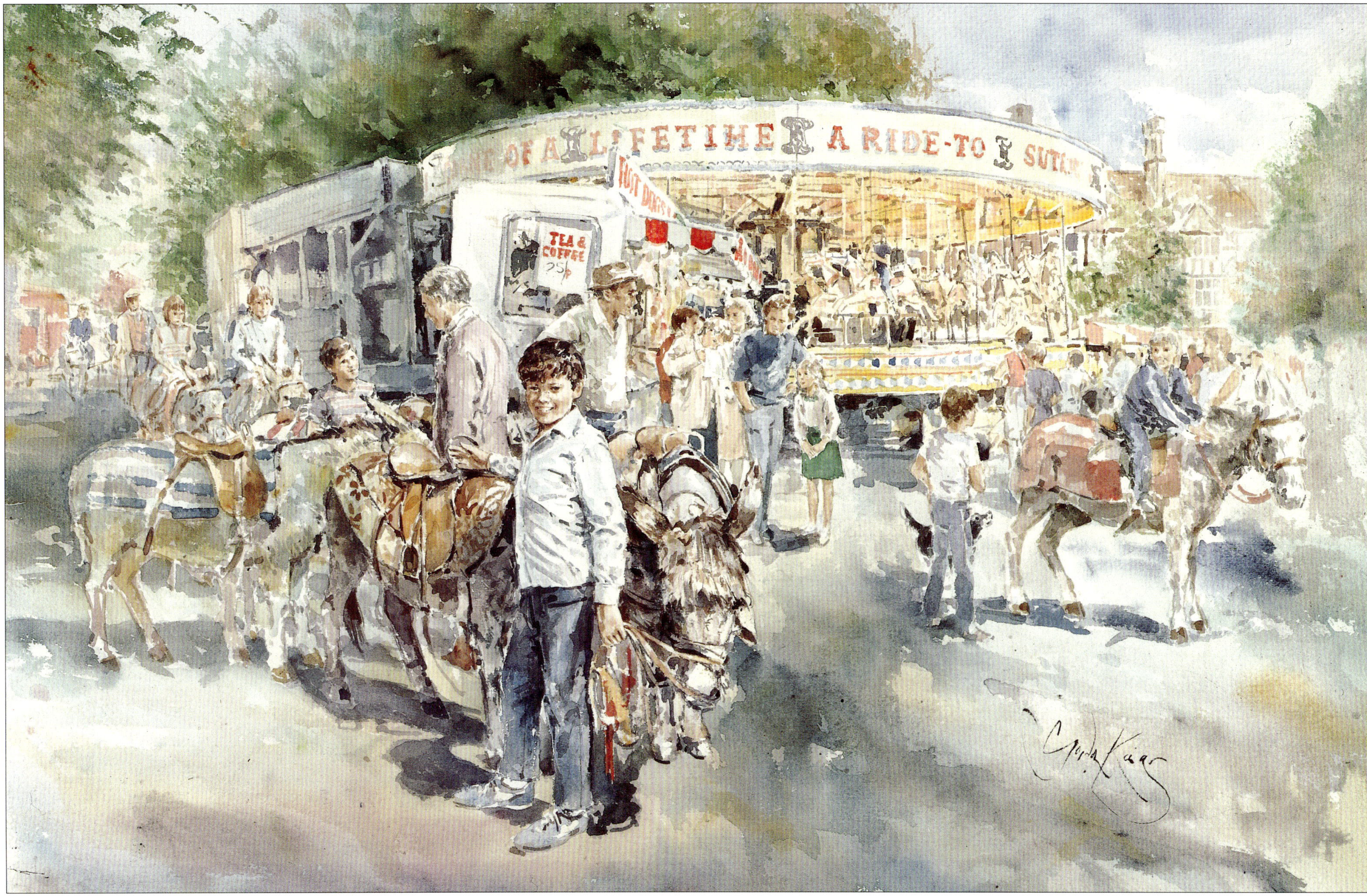

CAROUSEL

All the fun of Pinner Fair and ever popular donkey rides.

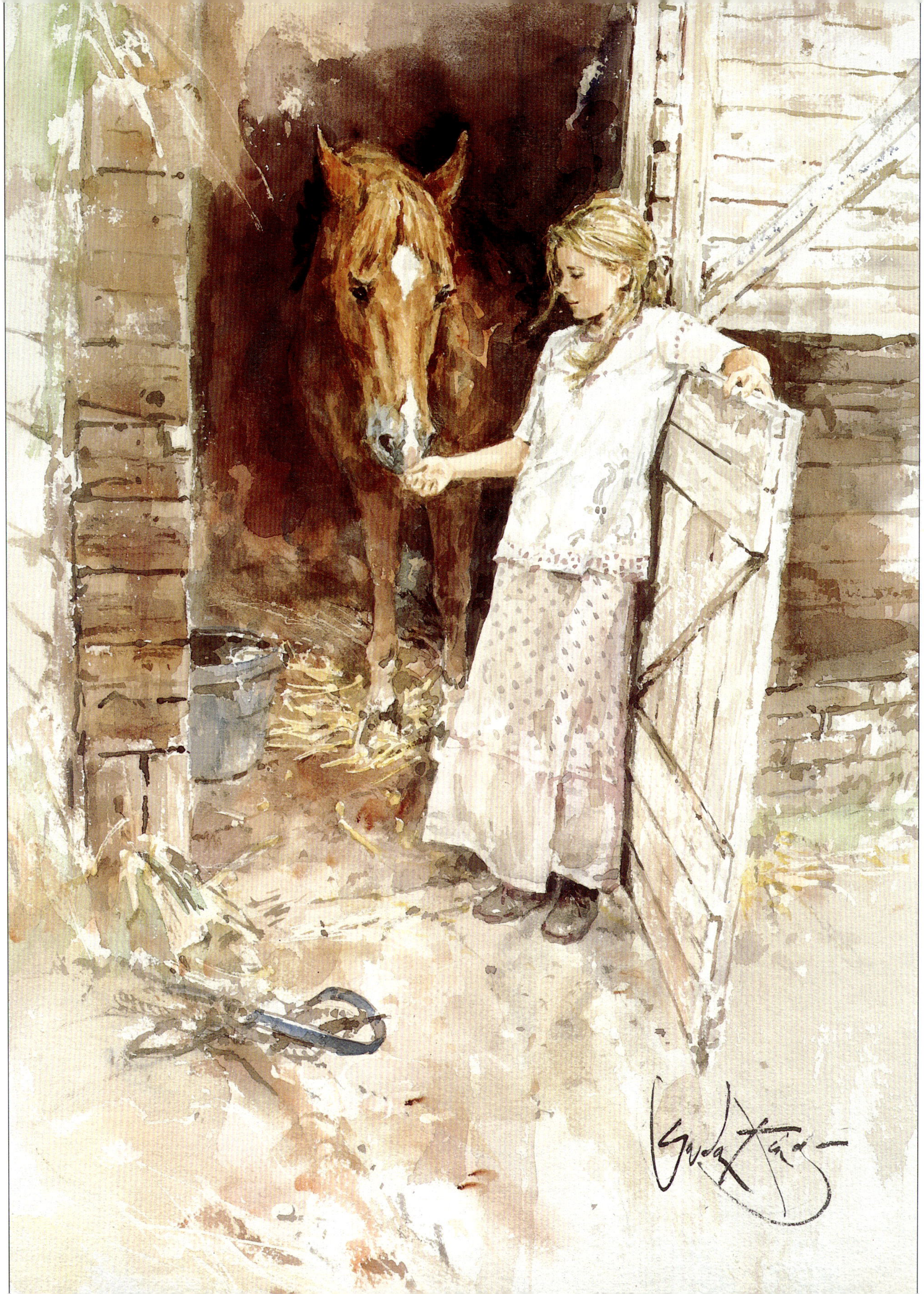

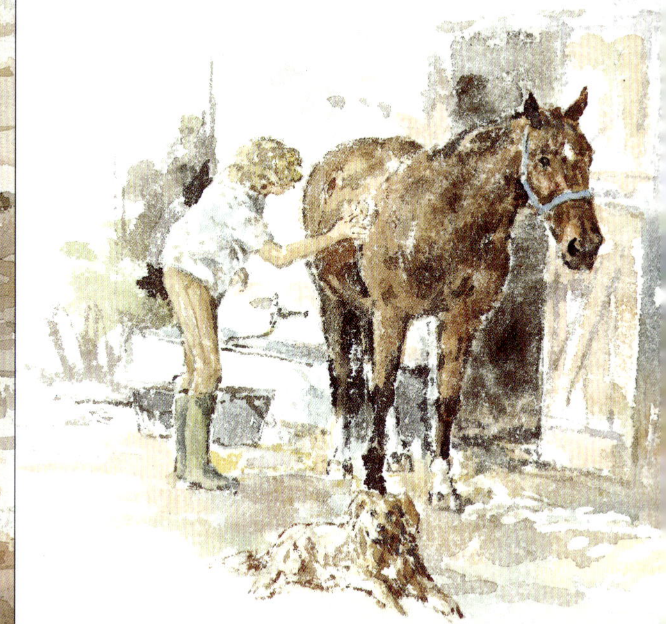

I spent a day at these stables
with Tania and her pony.
They seemed totally at one
with each other. The
dramatic effects of light and
shade through the rafters
inside the stable were quite
stunning.

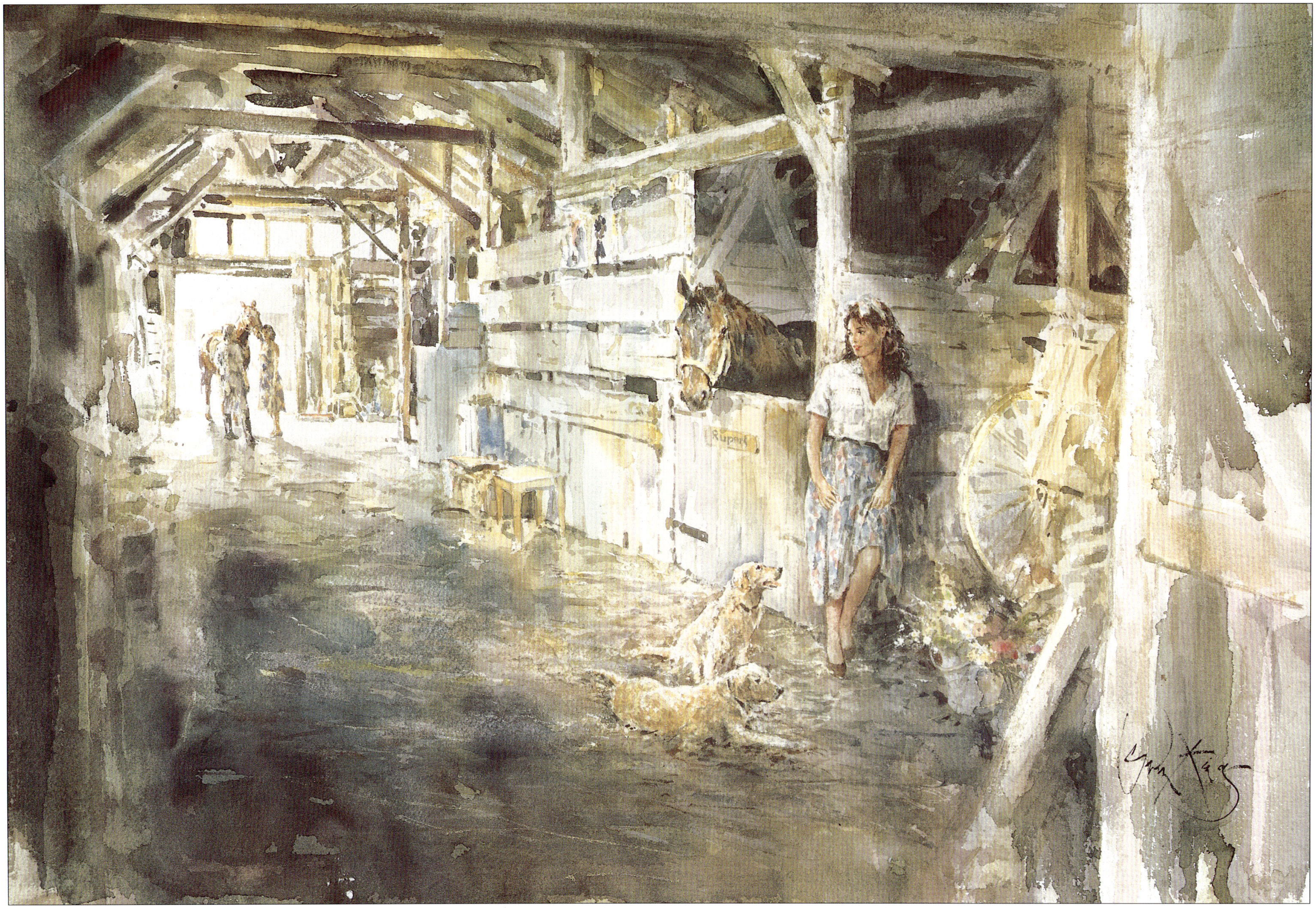

STABLE ENCOUNTER

Gallery 4

Painting to me is all about shape and movement combining together to portray a feeling of life. It seems only natural, therefore, that Music & Dance should be an inspirational subject for me.

Dancers, especially in the case of ballet, are trained to make pleasing shapes with their bodies telling a story in unison with the music. Some artists have found in it the complete subject and never look to anything else.

As with the dancers, musicians, whatever their instrument, also create a composition of interest just in the way they play, the position they adopt and the emotion they portray.

The challenge is to conjure up that additional dimension, to let you actually hear the music in the painting created by that particular shape and movement.

It's a subject I'll go back to again and again.

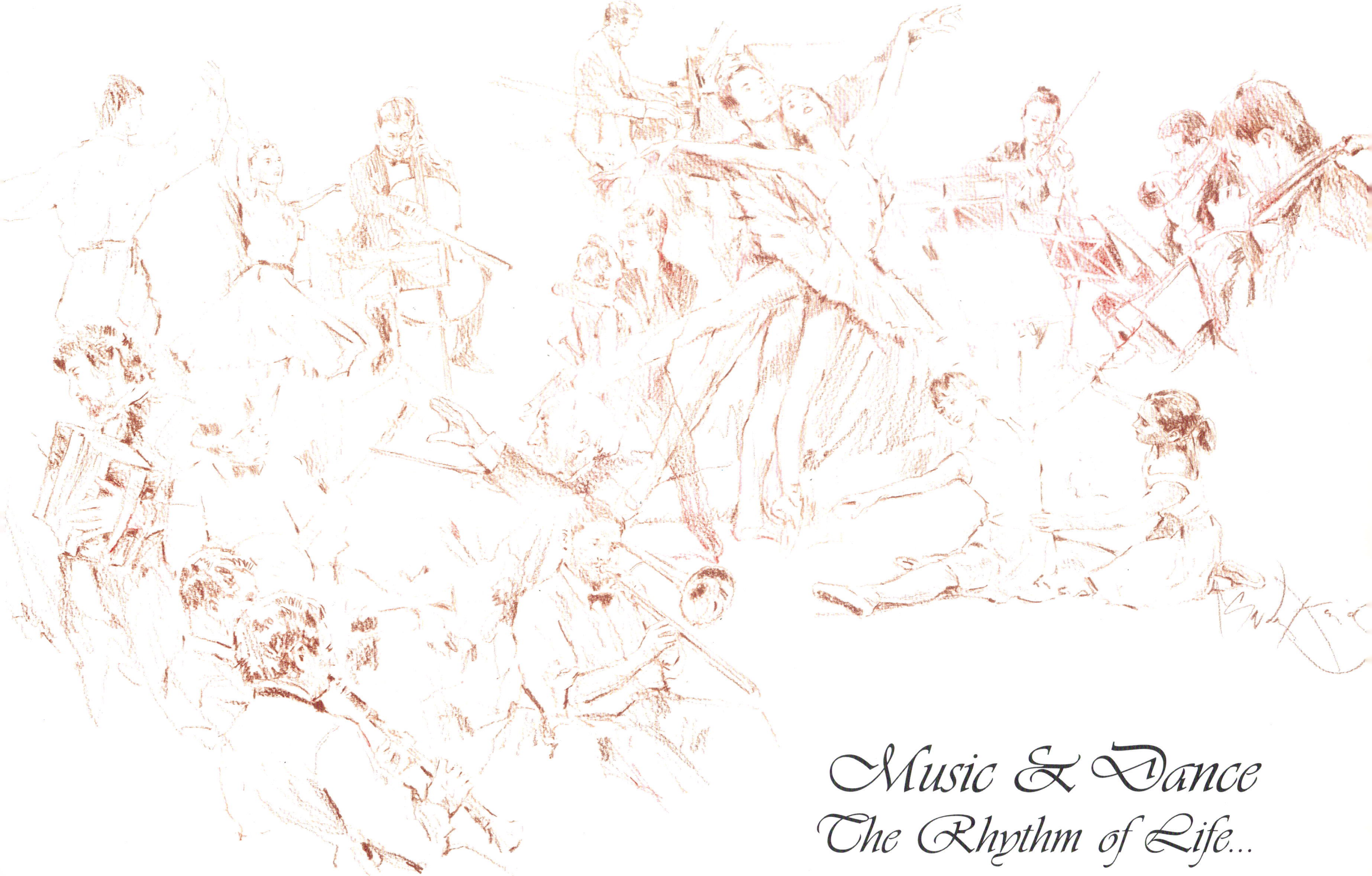

Music & Dance
The Rhythm of Life...

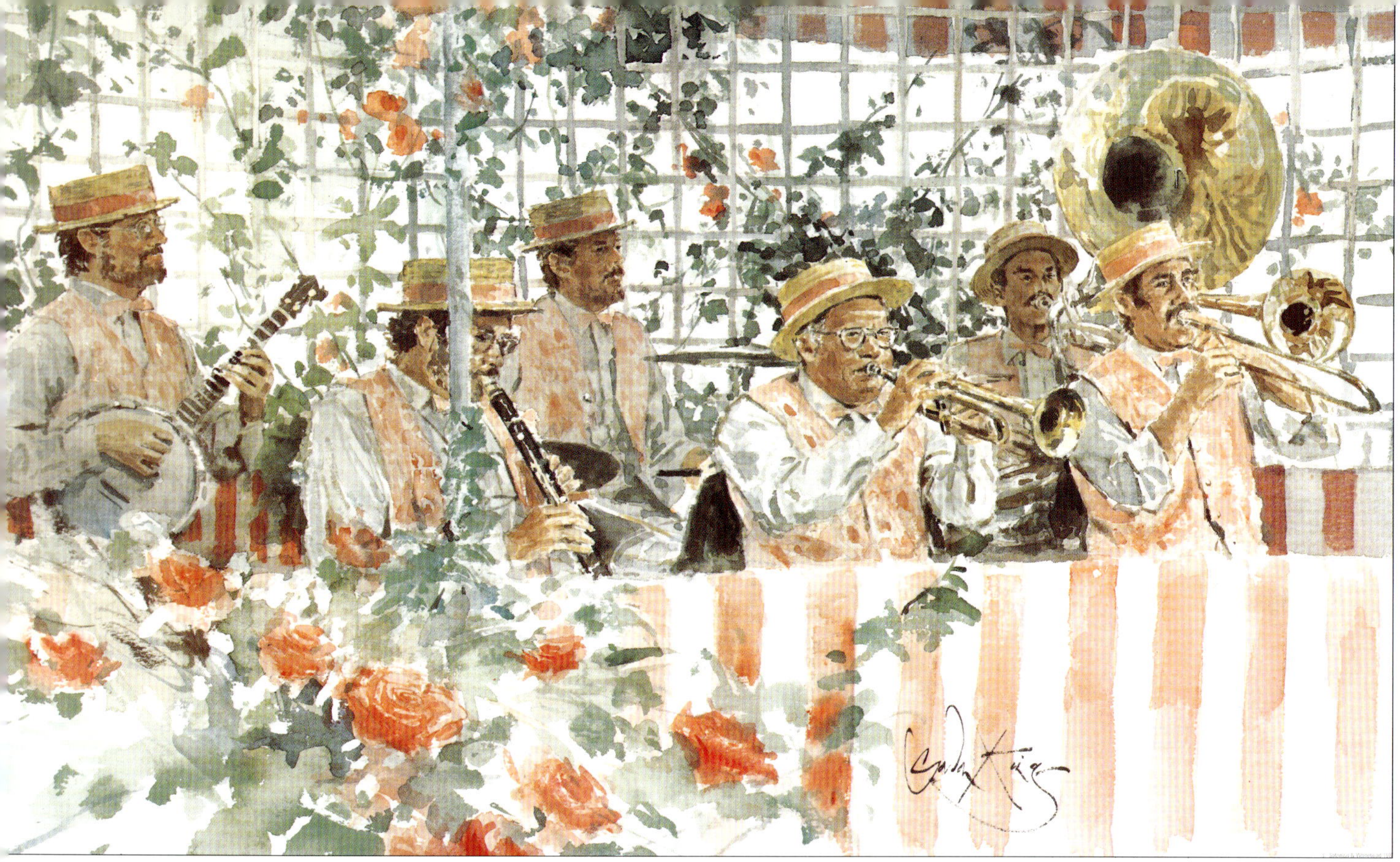

MY ROSALEE

This is a subject dear to my heart. Ever since I first heard jazz as a teenager I have enjoyed its particular sound, especially the traditional rendering. With the jazz bands featured here, hopefully I have captured something of the excitement and sheer enjoyment of their performance.

By kind permission of Solomon & Whitehead (Guild Prints) Limited

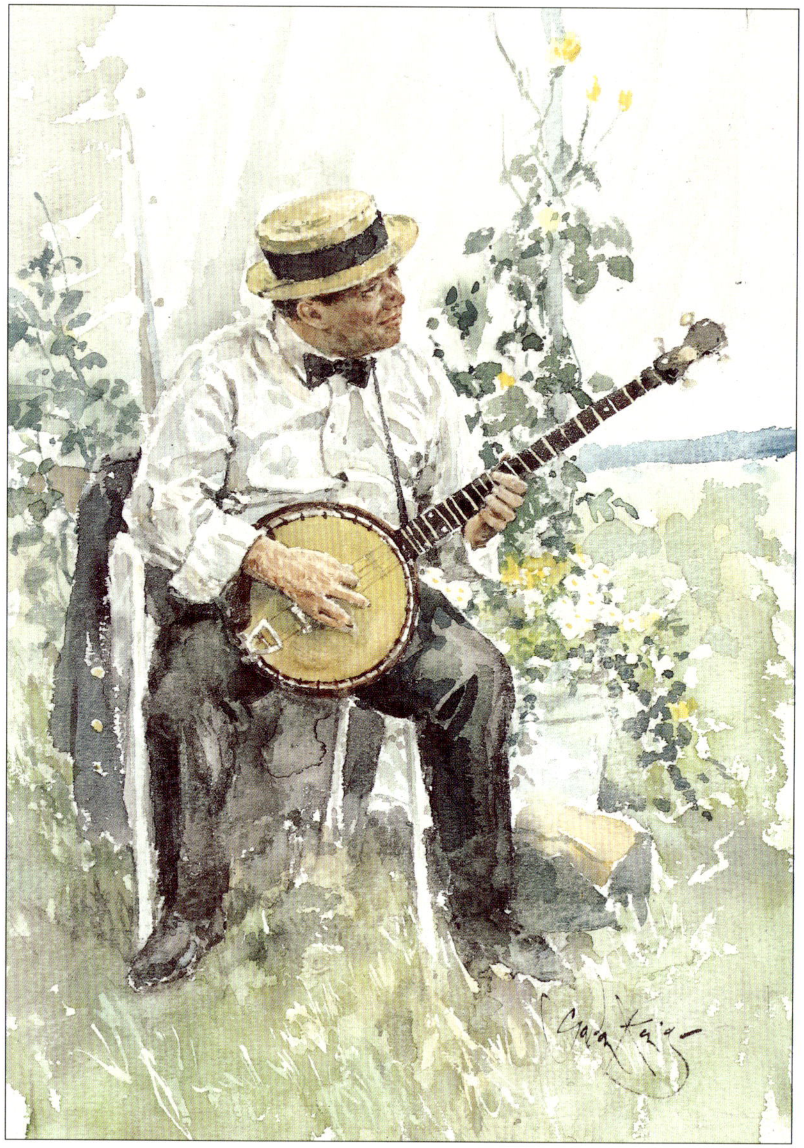

TUNING UP

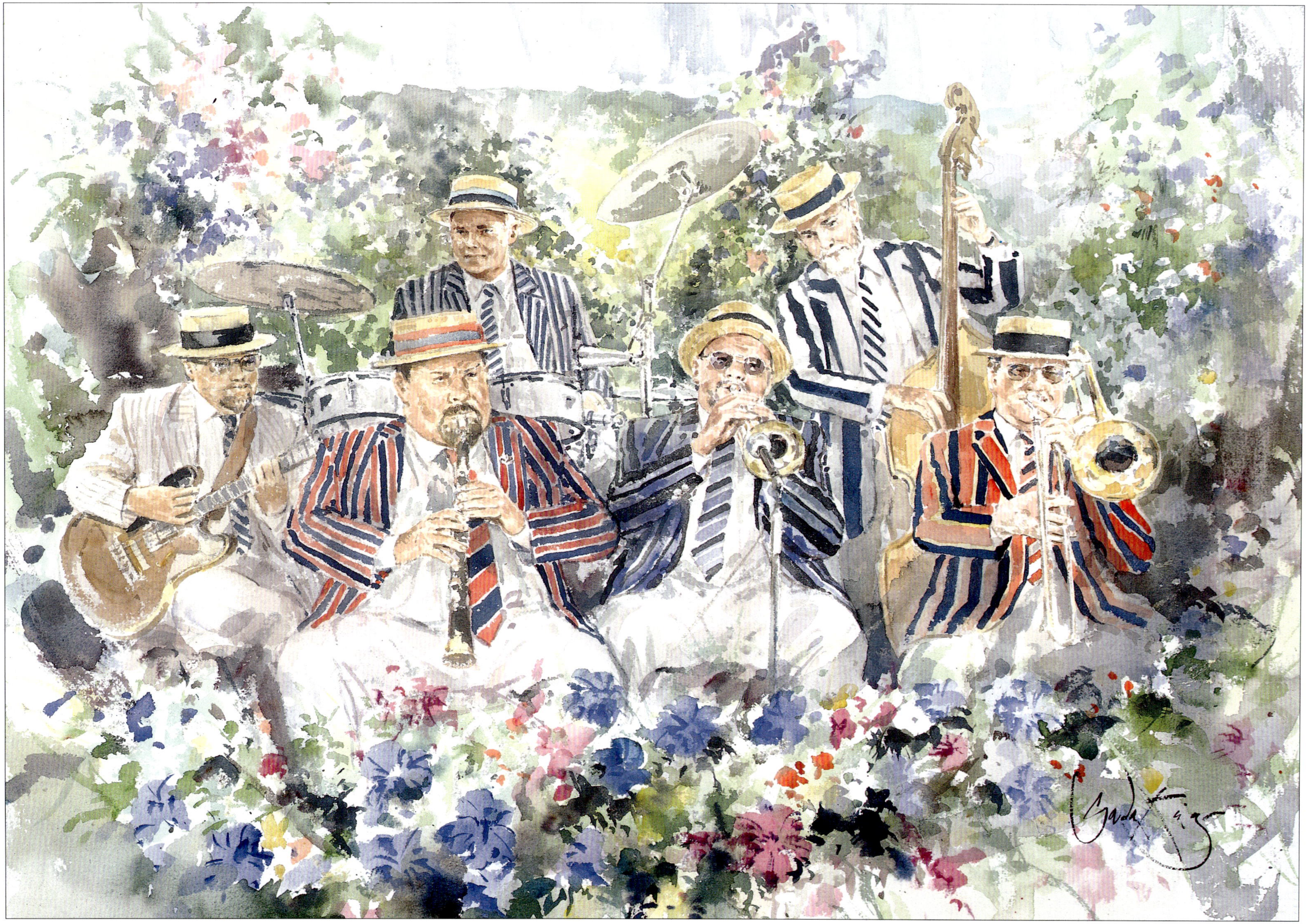

SUMMERTIME BLUES

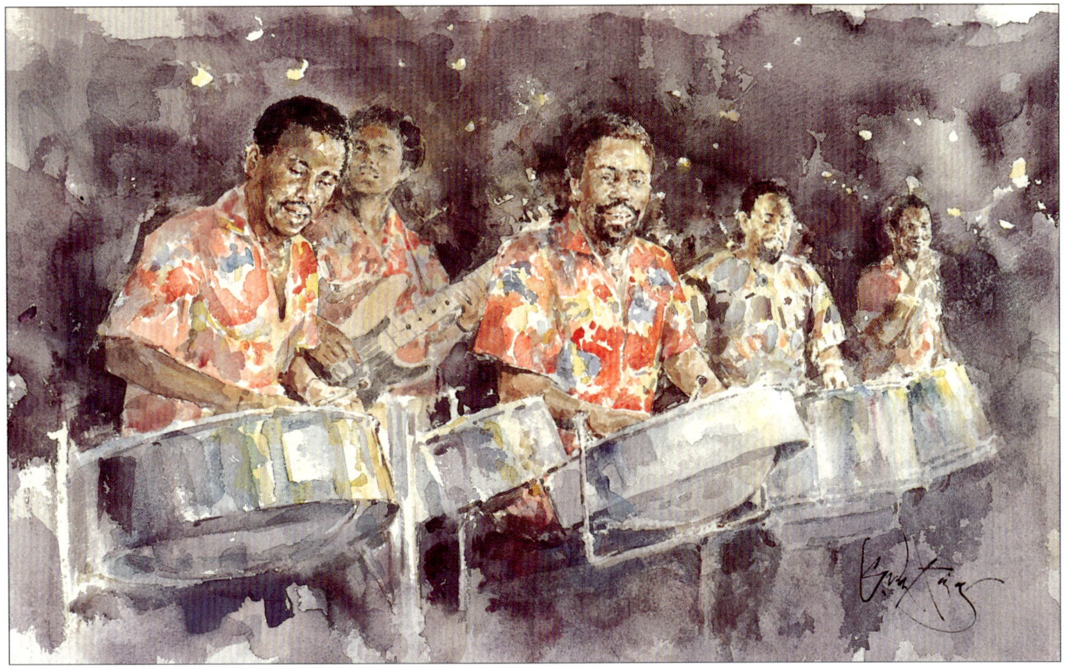

BAND OF STEEL

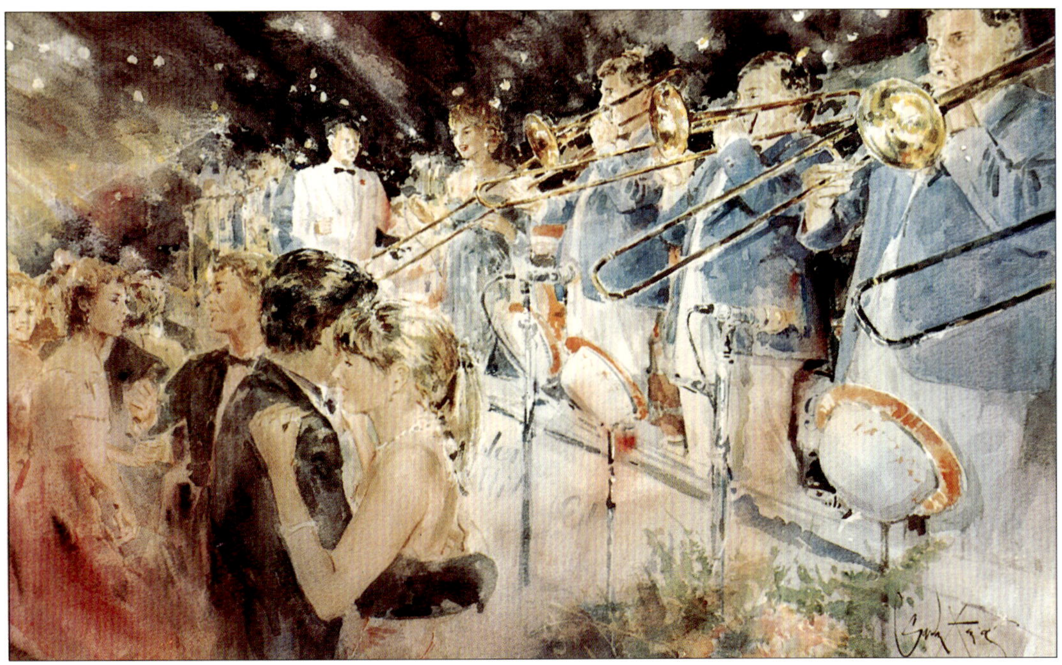

SOUND OF SWING

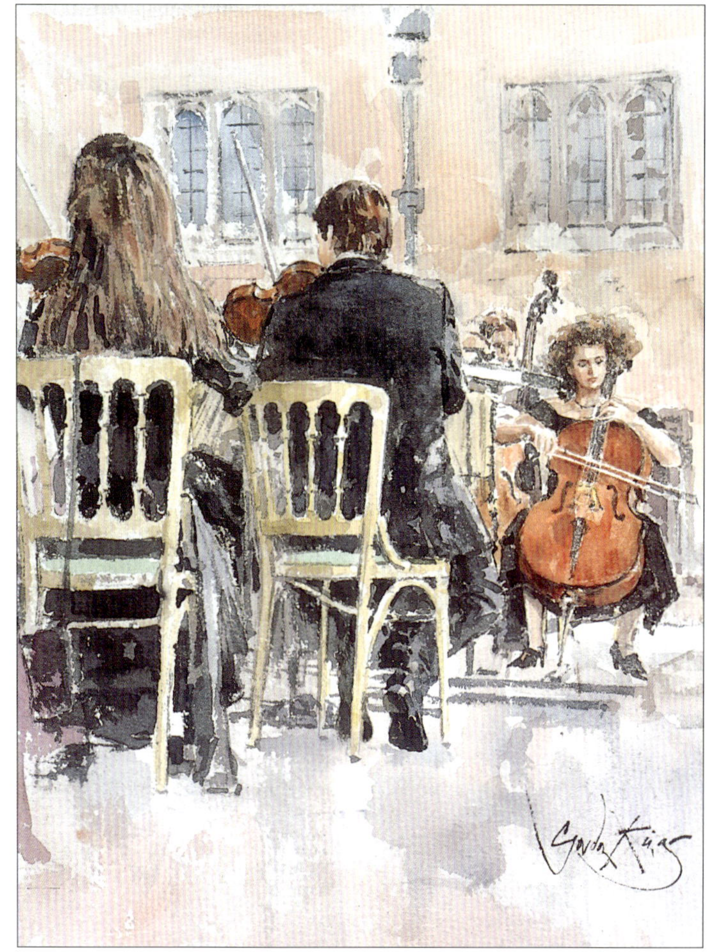

MUSIC AT HAMPTON COURT

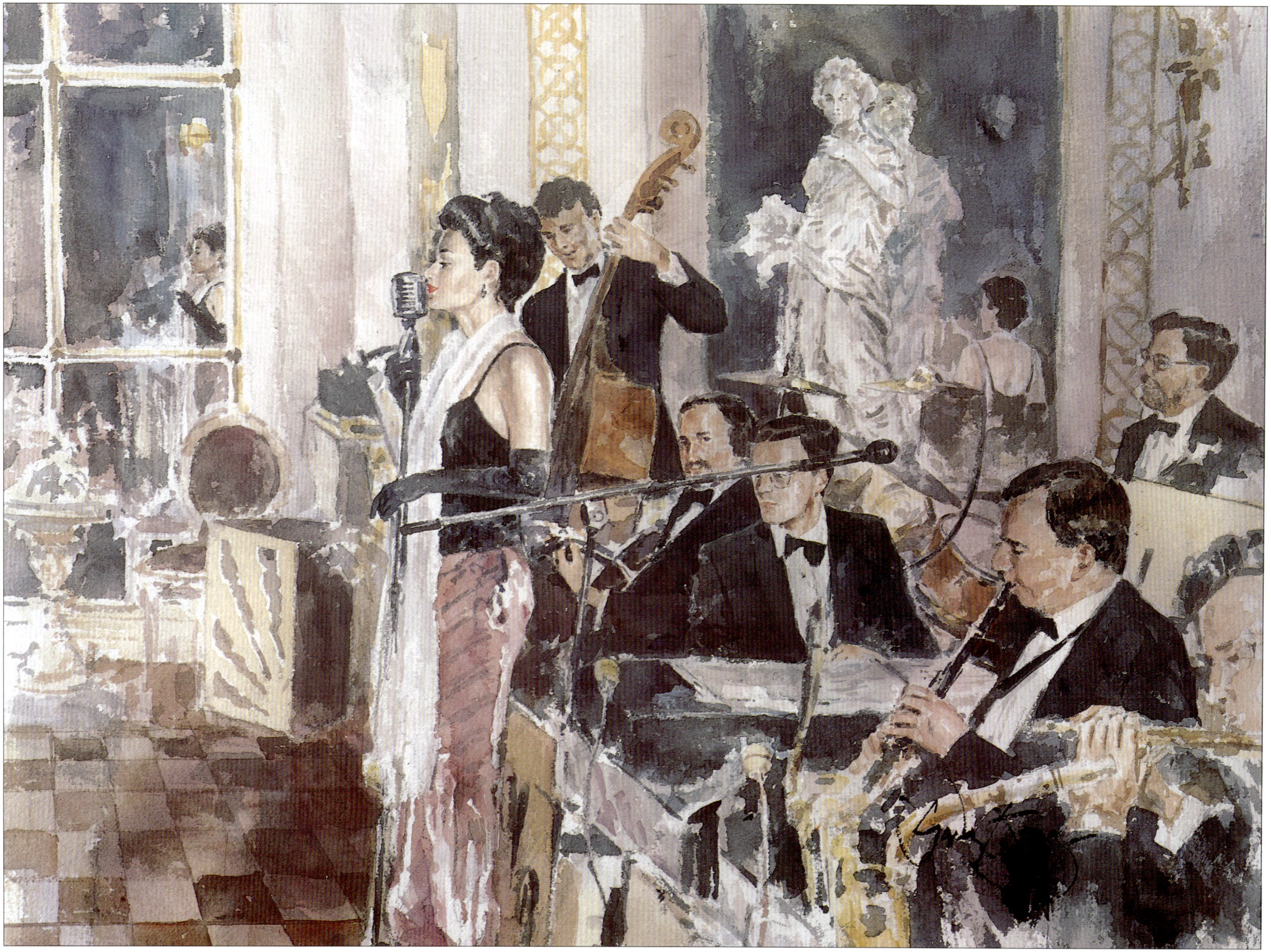

EVENING AT THE RITZ

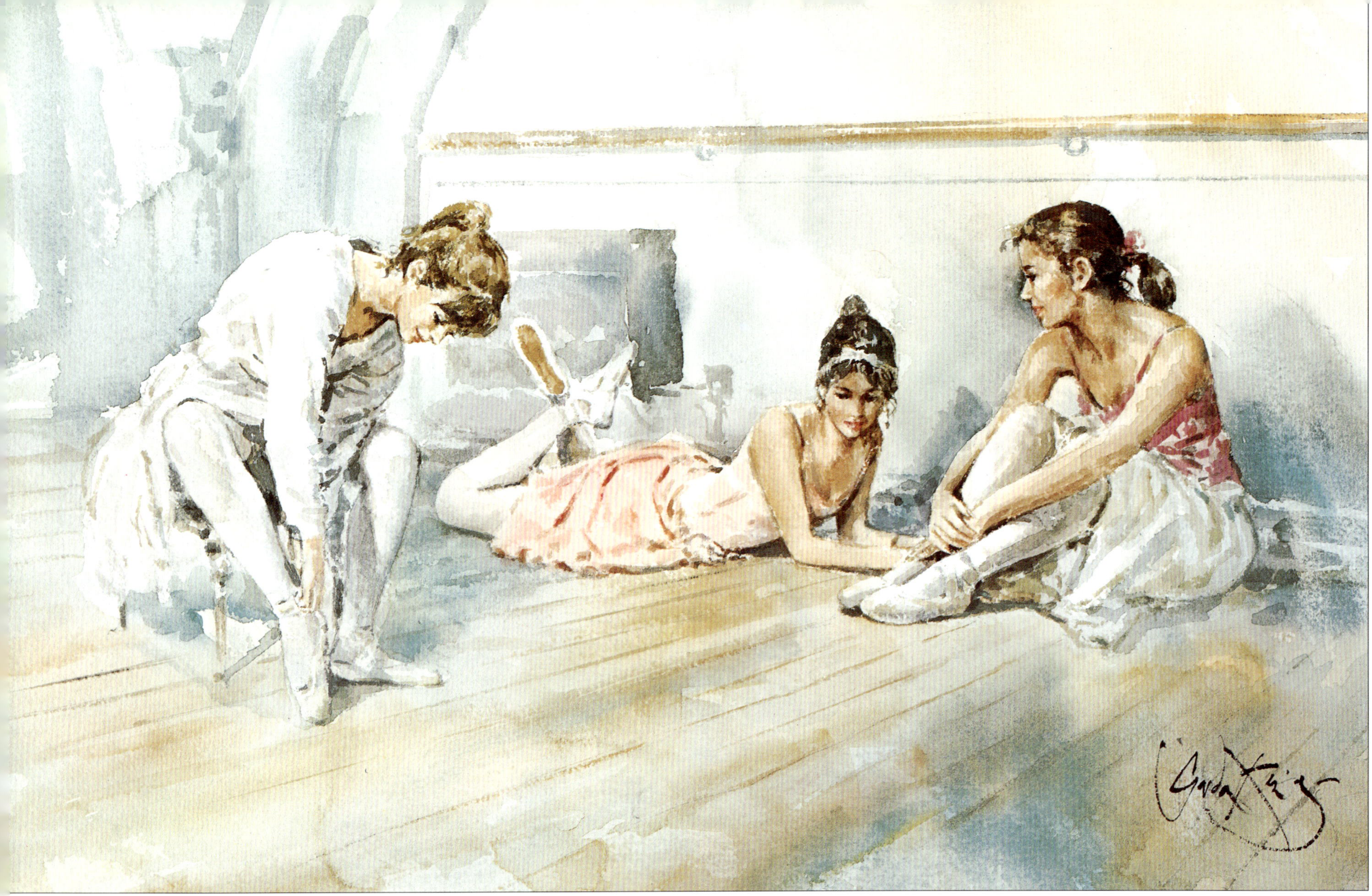

BETWEEN REHEARSALS

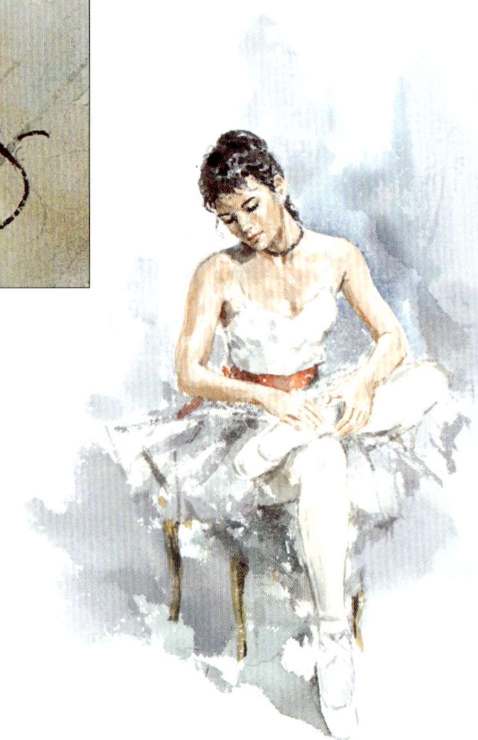

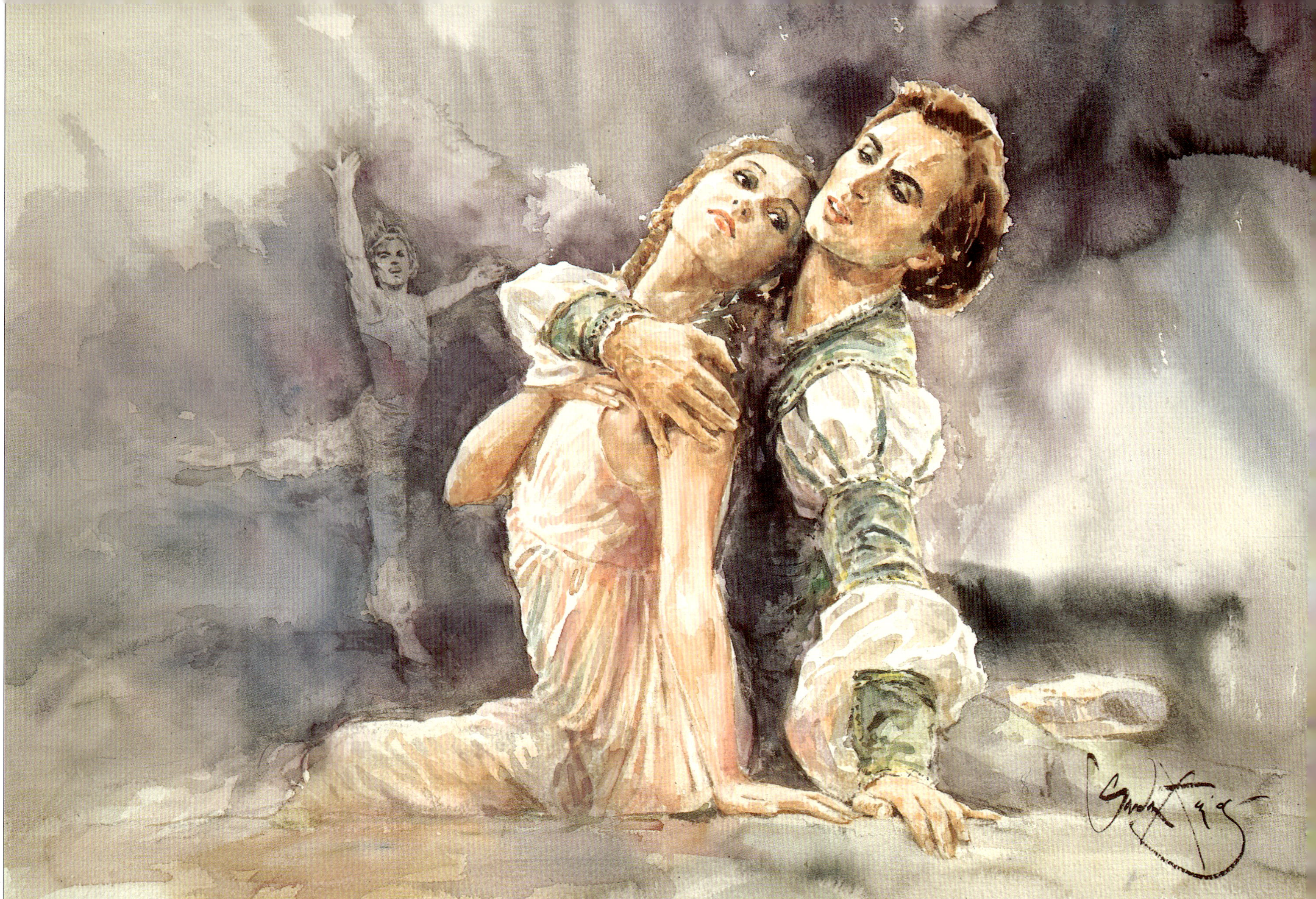

NUREYEV THE LEGEND

Having been captivated by the Bolshoi Ballet at one of their performances at the Royal Albert Hall, I shared the feeling of sorrow that ensued following the death of Rudolf Nureyev, the Bolshoi's most famous son. For such talent to be so sadly extinguished seemed tragic and I found myself painting him just for myself, as a kind of tribute. In the end I did quite a number of sketches and paintings and this one was reproduced as a Limited Edition print.

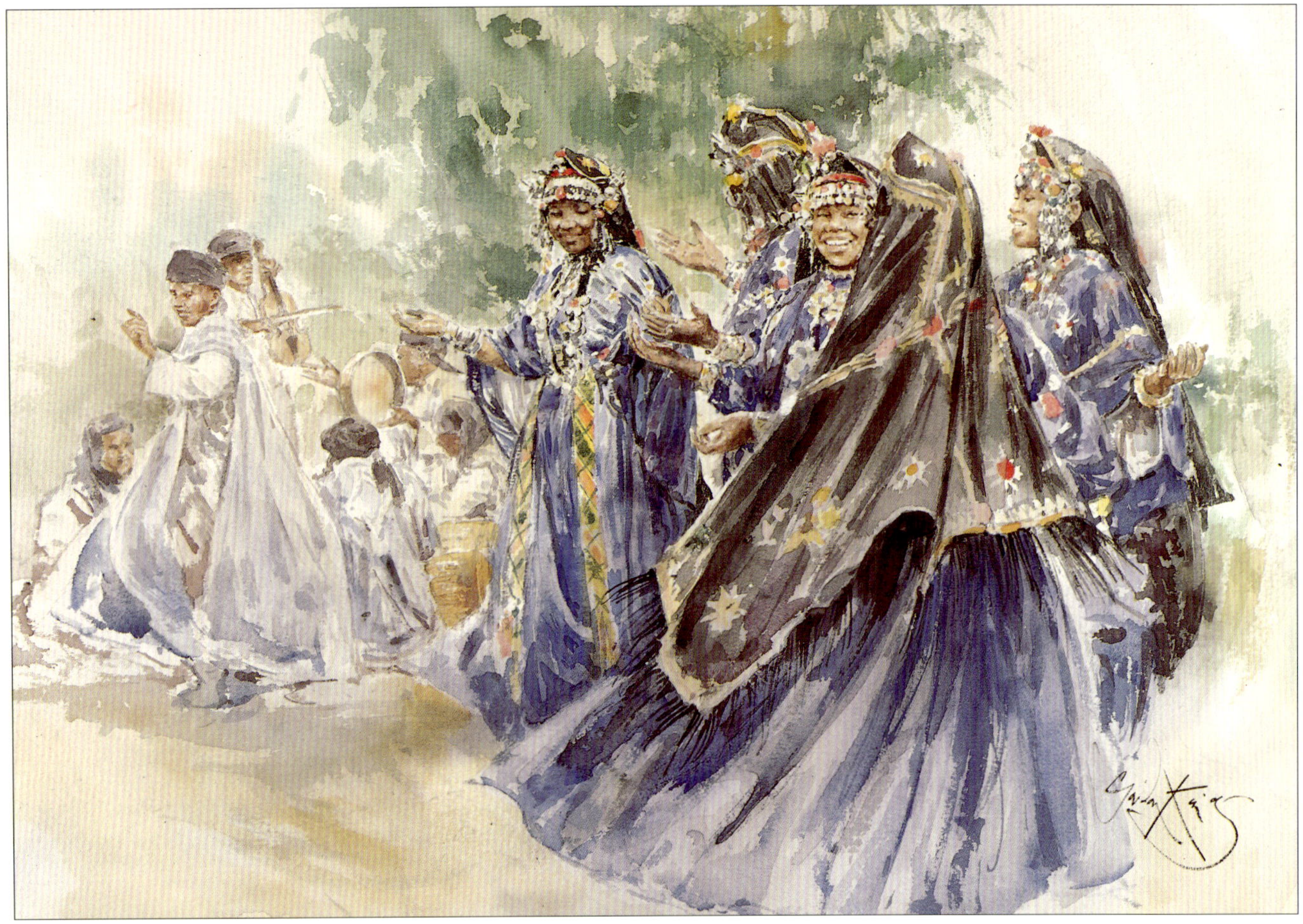

MOROCCAN DANCERS

MASAI SINGERS

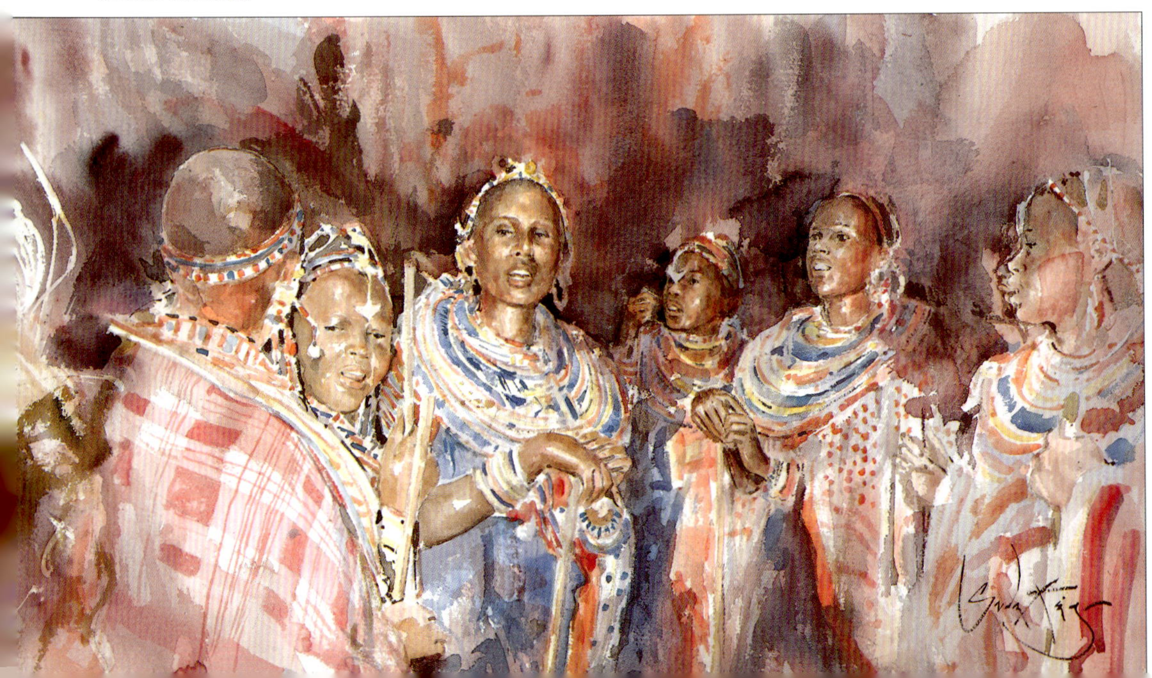

These women were singing and dancing in a local village with their multi-coloured robes and jewellery. I have tried to conjure up the colourful atmosphere as well as the sound of their ritual dance.

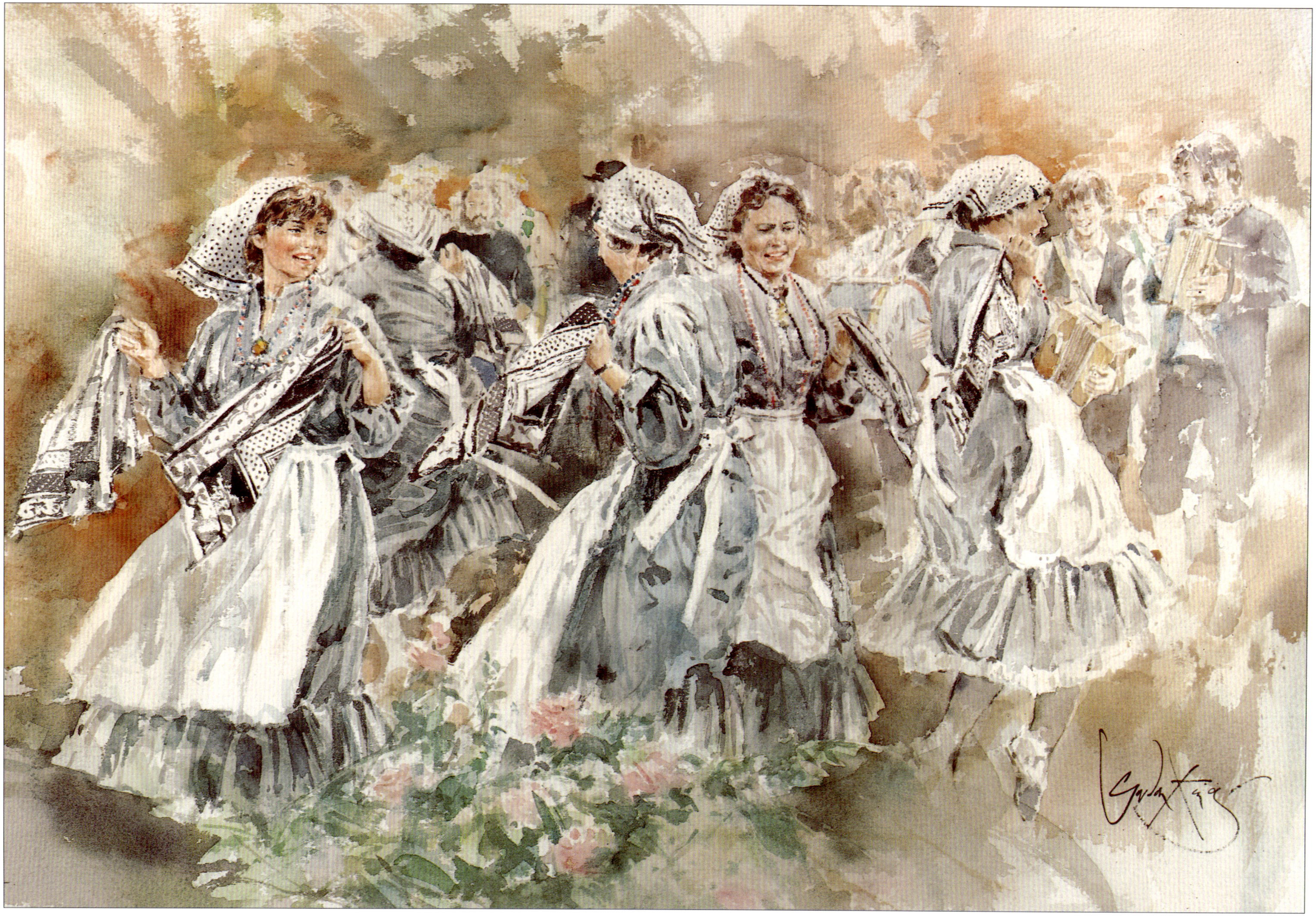

VILLAGE DANCERS

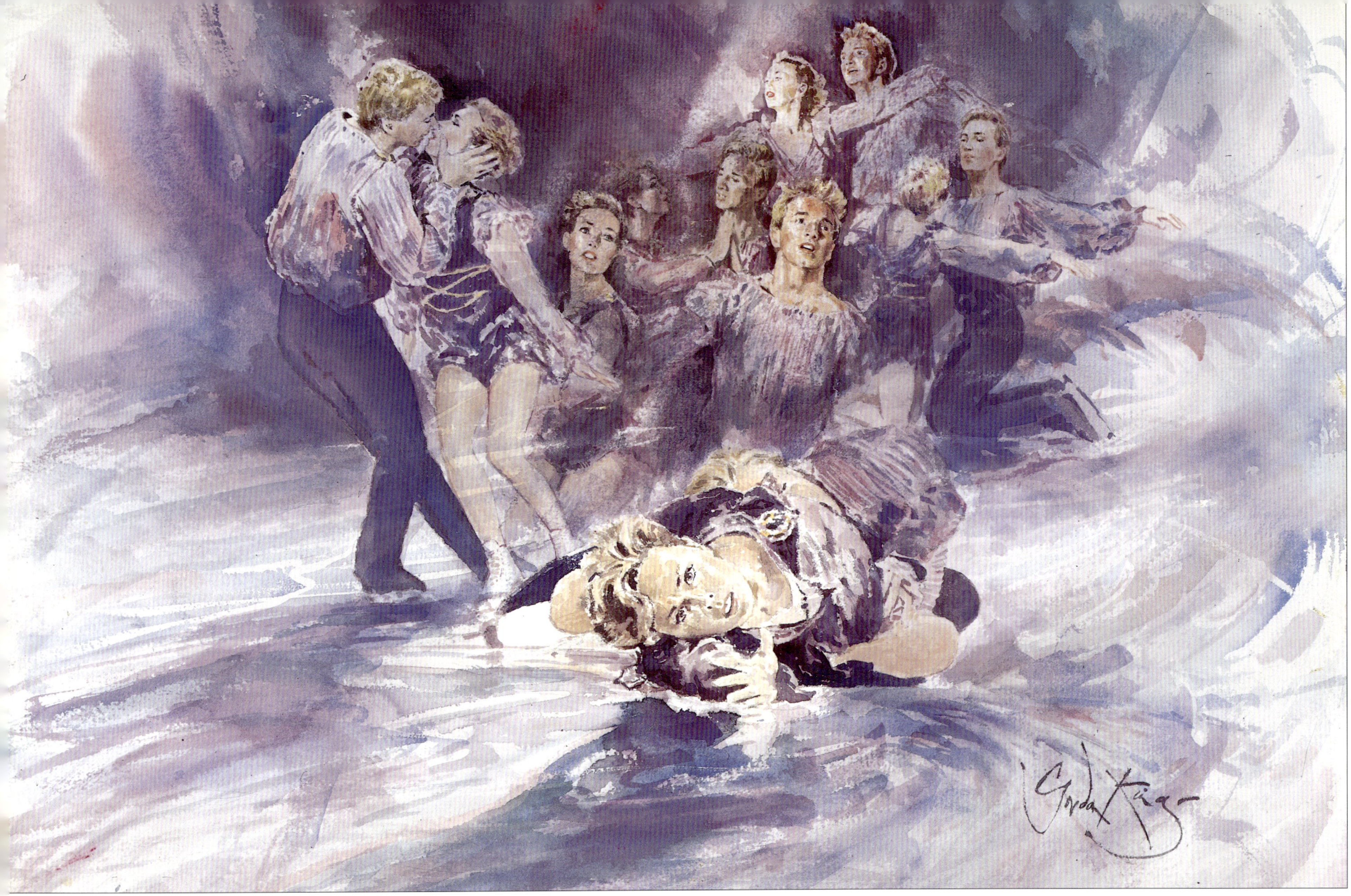

BOLERO

This was dreamland for the British, watching Jayne Torville and Christopher Dean skating with such harmony and excellence, enthralling their audience.

When they came back from the professional ranks to compete at Lillehammer in the '94 Winter Olympics, I was with them on every edge, turn and jump, but it was 10 years before that they reached the heights of perfection in ice dance with 'Bolero' the most captivating and moving of their performances.

It is this that I have tried to capture in these paintings after watching endless videos of their performances and also having a ringside seat at Wembley during their World Tour.

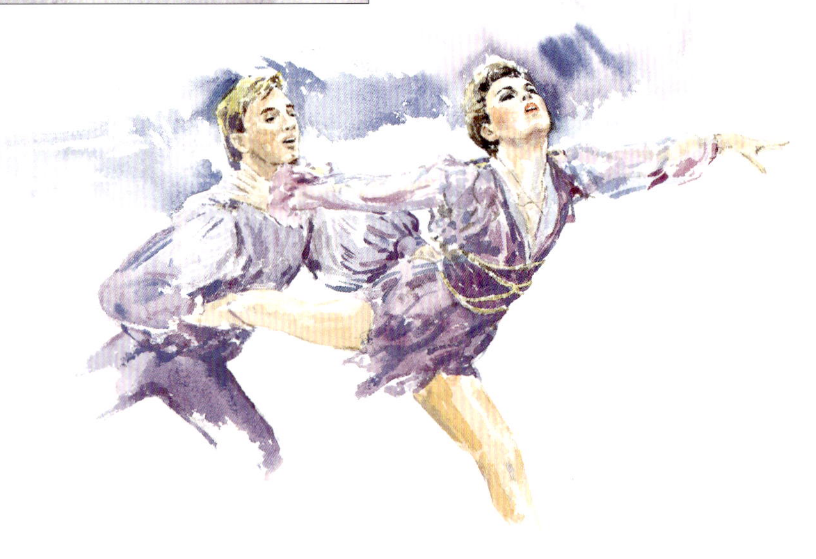

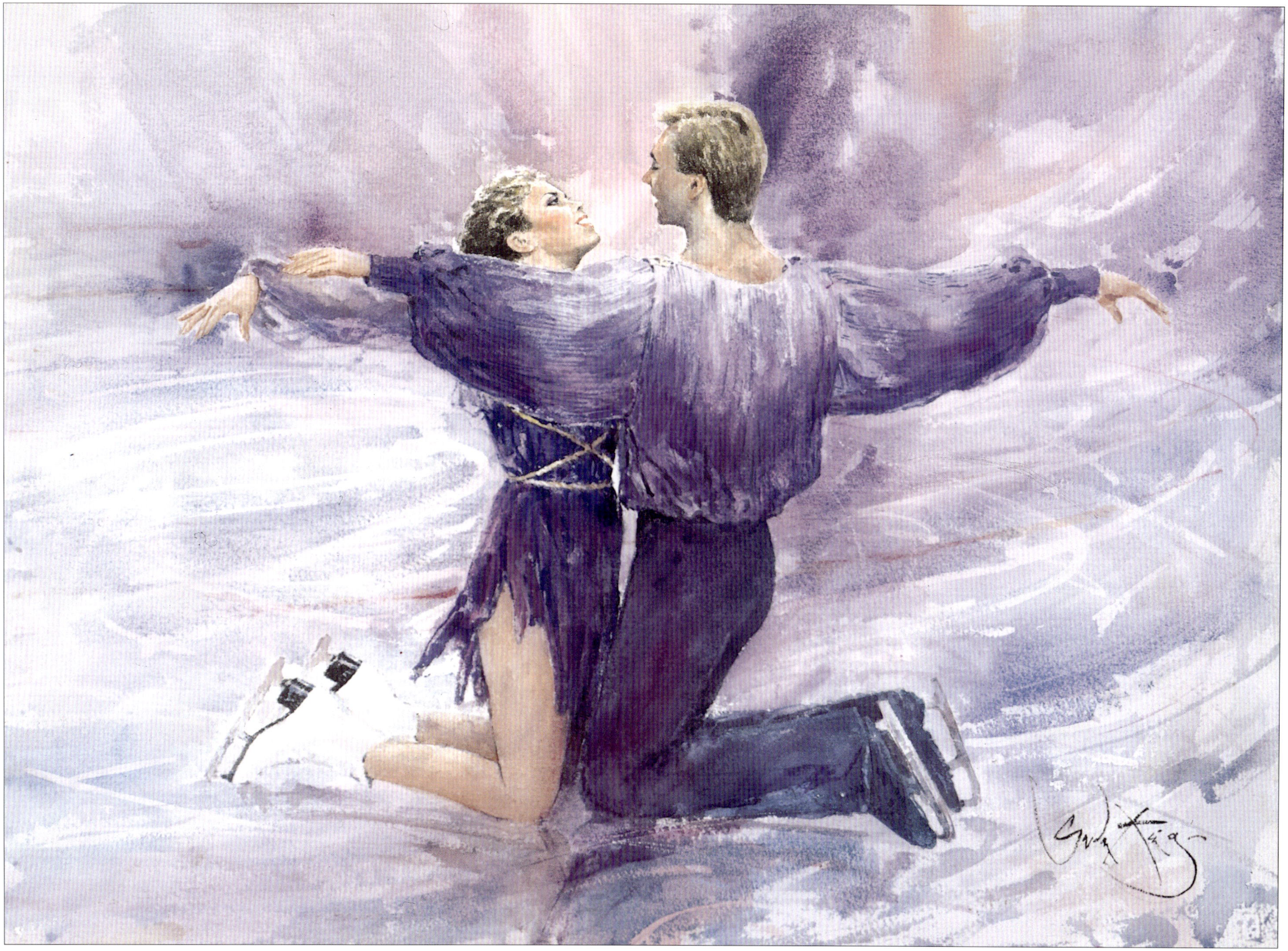

DREAM PERFORMANCE

Gallery 5

The chance of reliving a sporting occasion in my paintings is pure pleasure. Yes - I'm a sports 'nut'. Up half the night watching the cricket from Down Under, following the World Cup, or glued to tennis from Wimbledon.

I've been very fortunate to have experienced some of the great sporting occasions and have enjoyed the challenge of recreating the excitement in my paintings. I've been painting Ascot week and Henley Royal Regatta for a decade now, and both venues give me endless scope for my work.

At Ascot, I've been on the finishing line and in the Winner's Enclosure, soaking up the atmosphere so I can really feel my way into a painting. One year my press pass stated: "Gordon King: Artist up a Tree". They had made a platform high up in a tree for me to sketch from.

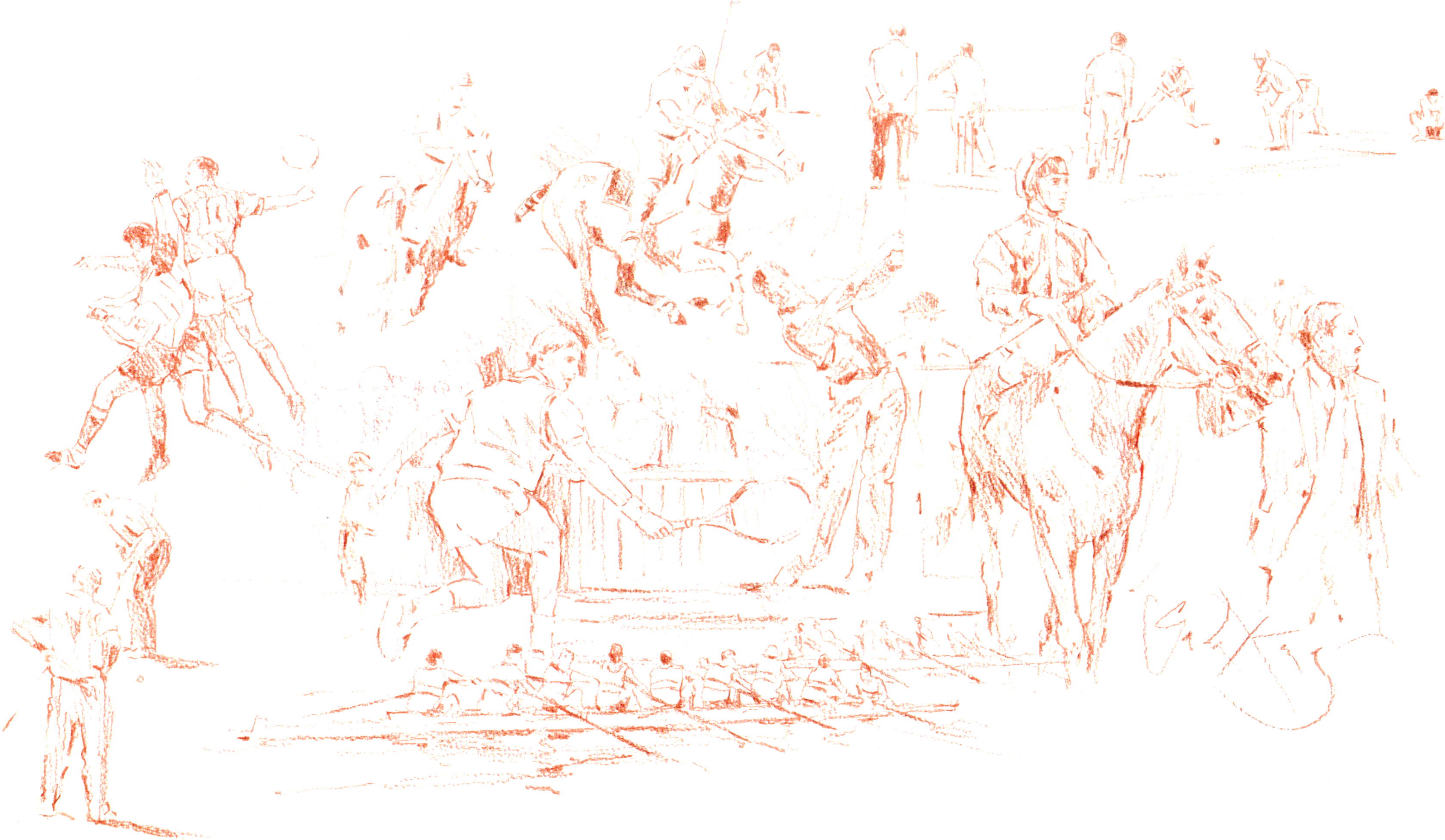

The Sporting Season

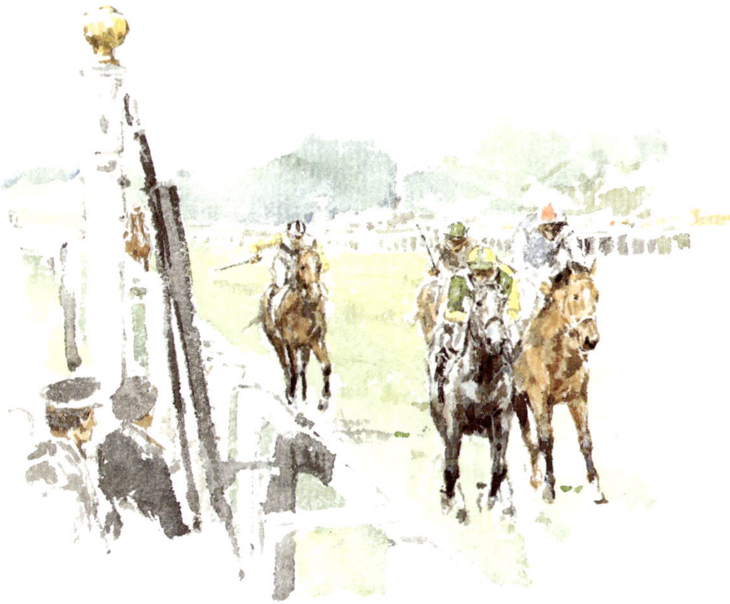

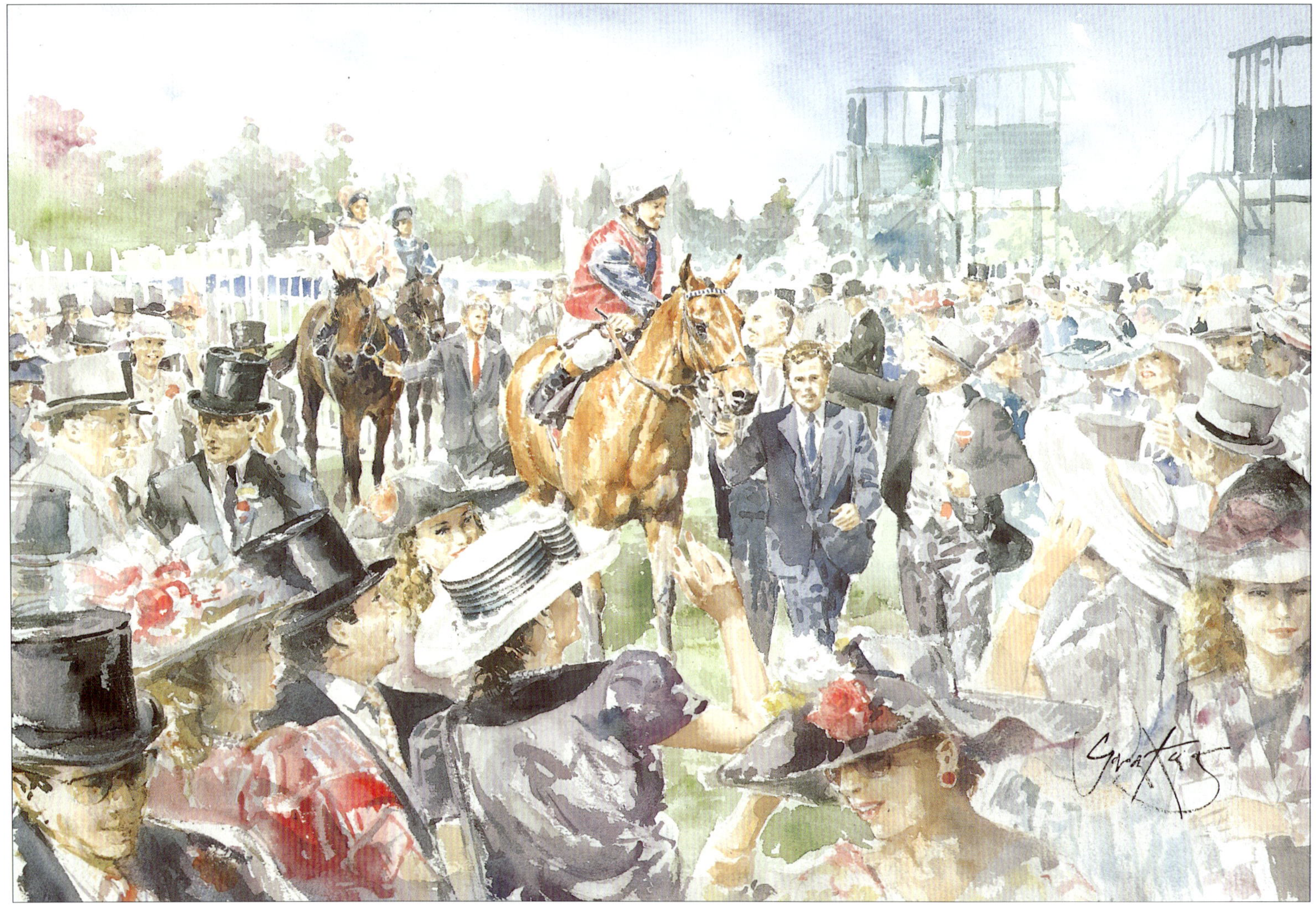

THE WINNER

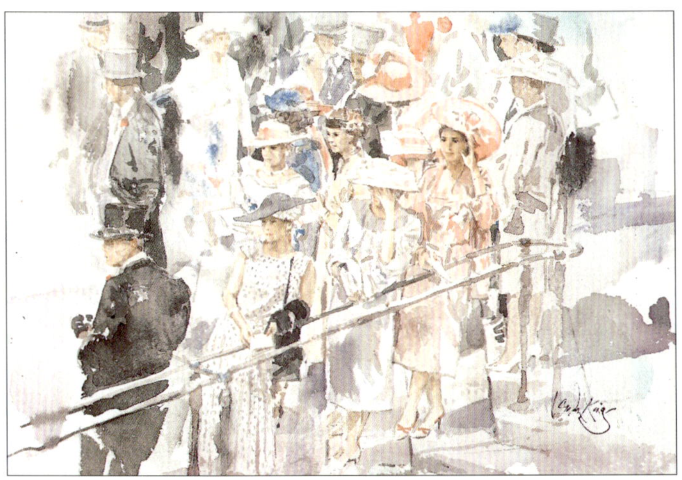

ASCOT LADIES

I have always loved Ascot as a subject, especially on Ladies Day when there is such a wonderful array of colourful hats and elegant outfits to complement the excitement of the racing and the Winner's Enclosure. I particularly like the idea of focusing in on a crowd of people and capturing a slice of life at that particular moment.

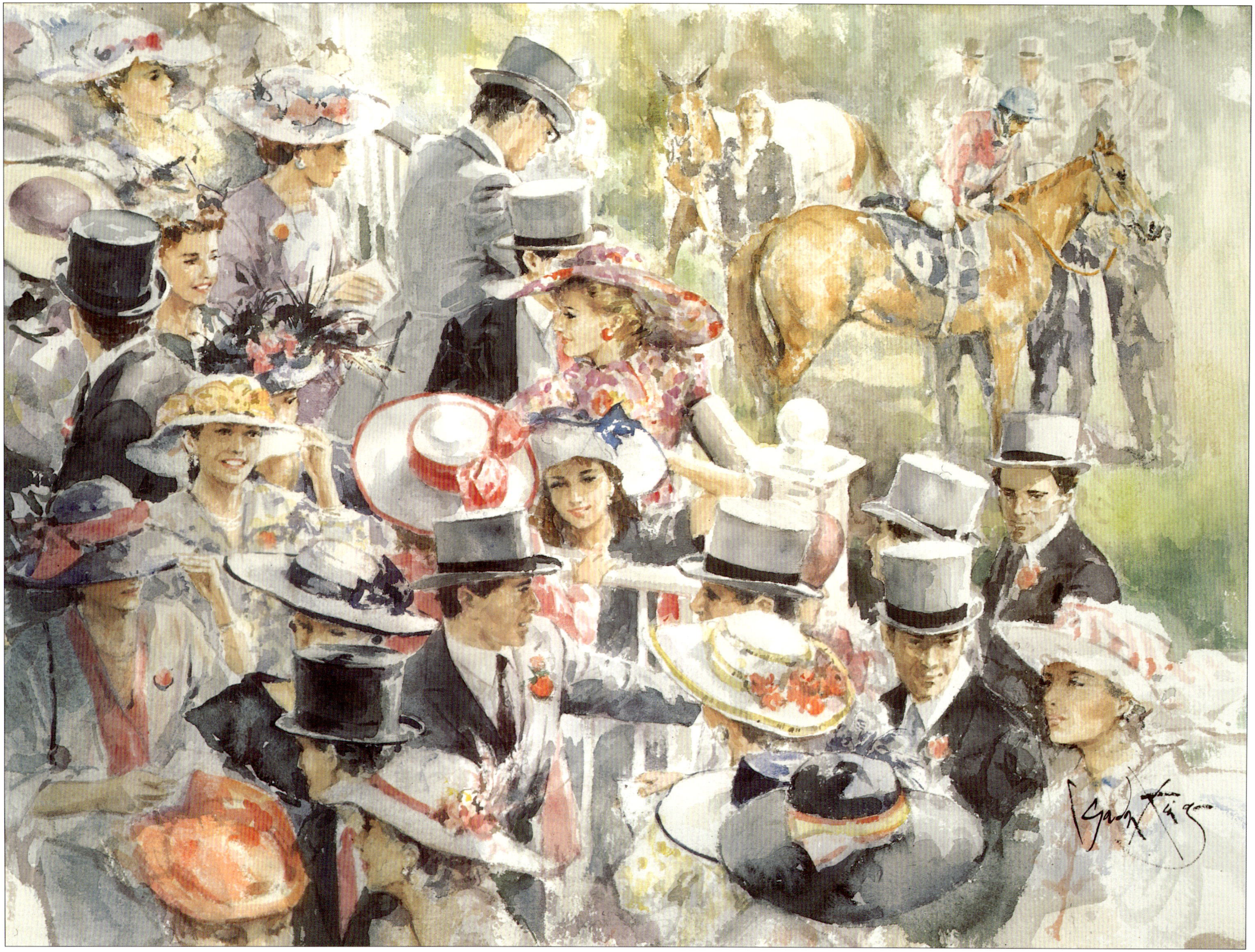

ASCOT HATS

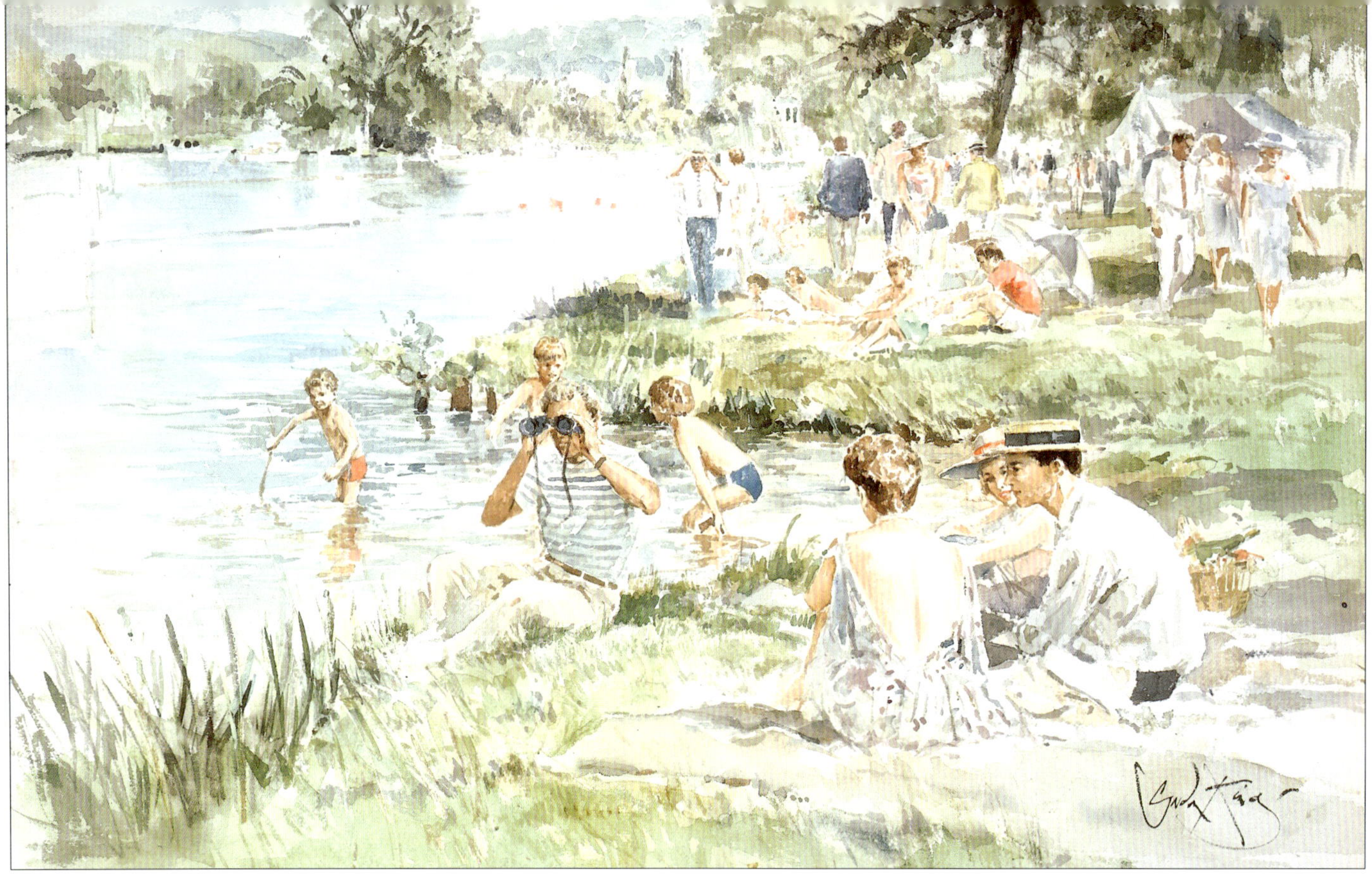

HENLEY RIVERSIDE

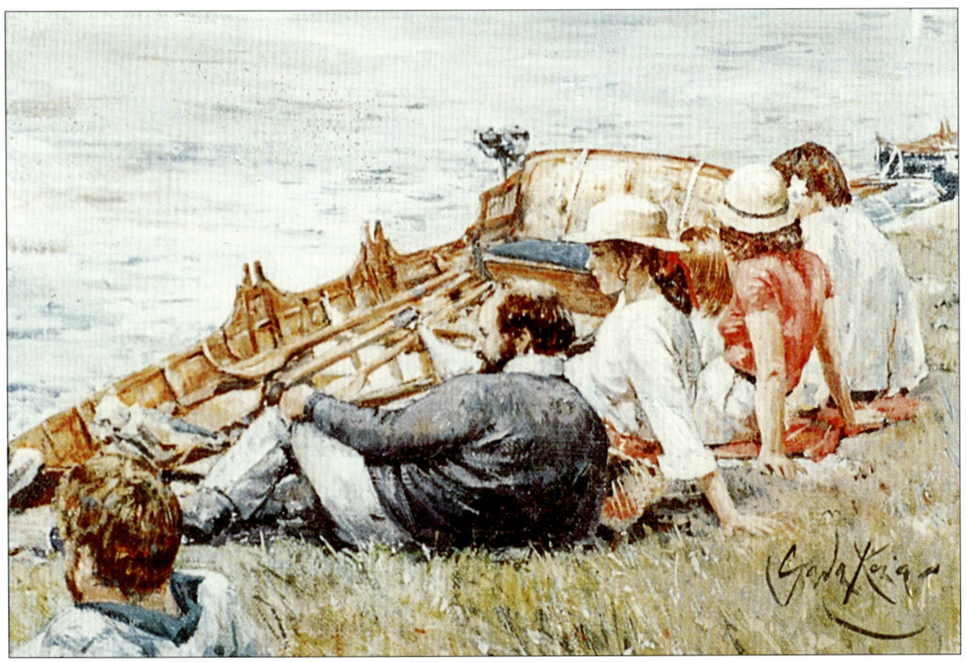

HENLEY RIVERBANK (OIL)

When I was young I used to cycle to Henley and it was a family tradition to go to firework night on Regatta Saturday.

The Regatta itself sometimes becomes a mere backdrop for many who are simply having fun and enjoying themselves on a warm day by the river. The occasion provides a wonderful opportunity to indulge in extravagant picnics and pop a champagne cork - or two!

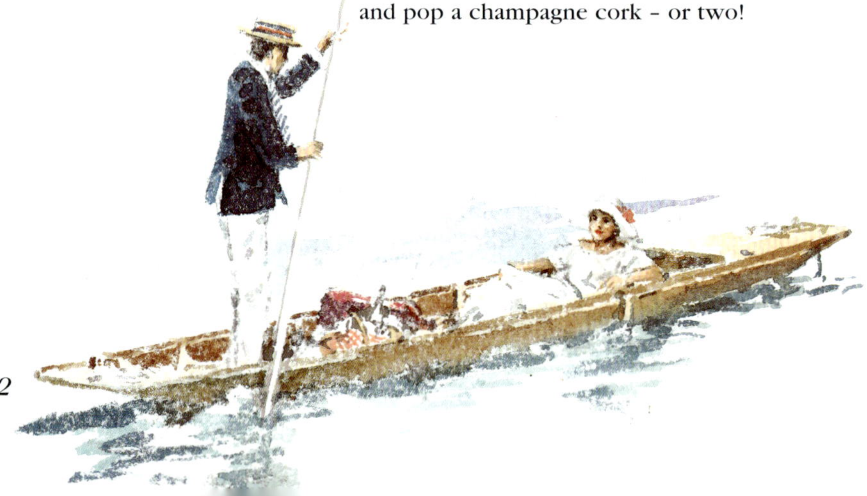

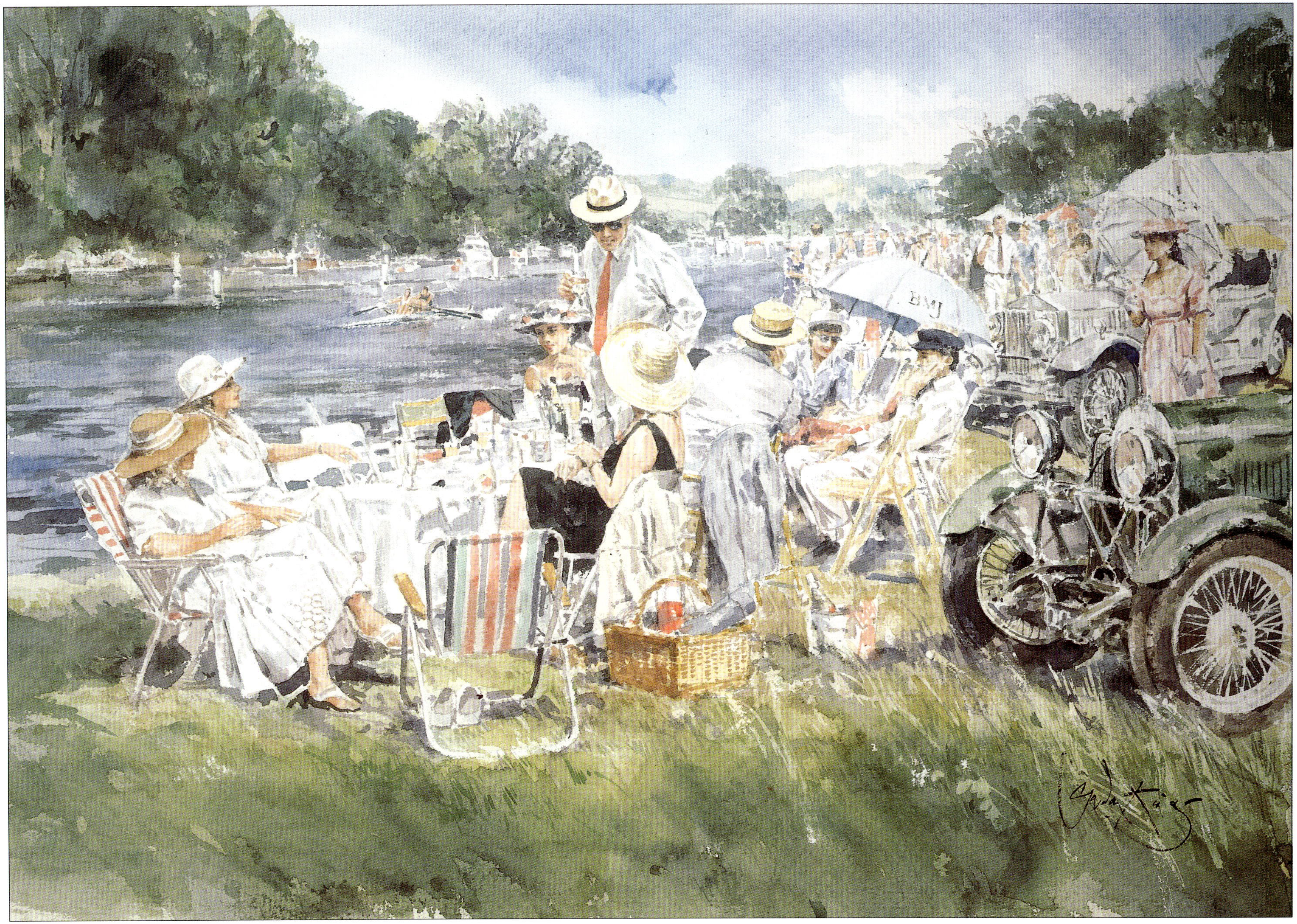

VINTAGE PICNIC

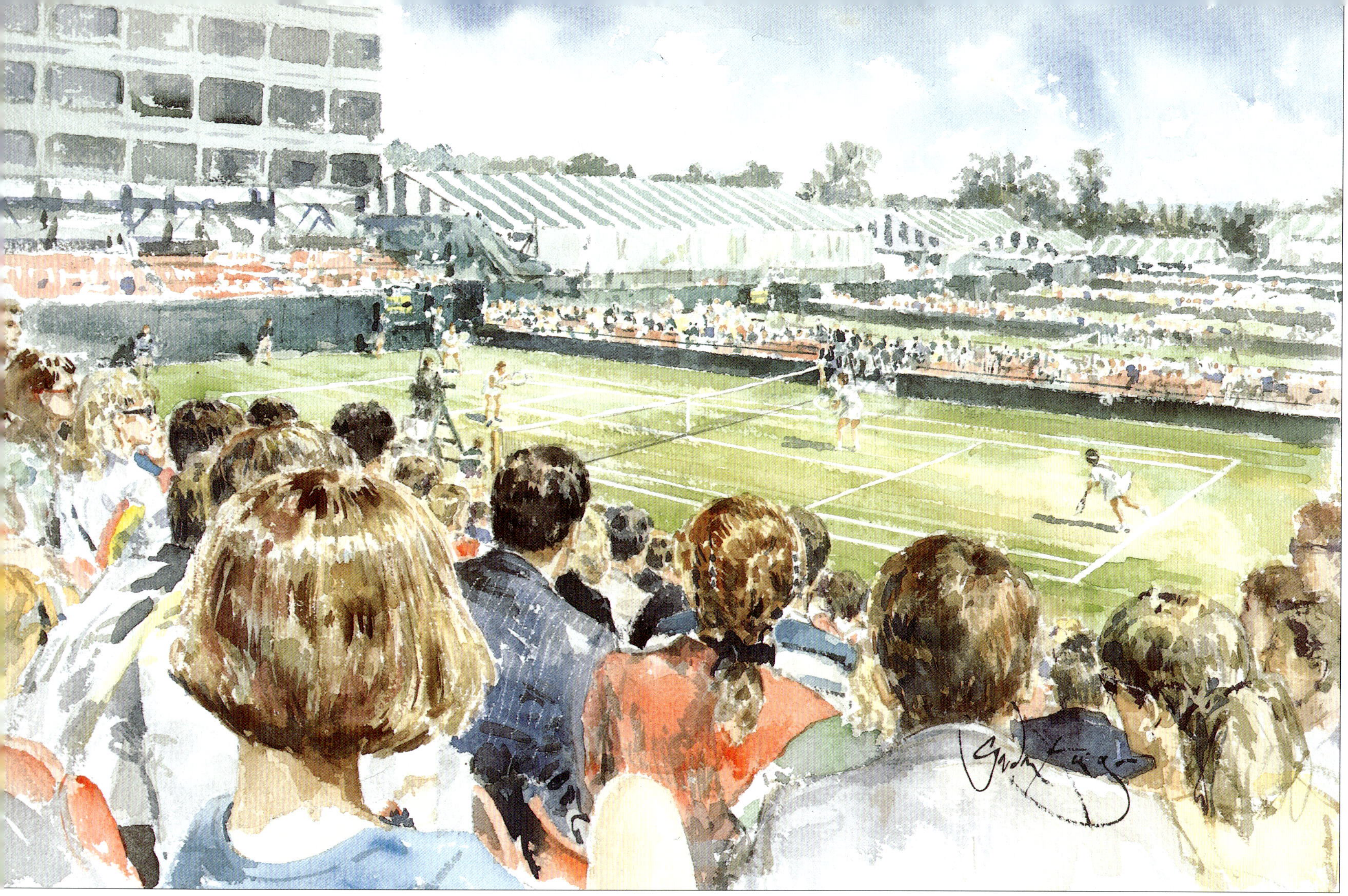

COURT FOURTEEN

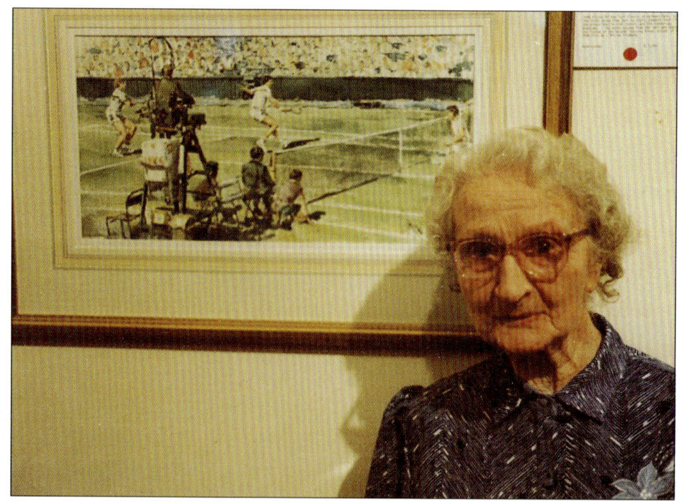

Kitty Godfrey, an early Wimbledon Singles Champion, opened an exhibition of sporting paintings in which I was involved.

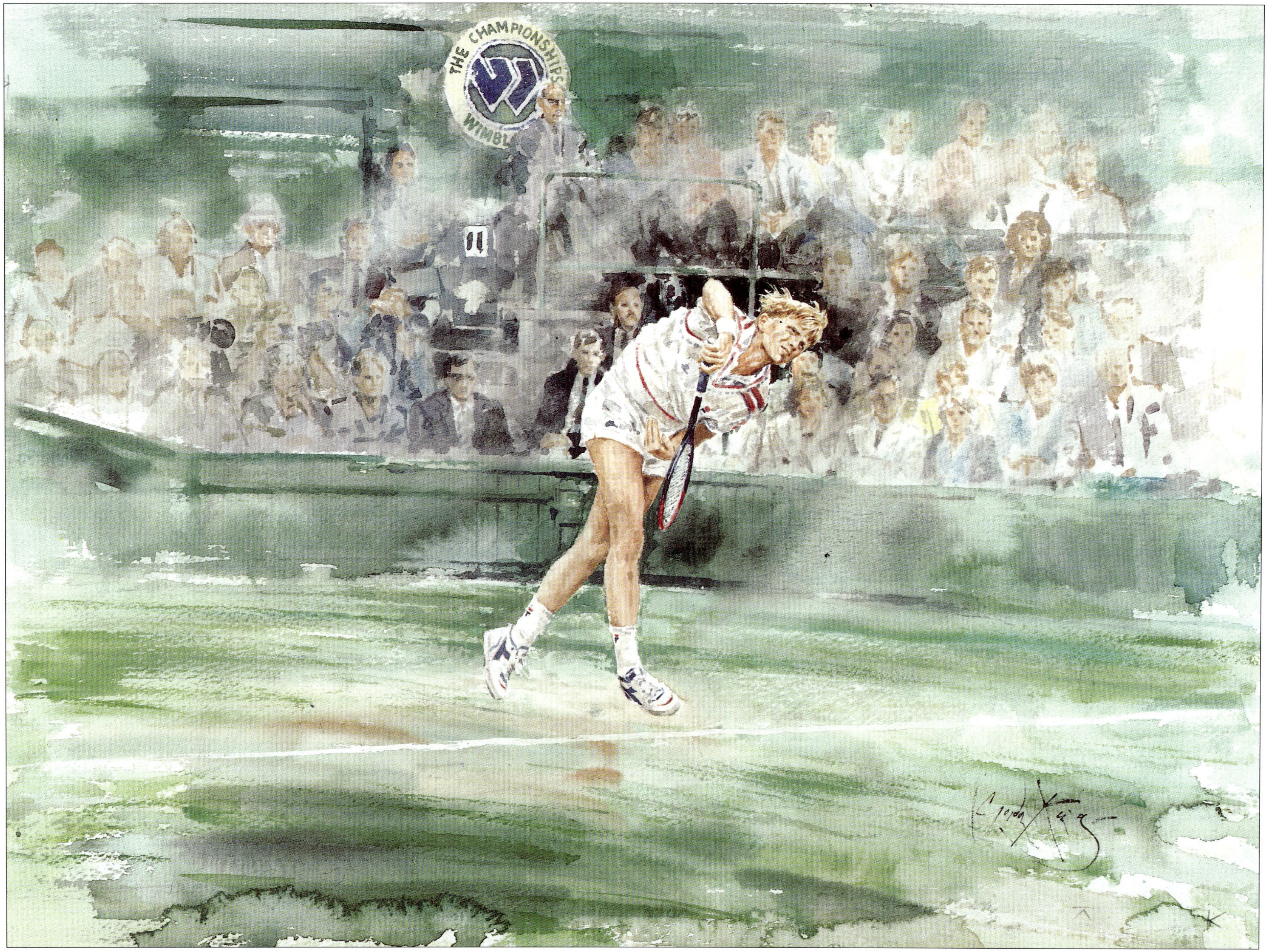

BECKER'S WIMBLEDON

Tennis is one of my favourite sports. As a keen amateur it was a pleasure to sit for a day in the warm July sun and sketch one of the world's finest grasscourt players.

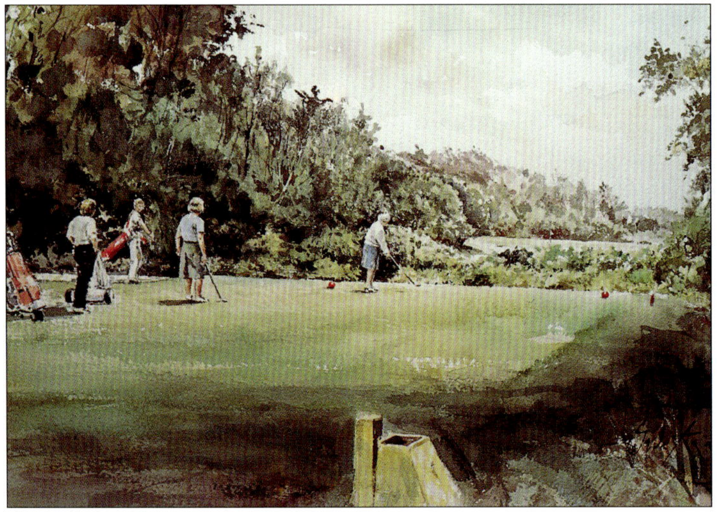

LADIES FOUR TEE OFF

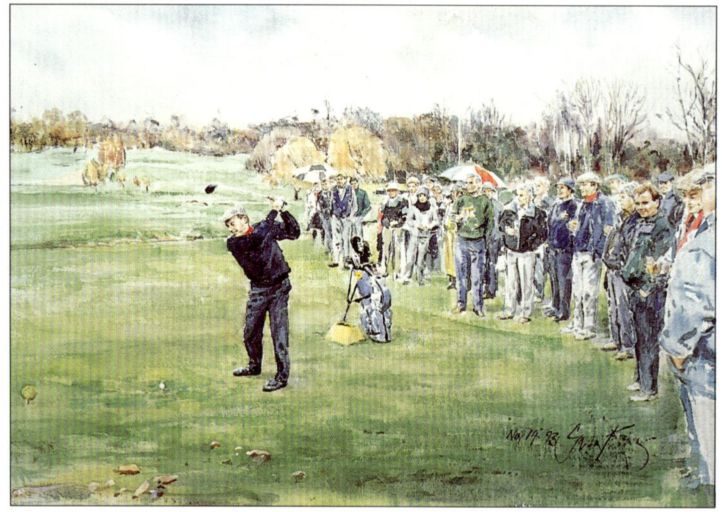

PLAYING IN THE CAPTAIN

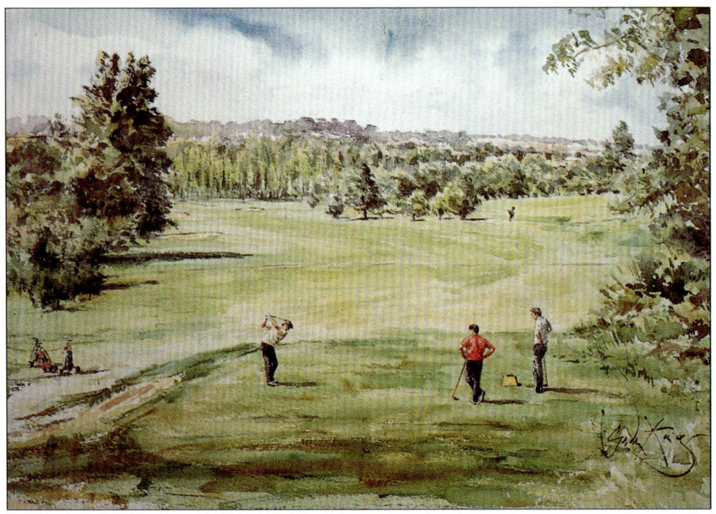

THE SECOND HOLE

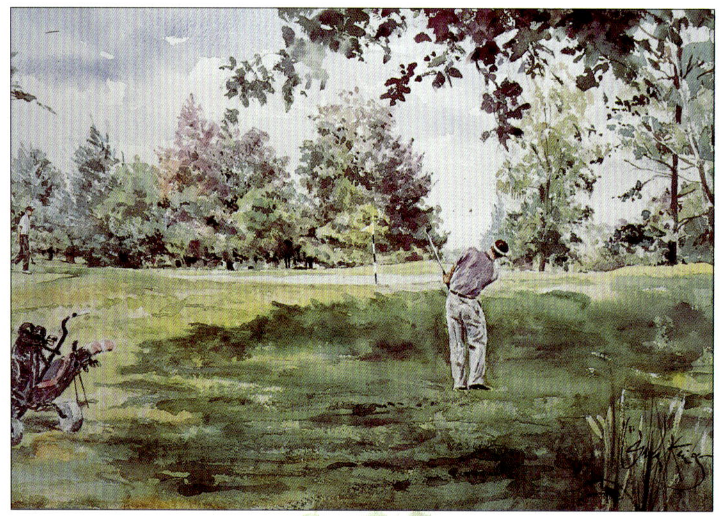

CHIPPING ONTO THE GREEN

My son, Richard, and I are both members of Gerrards Cross Golf Club, a beautiful course in the wooded Buckinghamshire countryside.

These paintings hang in the Clubhouse and are very much a labour of love. I've tried to capture the personality of the golf course as well as the golfers in play.

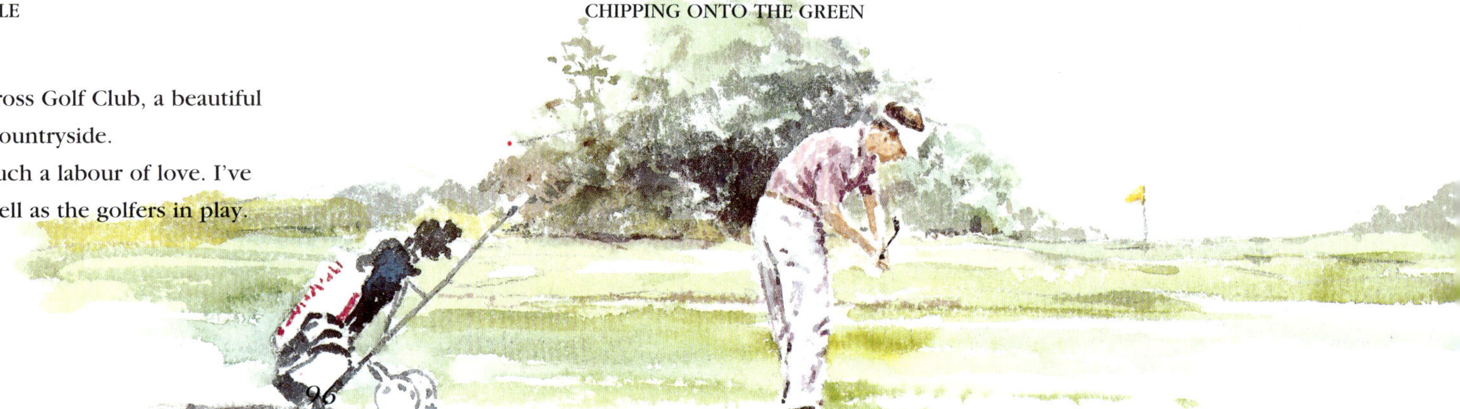

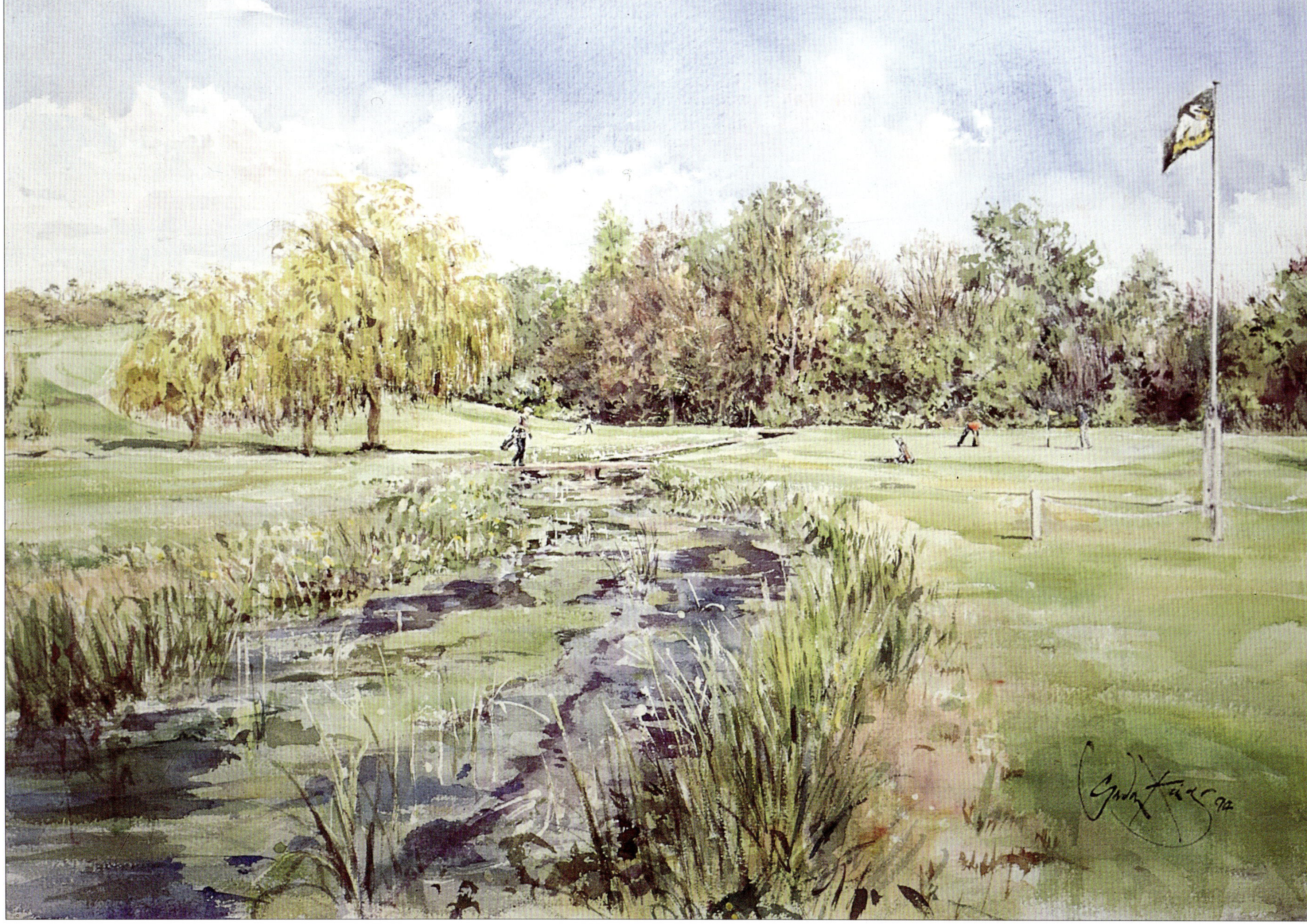

THE EIGHTEENTH HOLE

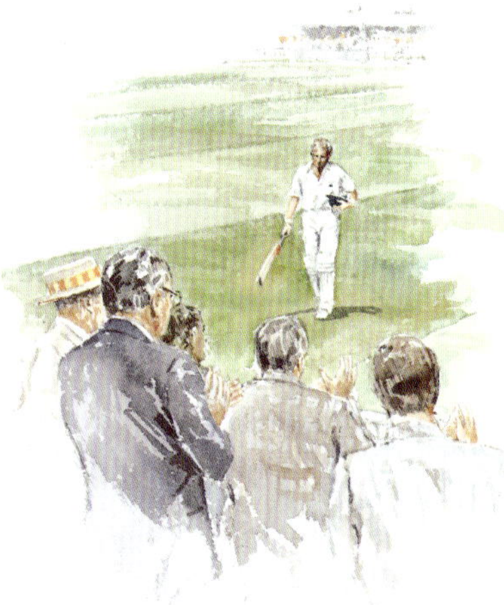

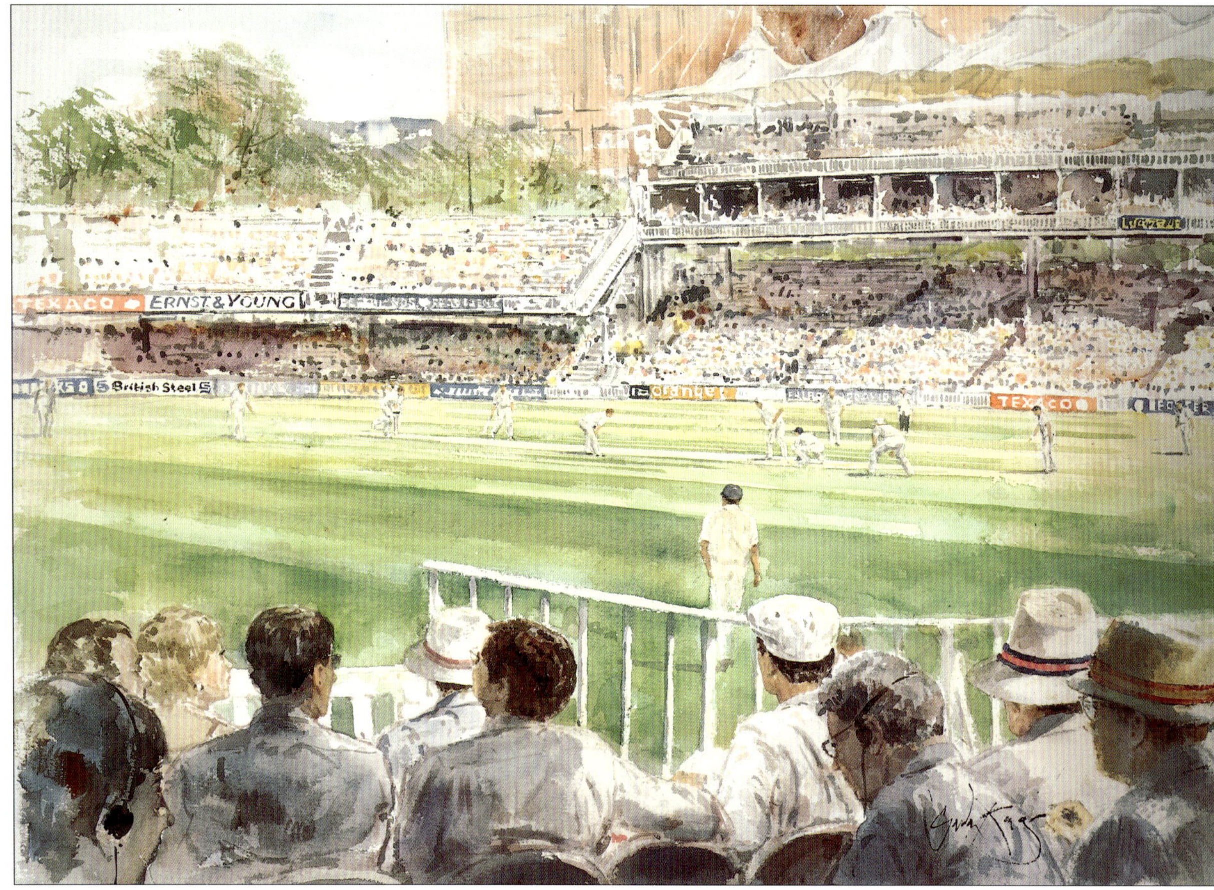

THE WARNER STAND

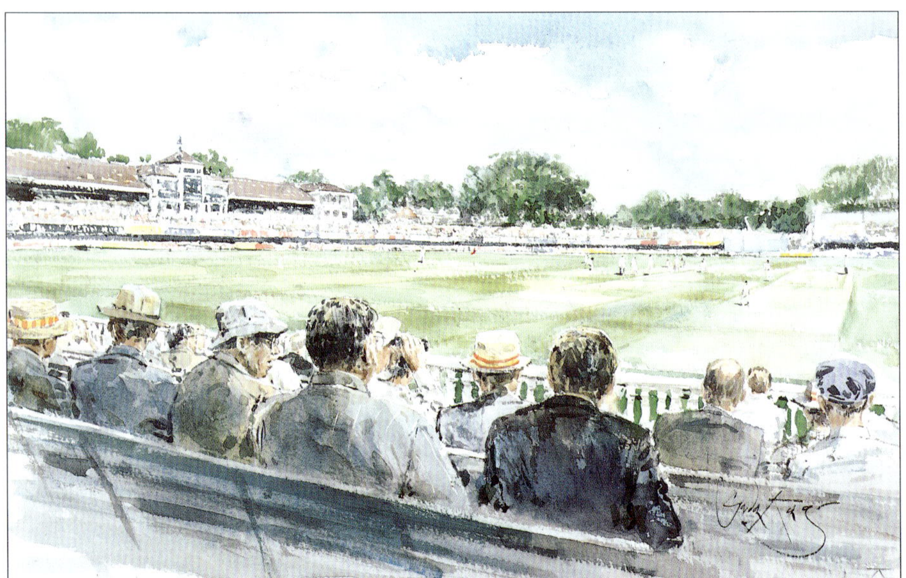

MEMBERS AT LORDS

As a schoolboy I used to travel up to London for the day with my sandwiches and a bottle of pop to watch players like Freddie Truman, Derek Statham and Denis Compton.
Television has made it so easy to watch sport in the comfort of your own home but it never quite captures the true atmosphere which can only be felt by joining the crowds live in the stands.
Both these paintings reflect specific vantage points I have had at Lords and hopefully portray a little of that special excitement produced by an absorbing Test Match on a warm summer's day.

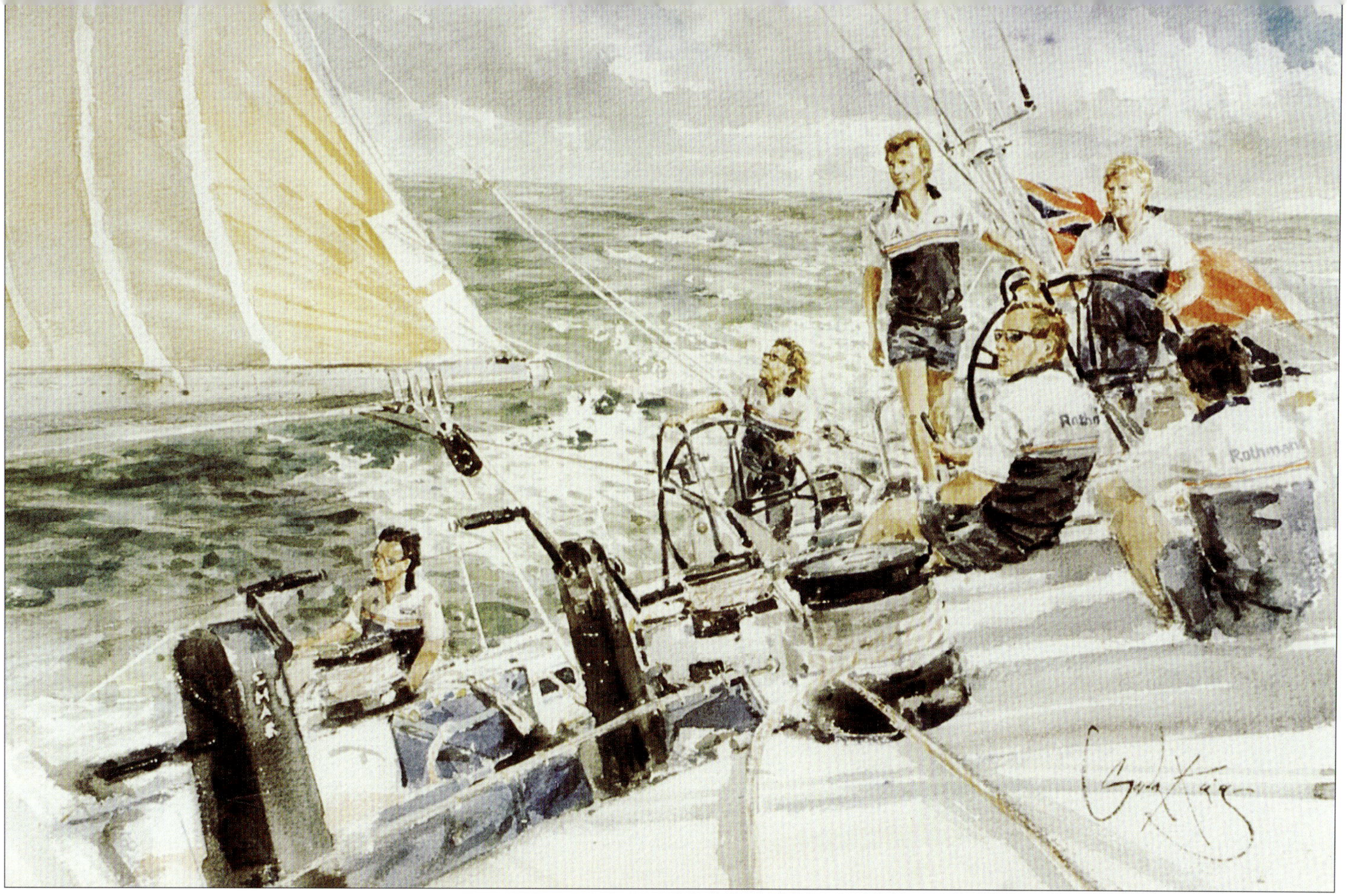

ROTHMAN'S YACHT

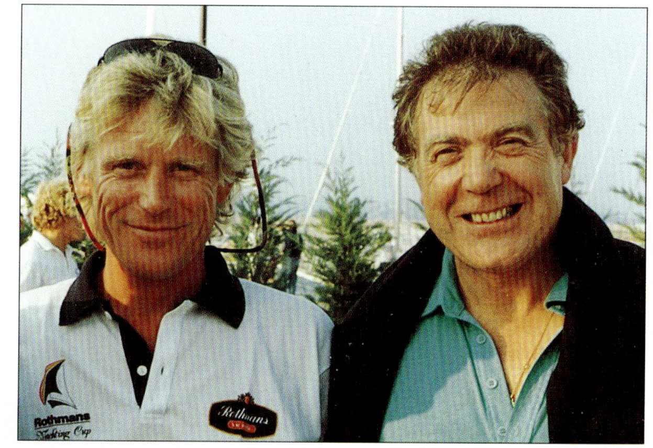

WITH LAWRIE SMITH AT ST. TROPEZ

Being invited to sail on the Rothman's maxi-yacht as it went through its paces in the Solent prior to the Whitbread Round the World Yacht Race was an experience I shall always remember.

POLO

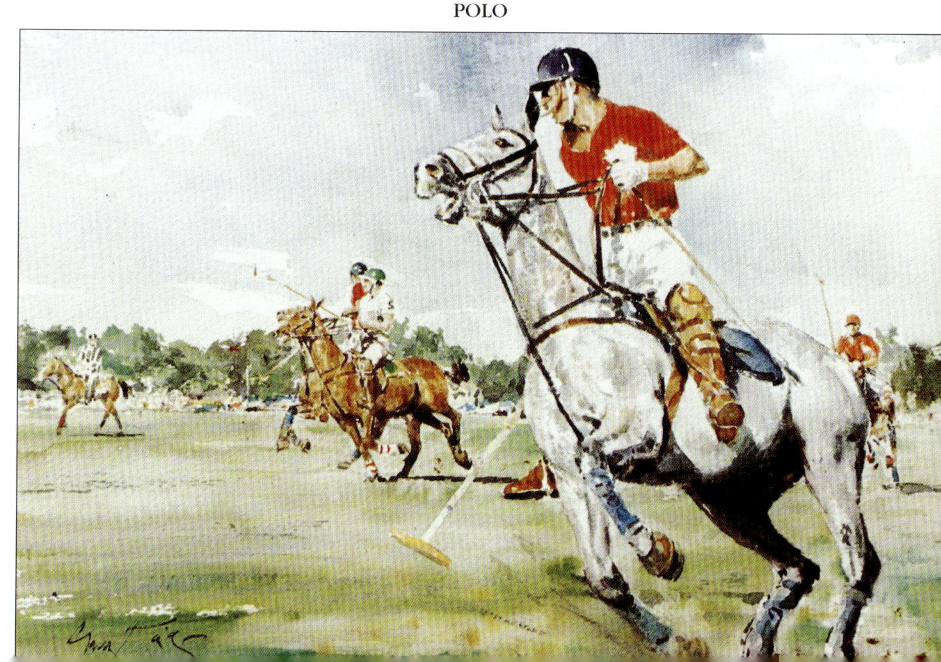

This is one of a series of polo paintings following several enjoyable visits to Smith's Lawn, Windsor.

Gallery 6

By it's very nature travelling will provide that new environment, that different light and colour, the inspiration for something new.

I have been lucky enough to see quite a lot of the world in the last few years inspiring paintings from Venice to the Far East, Paris to the West Indies, even a few miles down the road where a change of scene can provide the spur for something new and original.

I seem to spend my life looking and thinking about images, seeing pictures in my mind, waiting for that seed of an idea to flower, and travel can always be relied upon to provide a fascinating variety of interesting subjects - essential fuel for a creative mind.

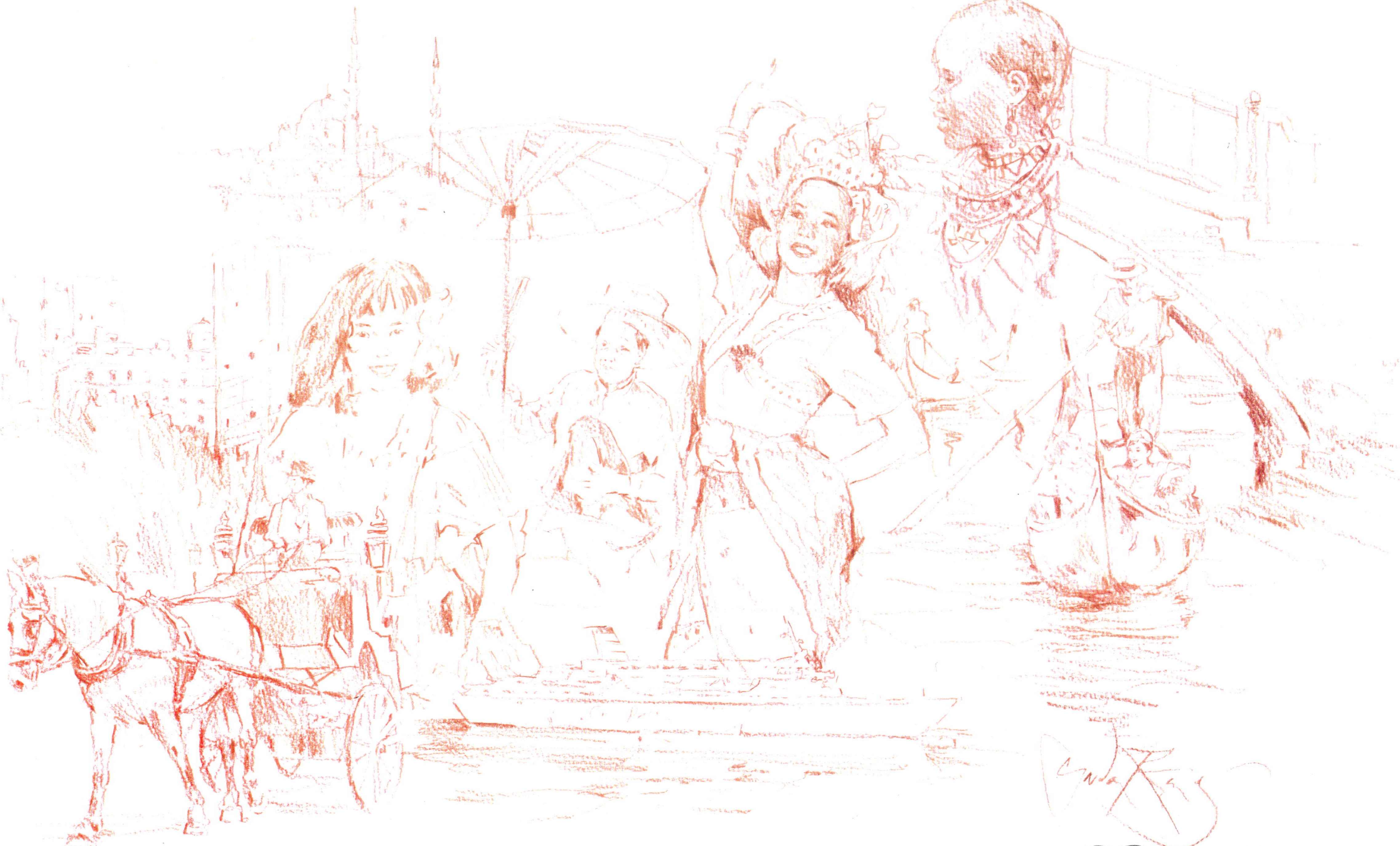

Travelling
The Artist's Escape...

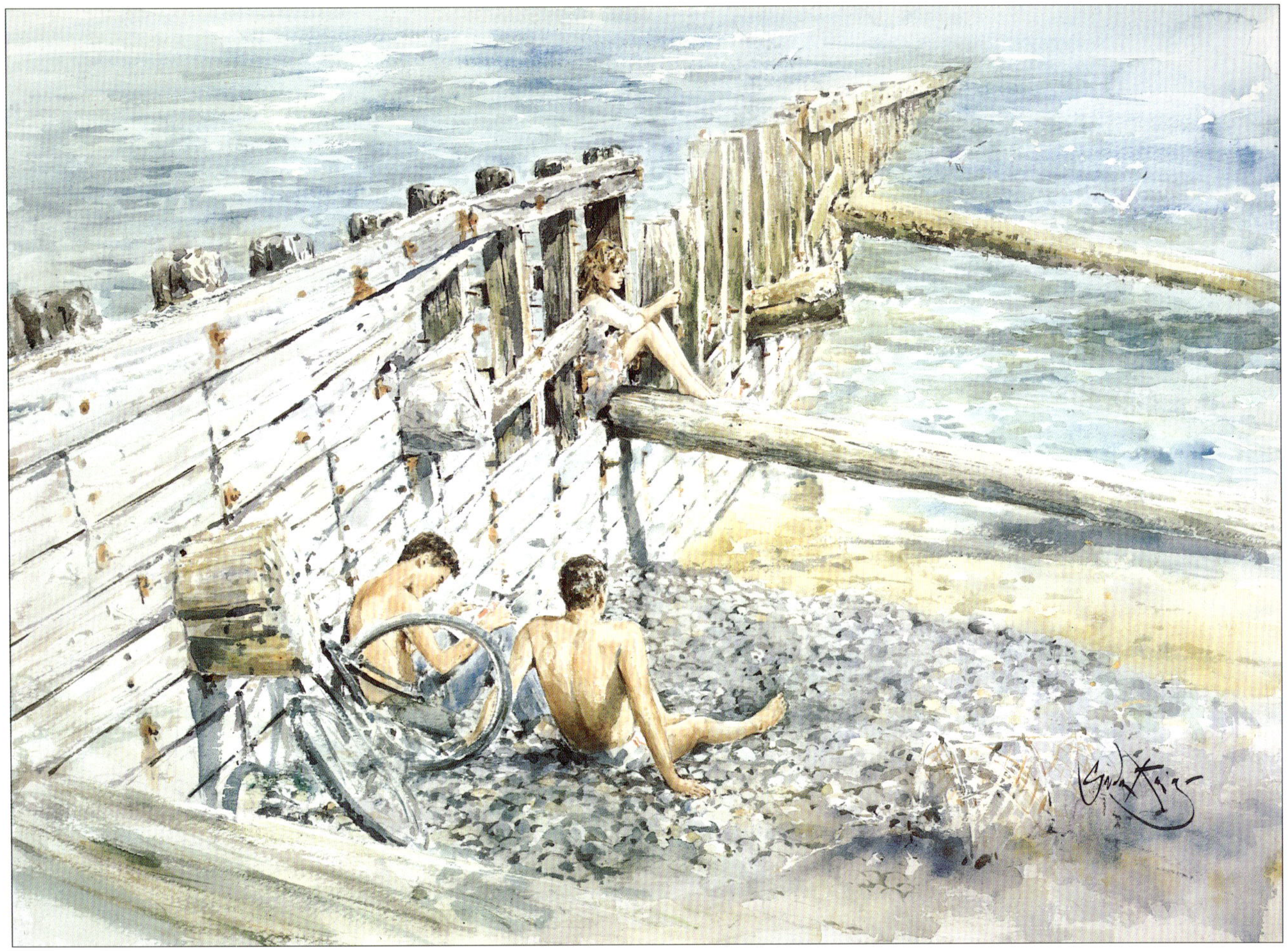

BREAKWATER AFTERNOON

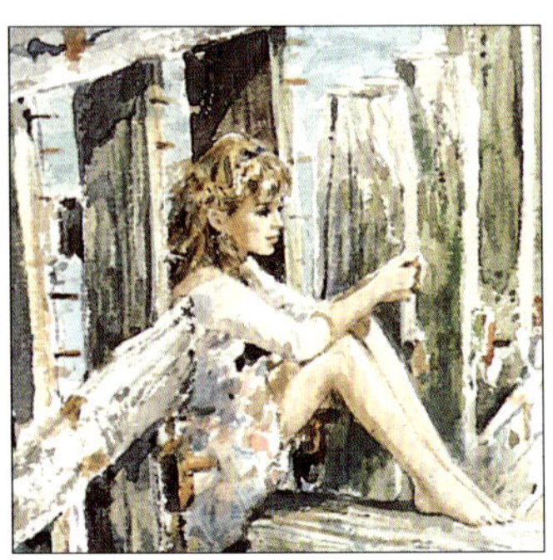

I caught sight of this confident young lady perfectly framed between the gnarled old timbers of the breakwater at Eastbourne during high tide.

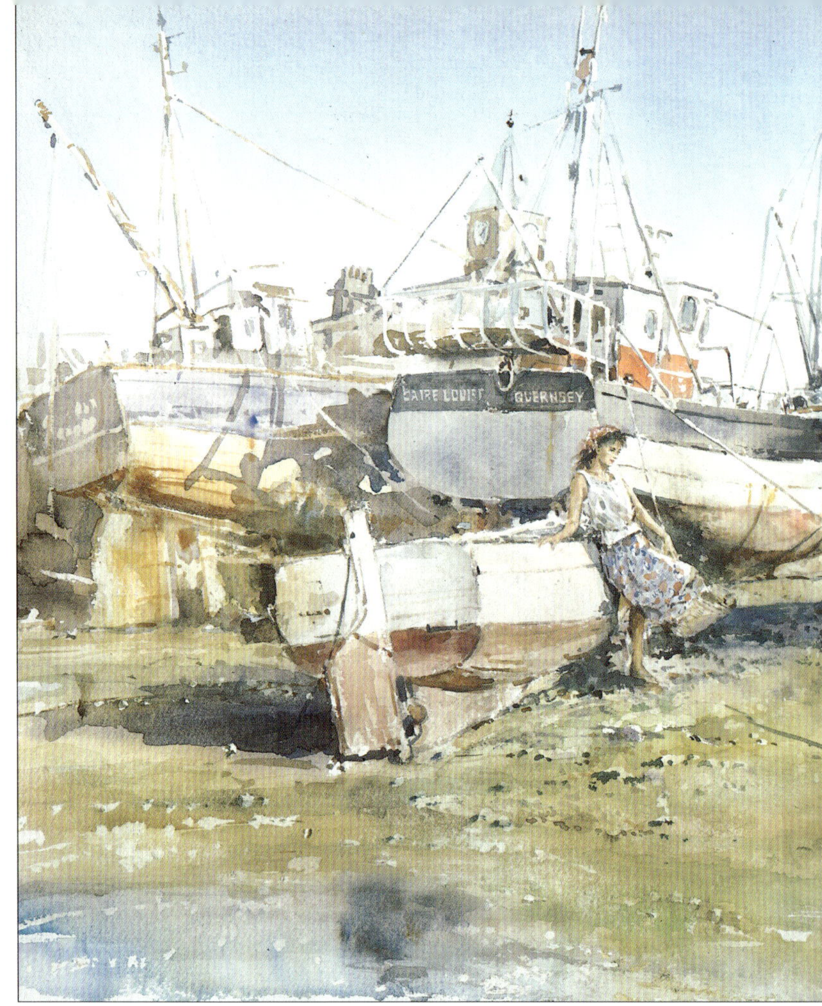

LOW TIDE IN THE CHANNEL I

THE BICYCLE

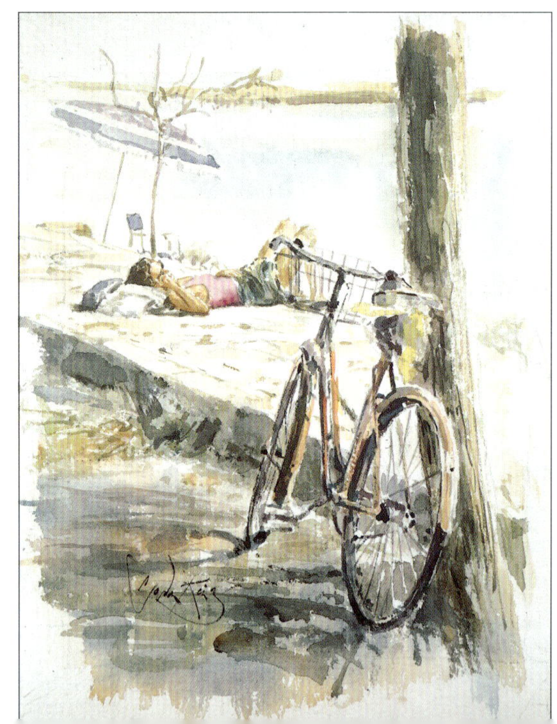

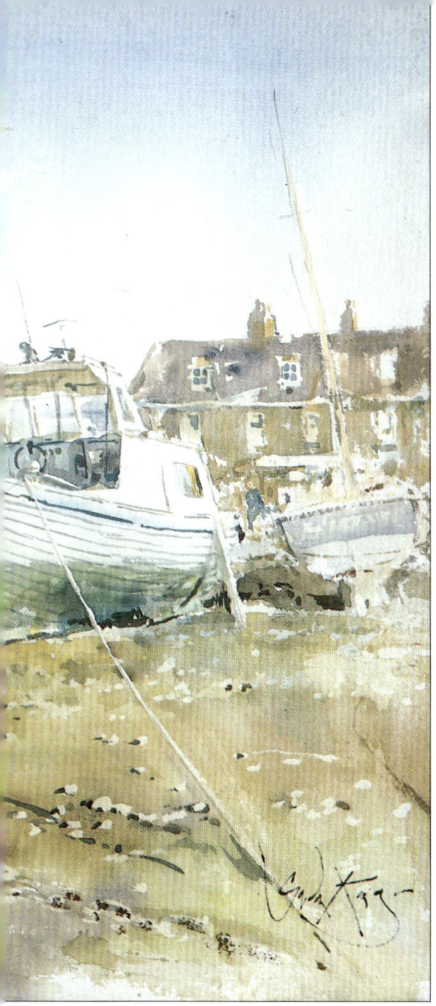

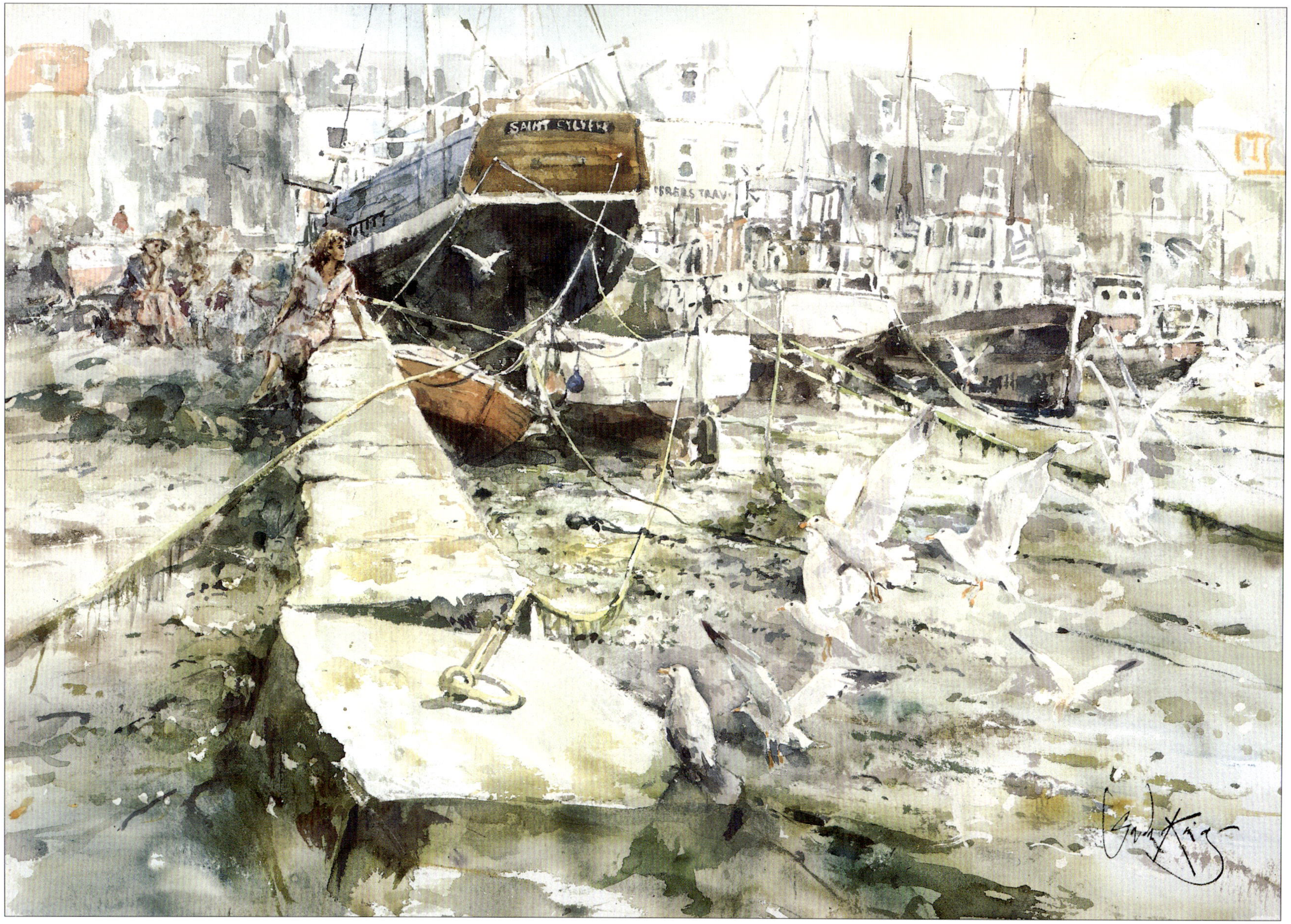

HARBOUR GULLS

This indulged my passion for old boats which I find very evocative.

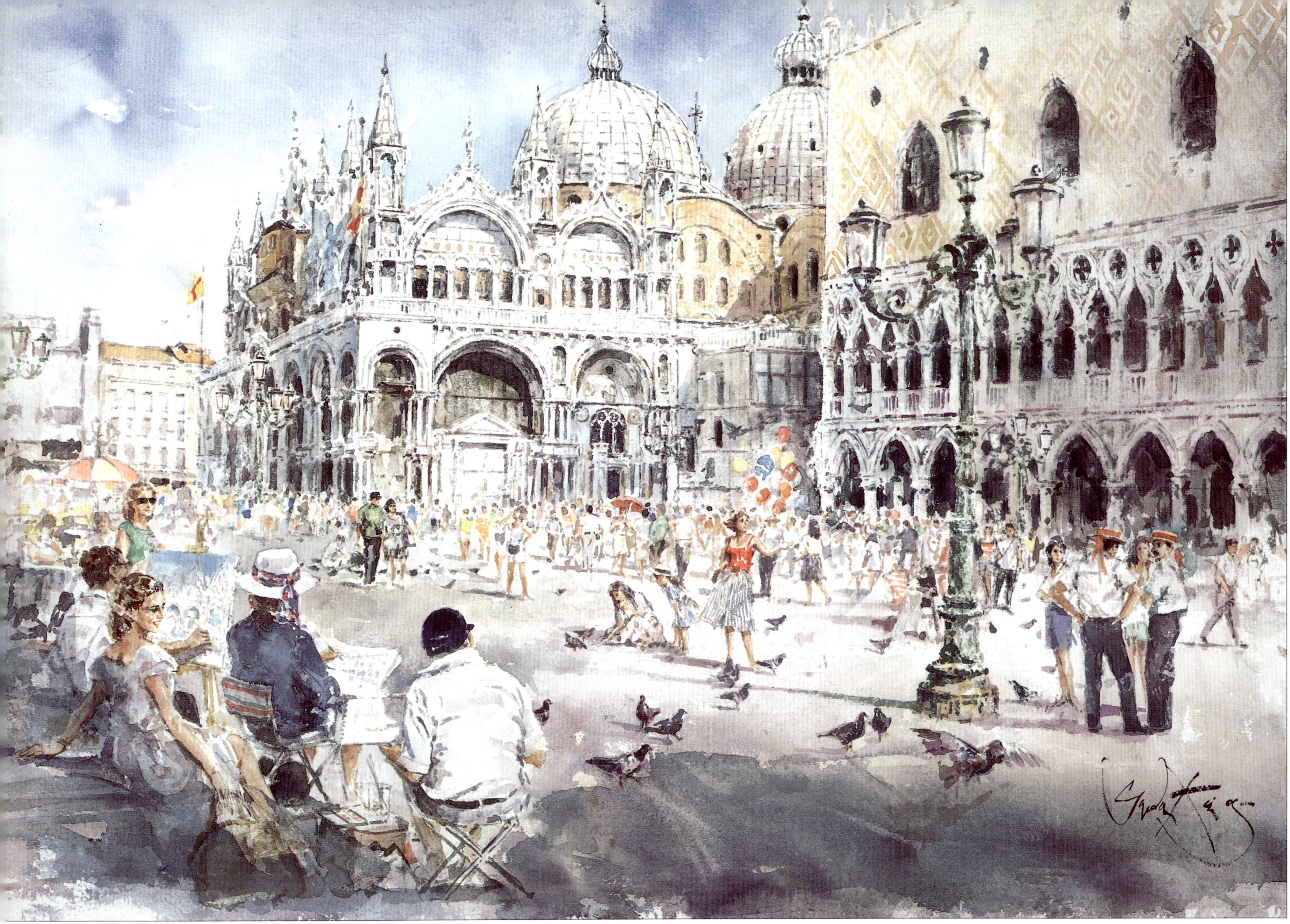

ARTISTS IN ST. MARK'S SQUARE

There's something exciting about watching artists paint, wherever it may be.

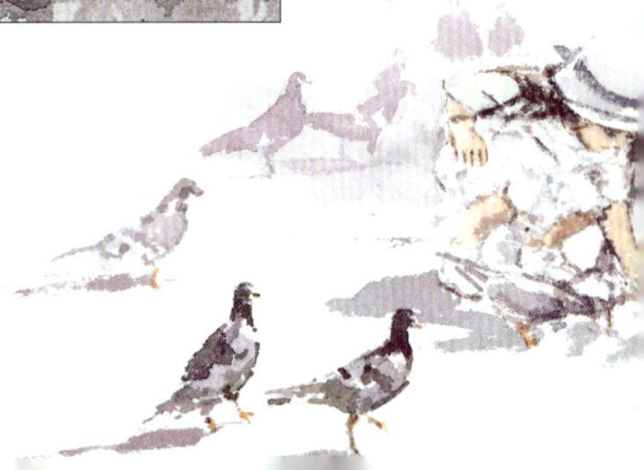

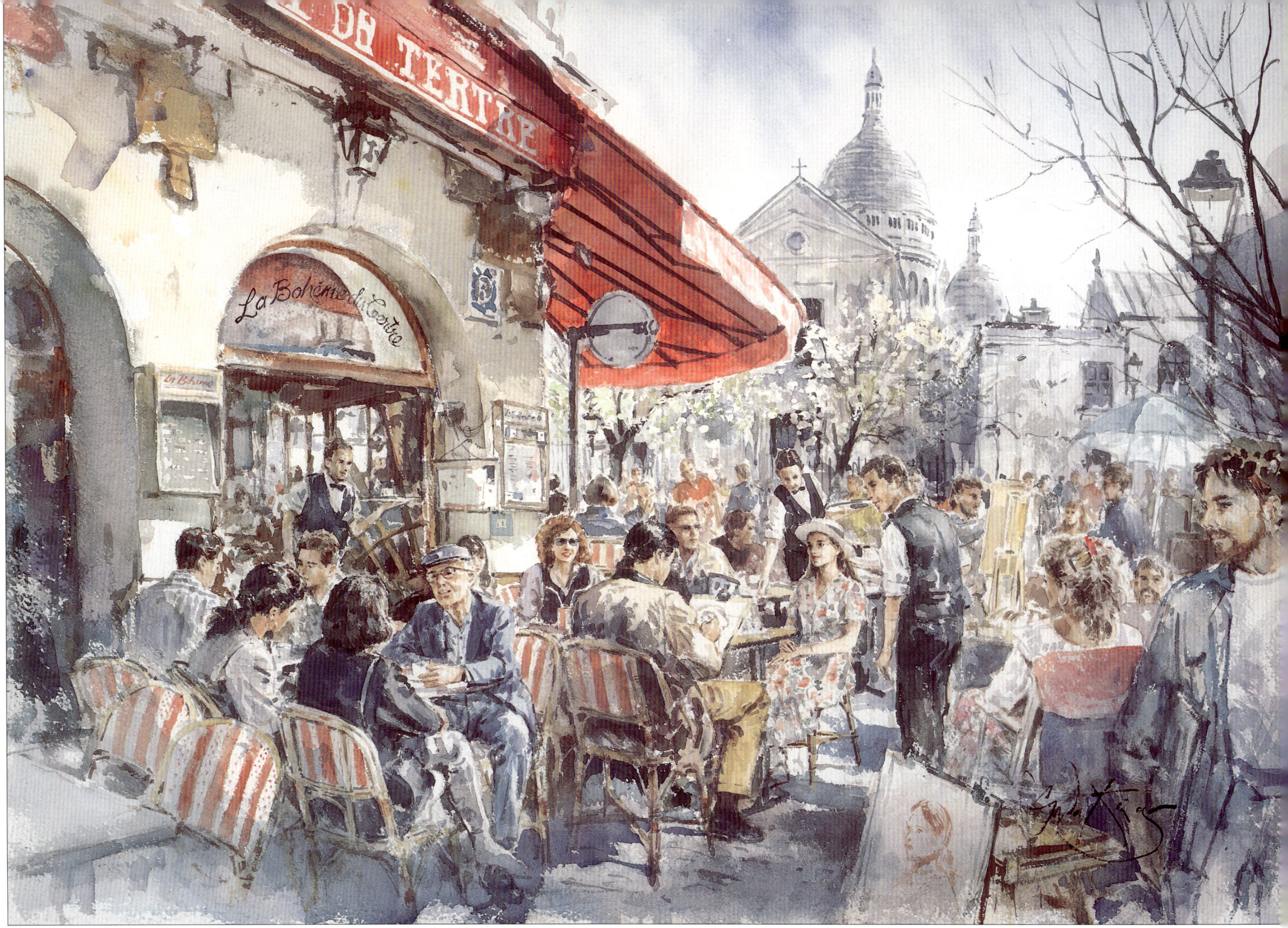

PORTRAIT OF MONTMARTRE

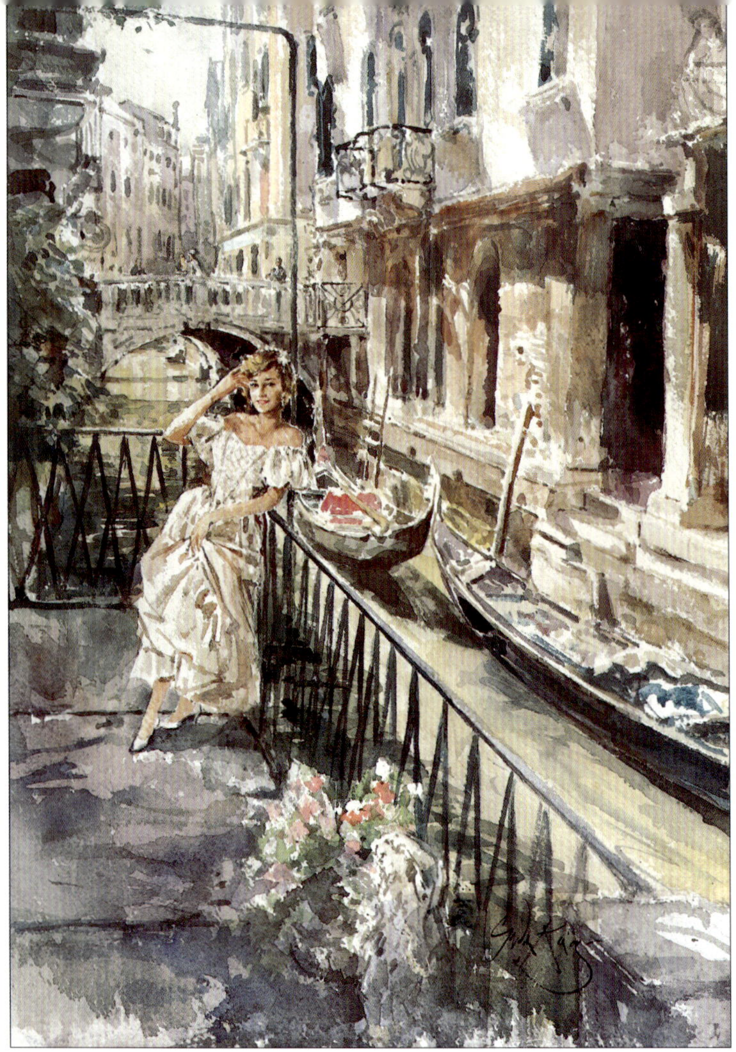

VENETIAN VERANDAH

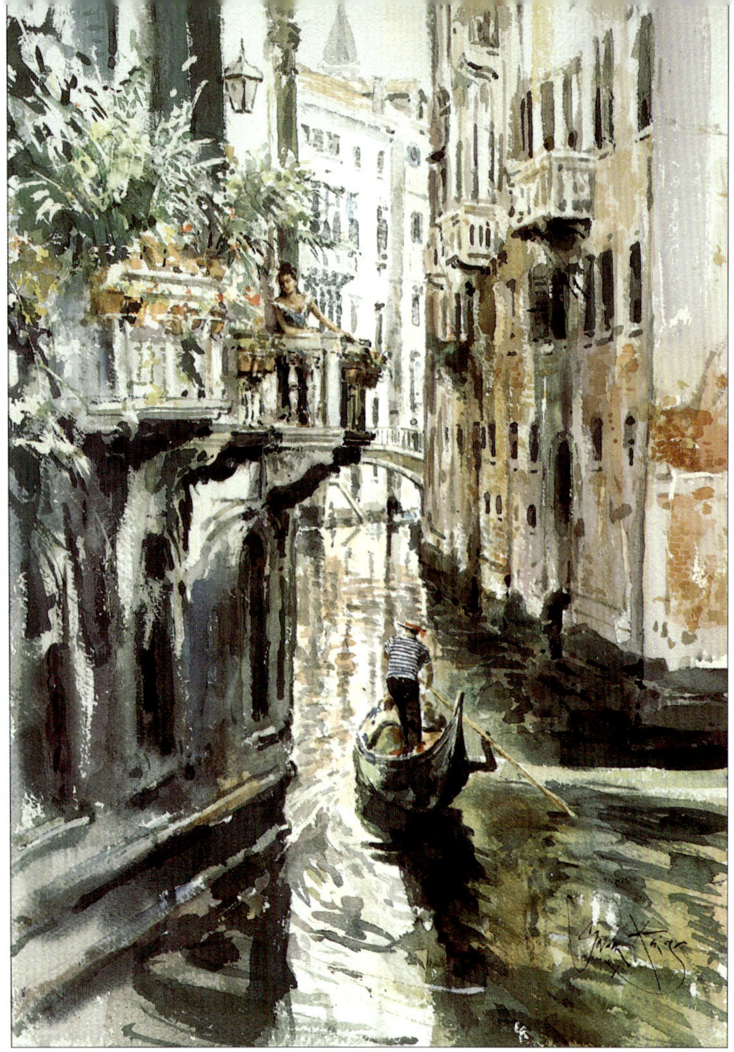

TIMELESS VENICE

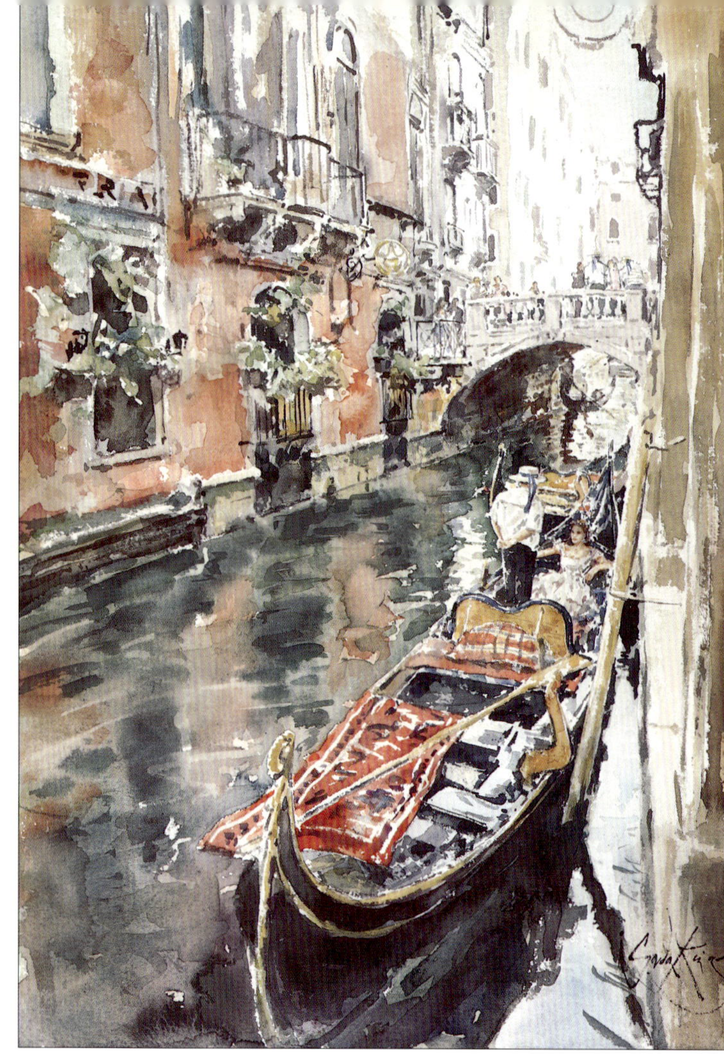

VENETIAN BACKWATER

From the minute I first saw Venice I understood the lure that it has had for generations of artists. I was captivated by the buildings and the reflections in the water. There is an air of tranquillity as the gondoliers steer their craft silently through the narrow backwaters, contrasting strongly with the hustle and bustle of the Grand Canal.

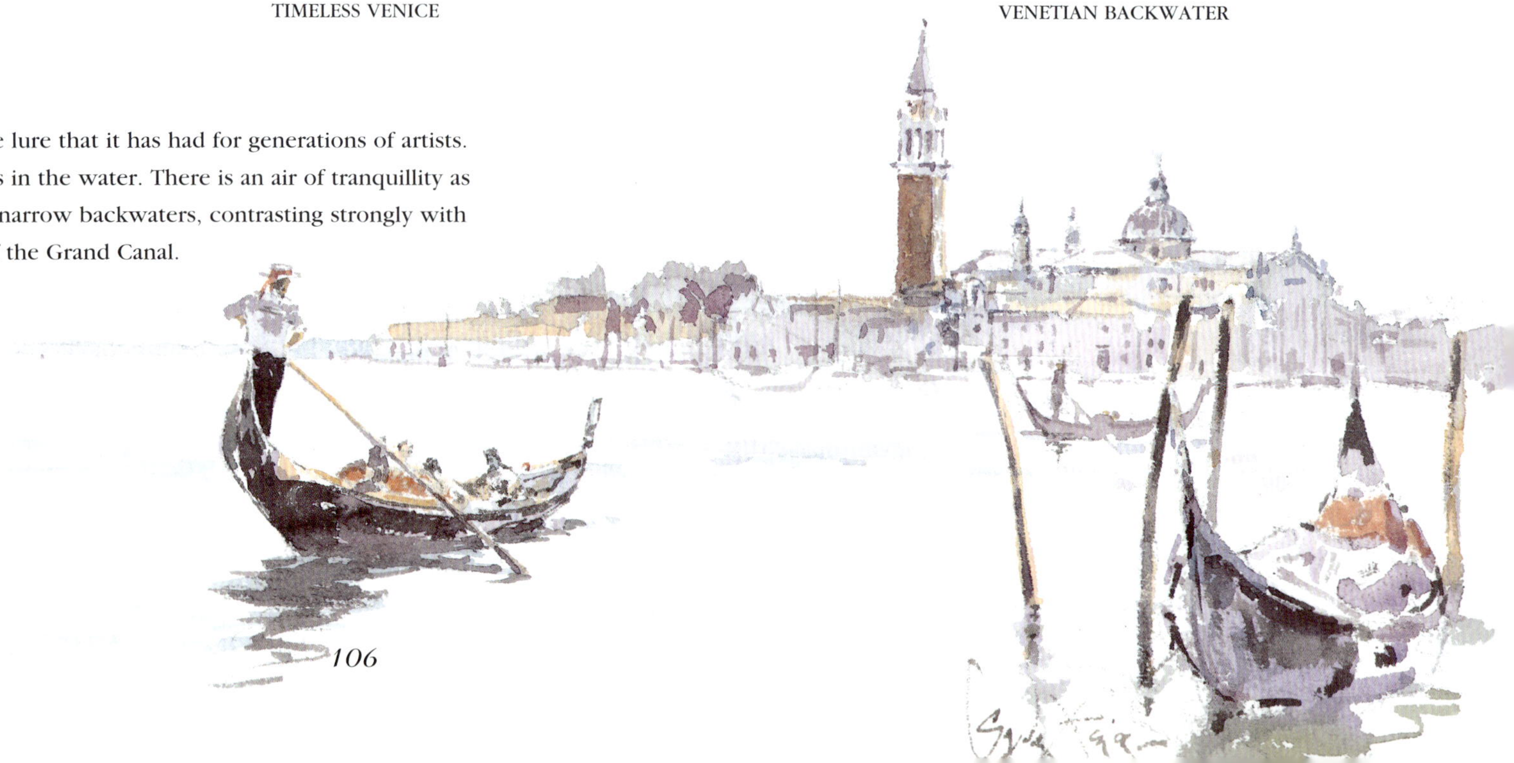

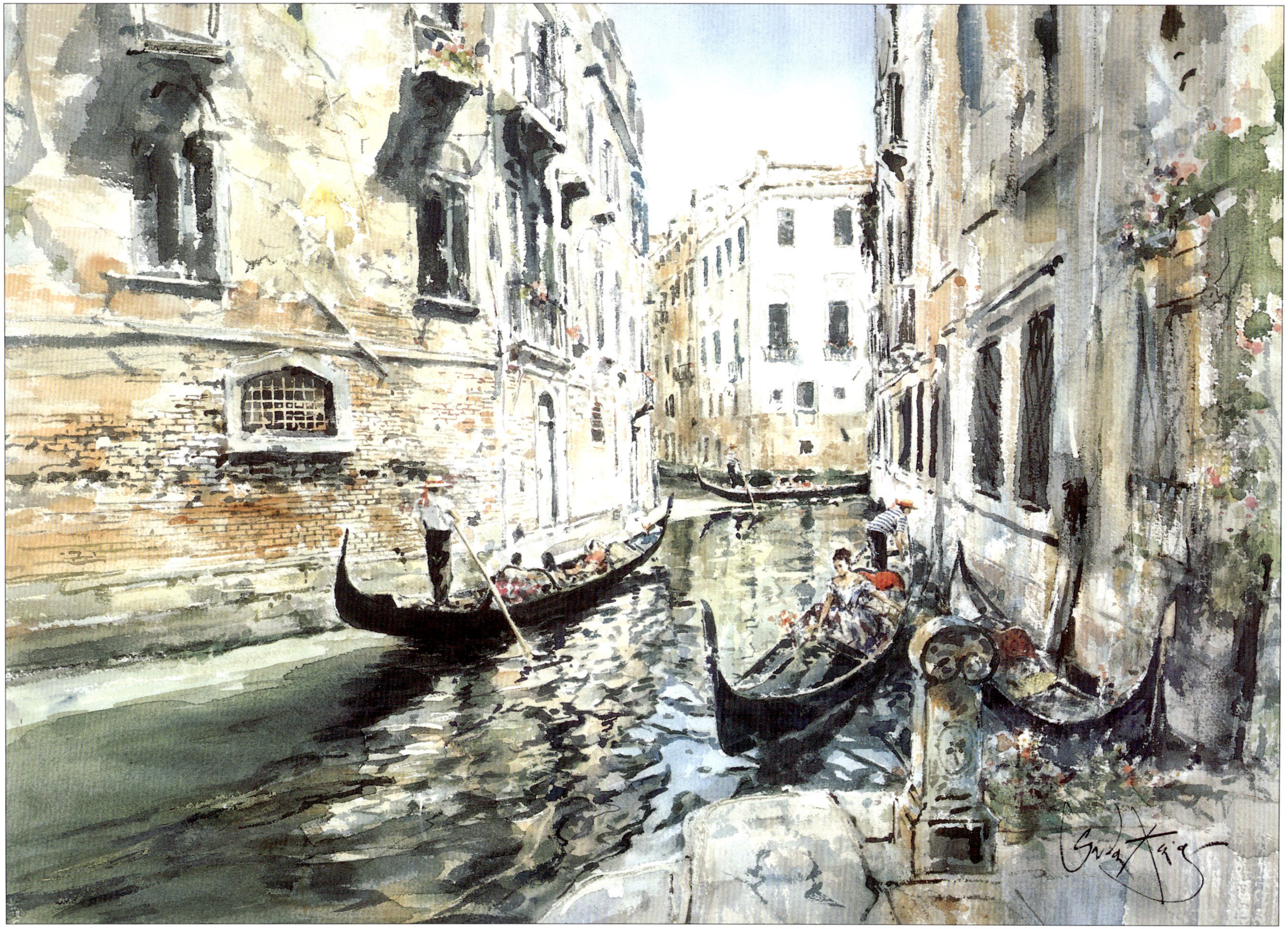

PASSING GONDOLAS

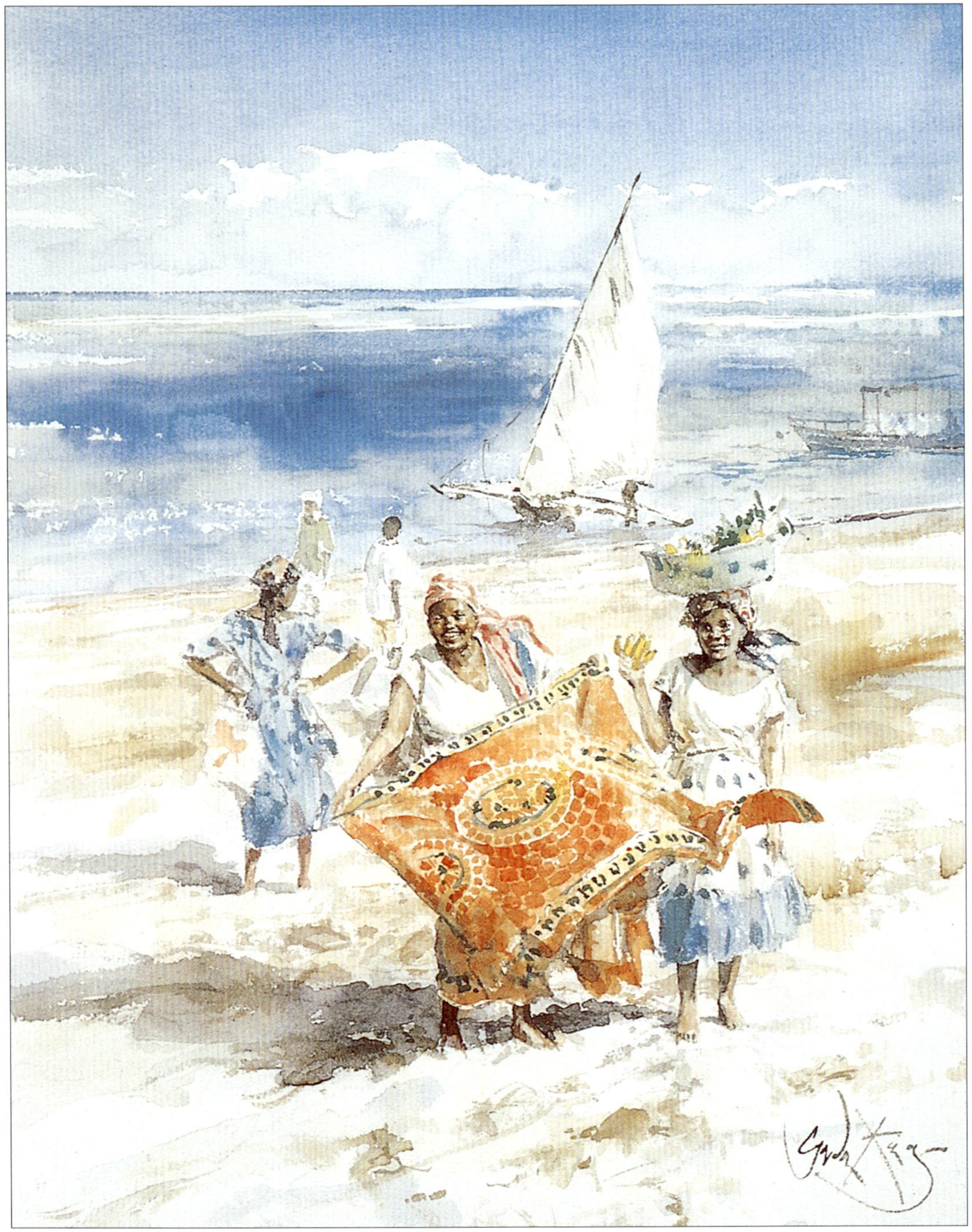

AFRICAN BEACH

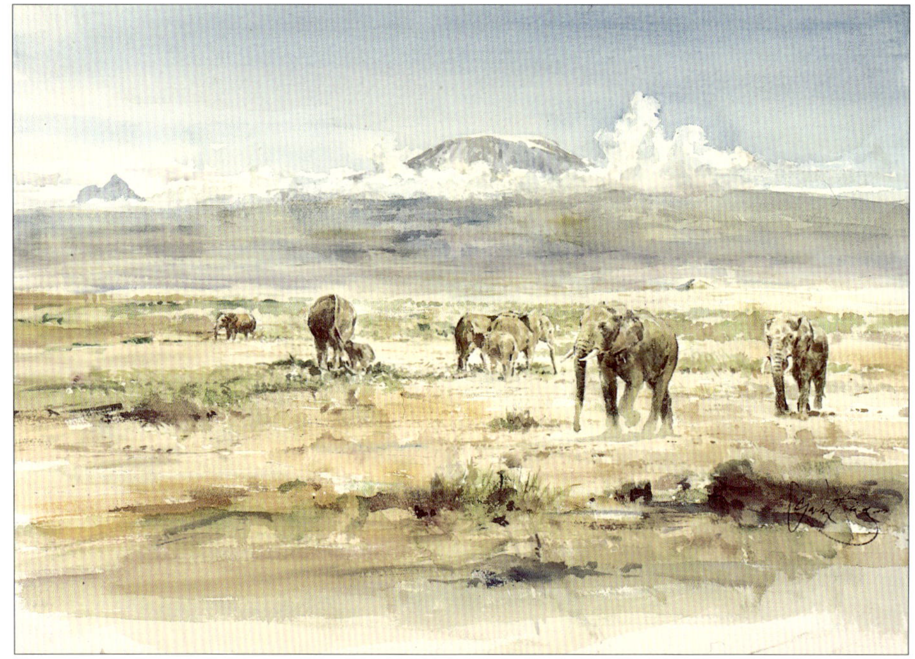

ELEPHANTS AT KILIMANJARO

These paintings all stemmed from my trips to Africa encompassing beautiful beaches, exciting safaris and fascinating people.

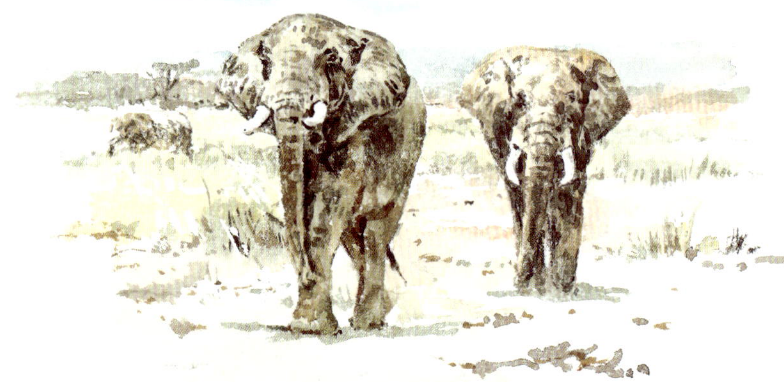

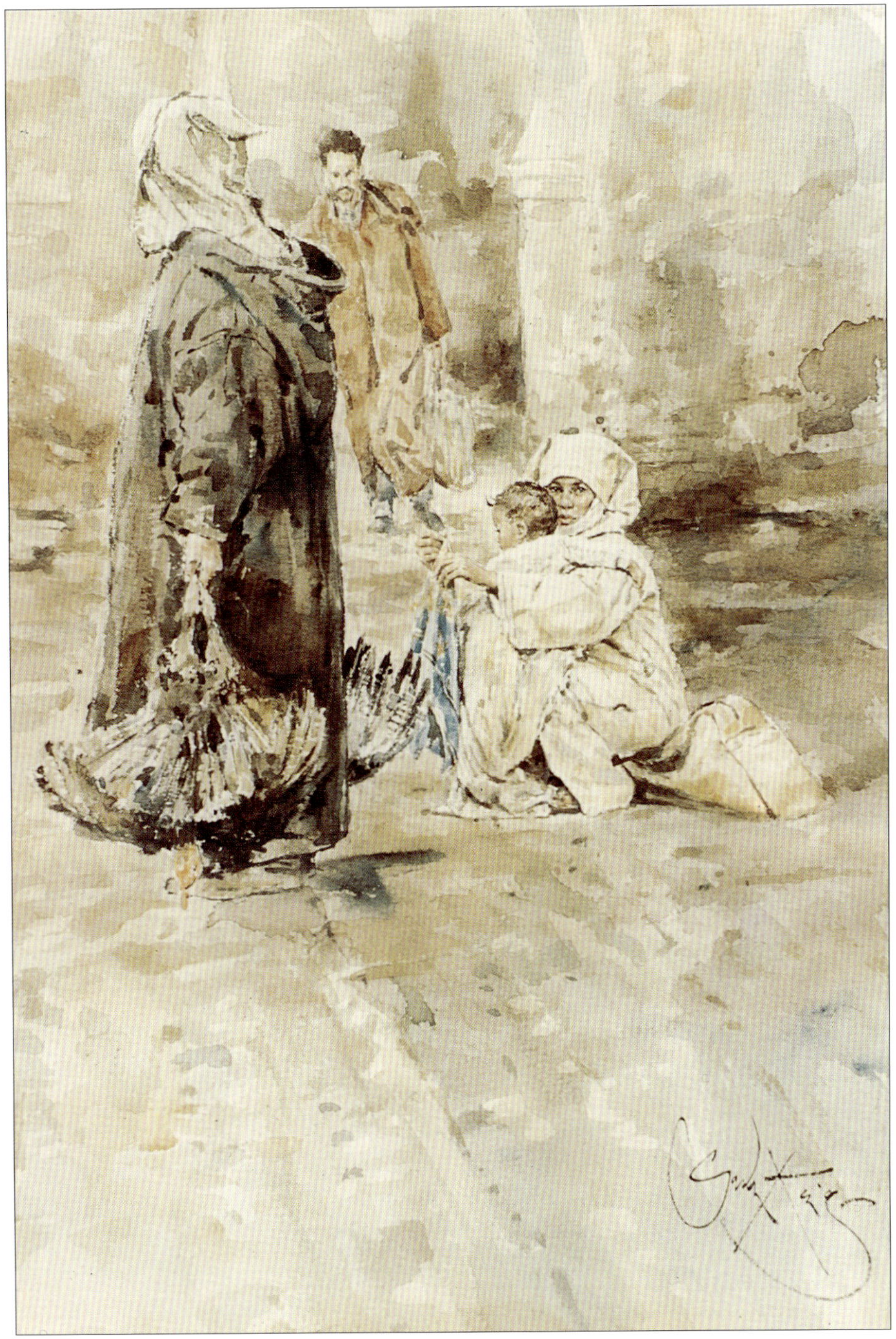

MOROCCAN FAMILY

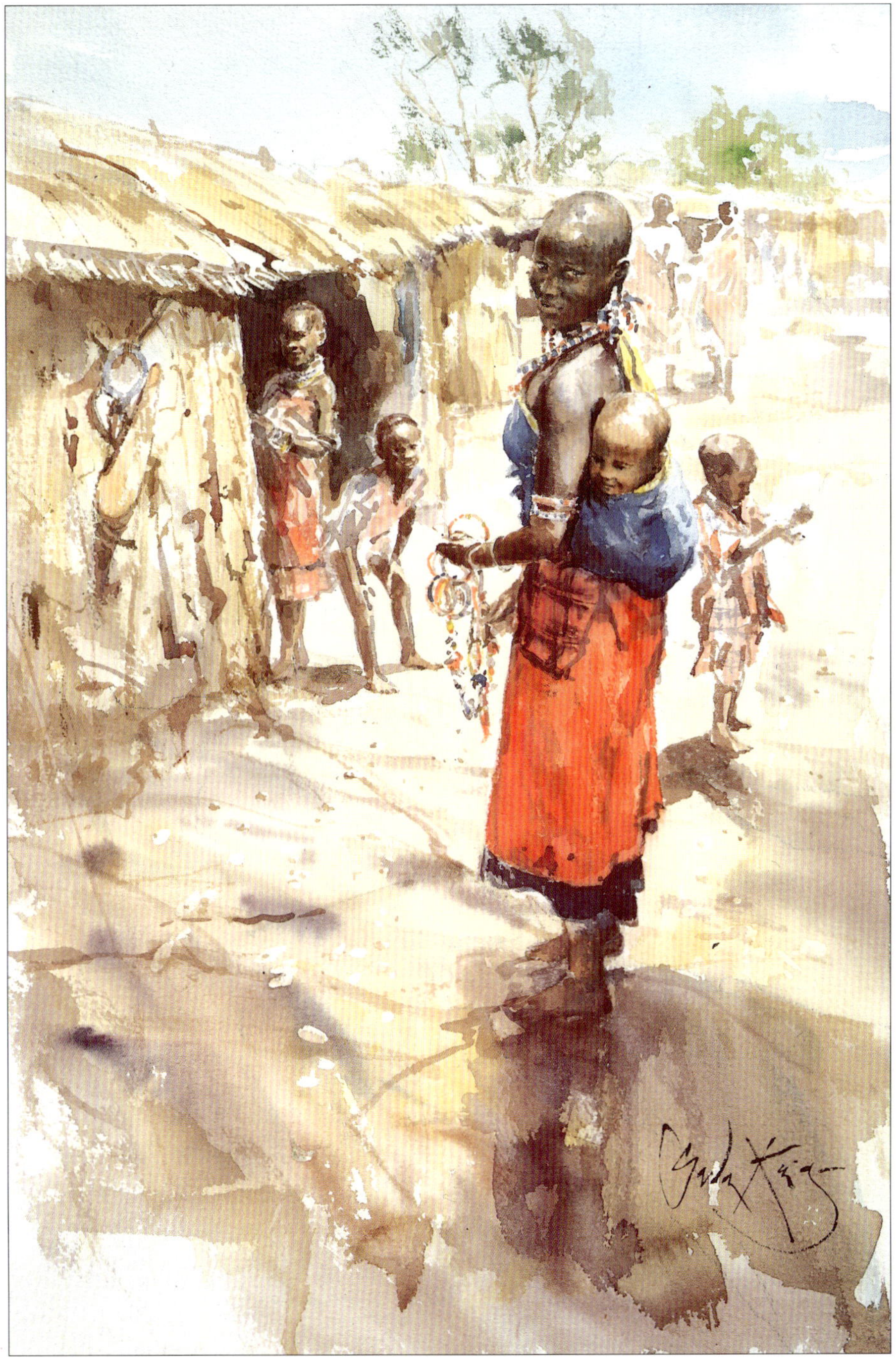

MASAI MOTHER & CHILD

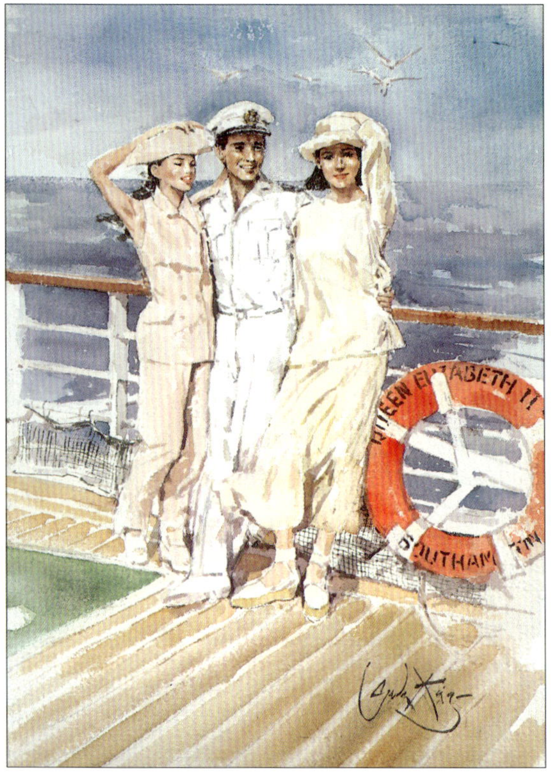

THREE ON BOARD

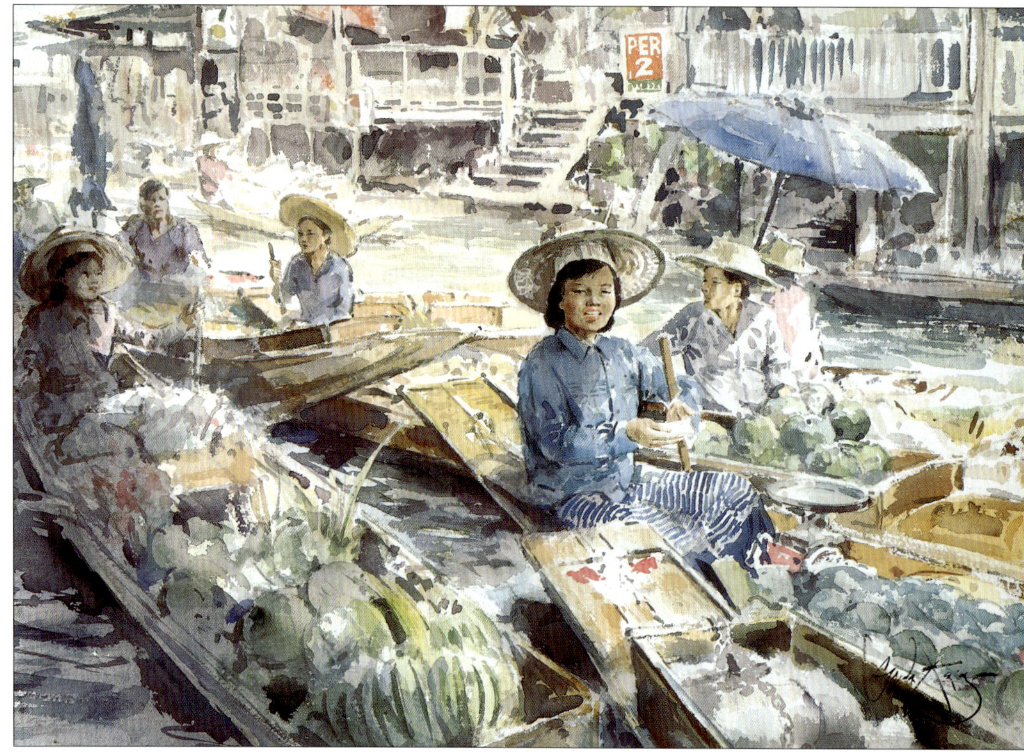

THE FLOATING MARKET

SUNSET PRINCESS

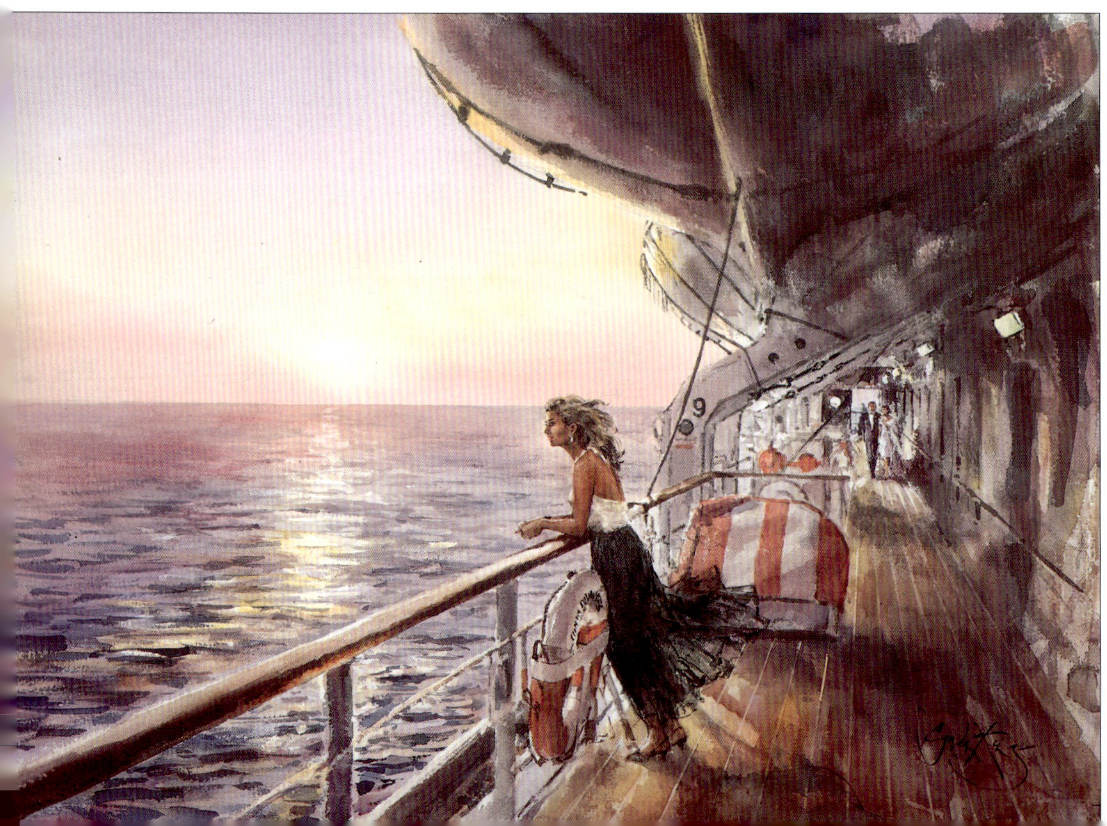

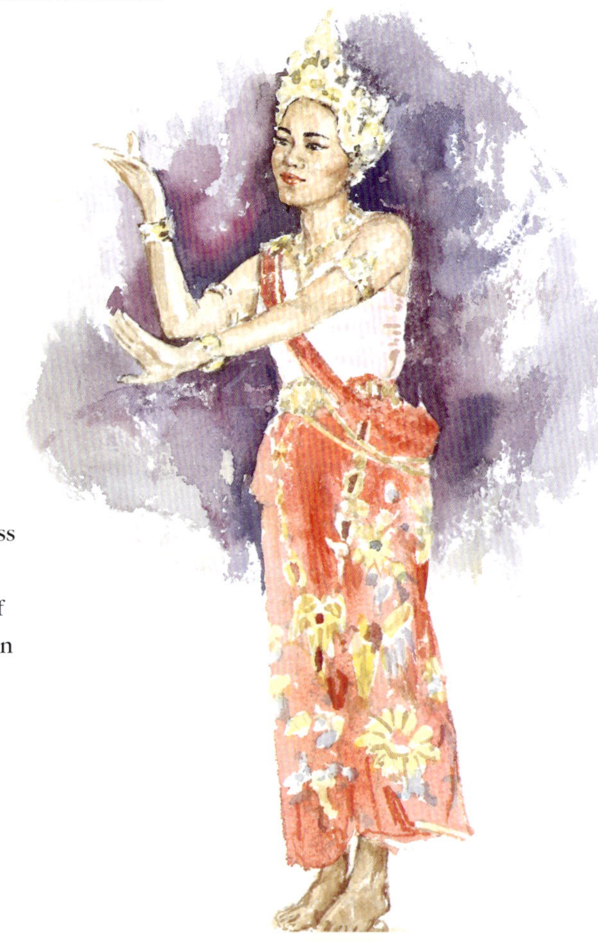

Being at sea with the vastness
of the ocean, wonderful
sunsets and the prospect of
new destinations is always an
exciting experience.

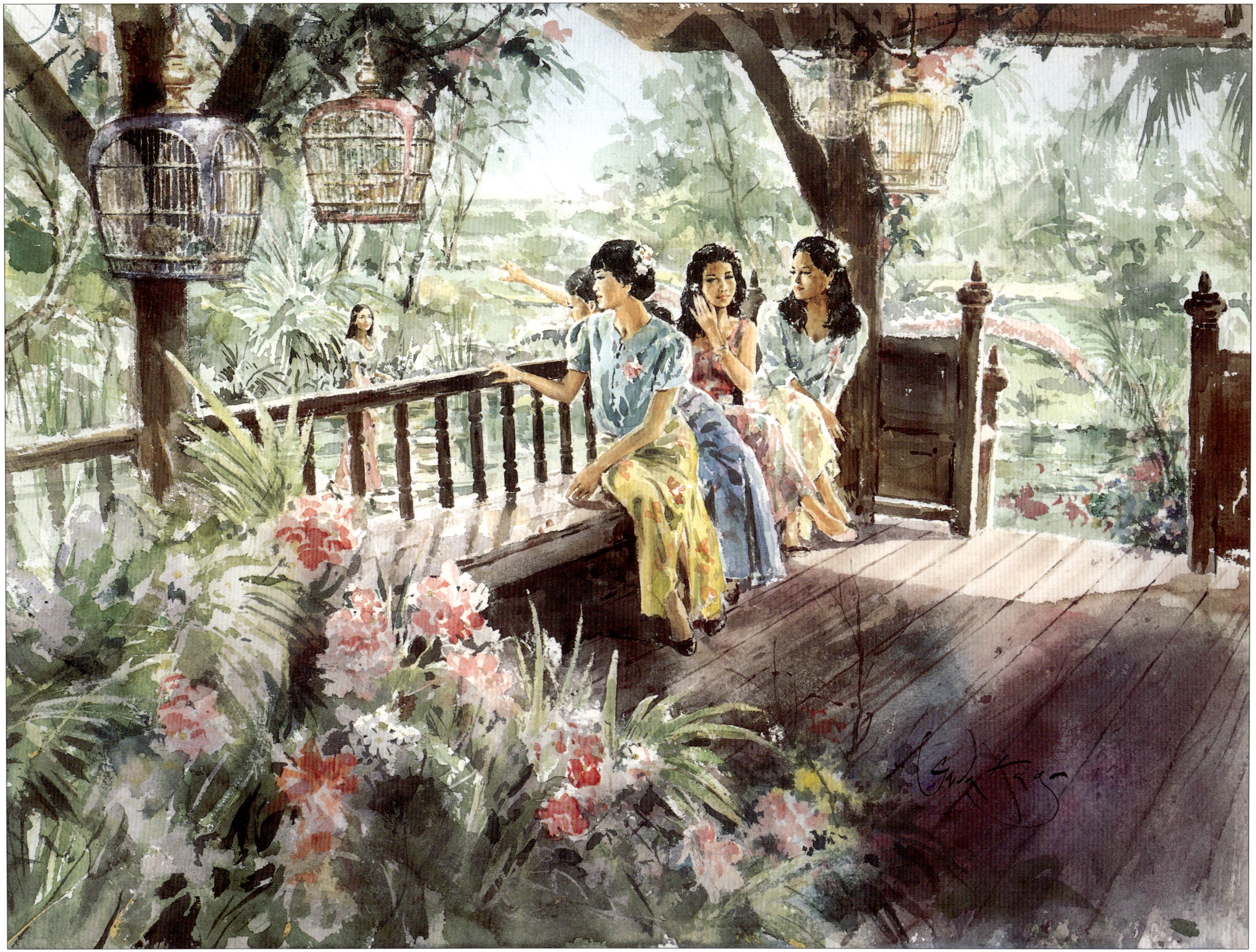

THE SUMMERHOUSE

Thailand was an absolute feast of colour and atmosphere.

Gallery 7

I've always tried to achieve the feeling that if you flick your fingers the characters in my paintings will spontaneously start moving and come to life.

Generally, in a painting, likeness is not a high priority. It's more a general look or feeling that I am concentrating on. However, in a portrait or character sketch the specific characteristics of the individual as shown by their facial features becomes all important.

I'm not just looking for a photographic likeness. Being an artist gives me the flexibility to enhance certain features and play down others. The technique both in oil and watercolour is to use confident brushstrokes with a degree of panache bonded by good drawing and observation.

With a portrait there is an additional challenge. By giving permanence to a memory the painting is making a statement for posterity, whether it be of children at a certain stage, of parents, of loved ones or of those who are sadly no longer with us. Reviving happy memories can be very rewarding.

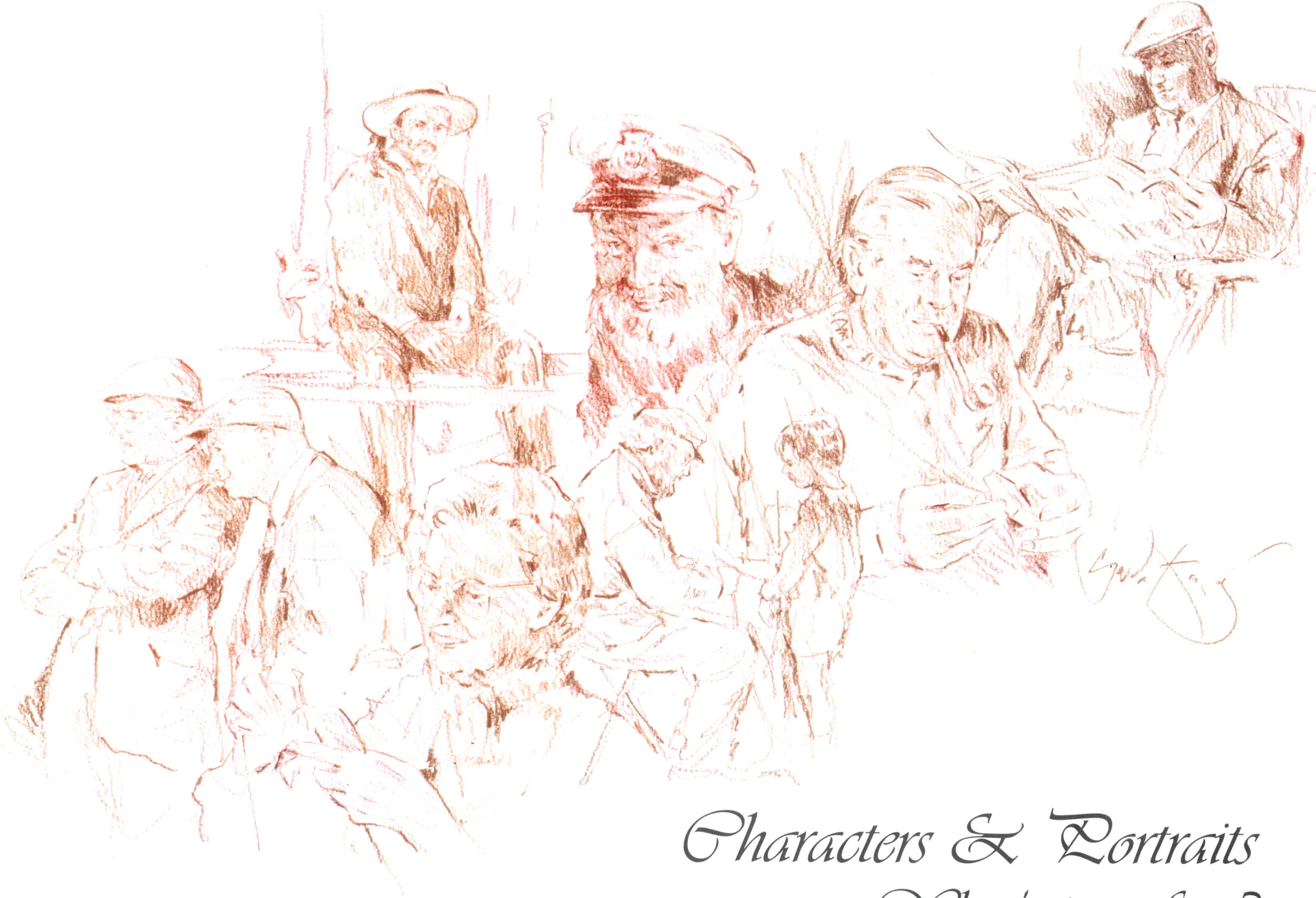

Characters & Portraits
What's in a face?

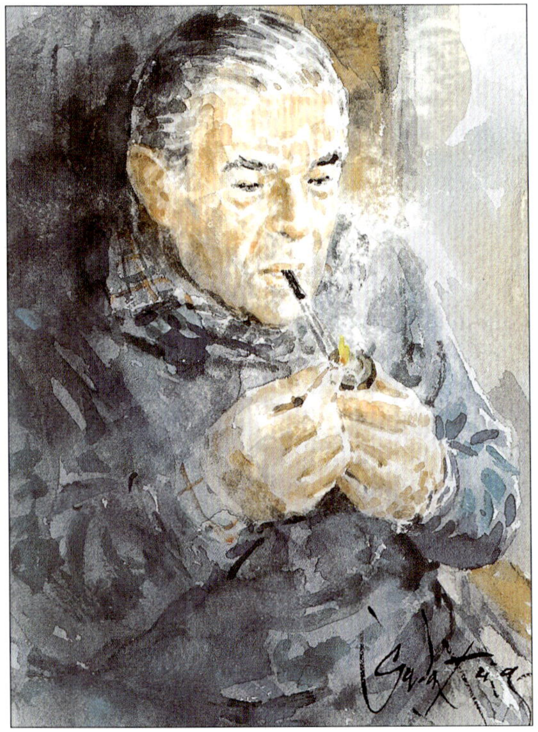

MY FAVOURITE PIPE

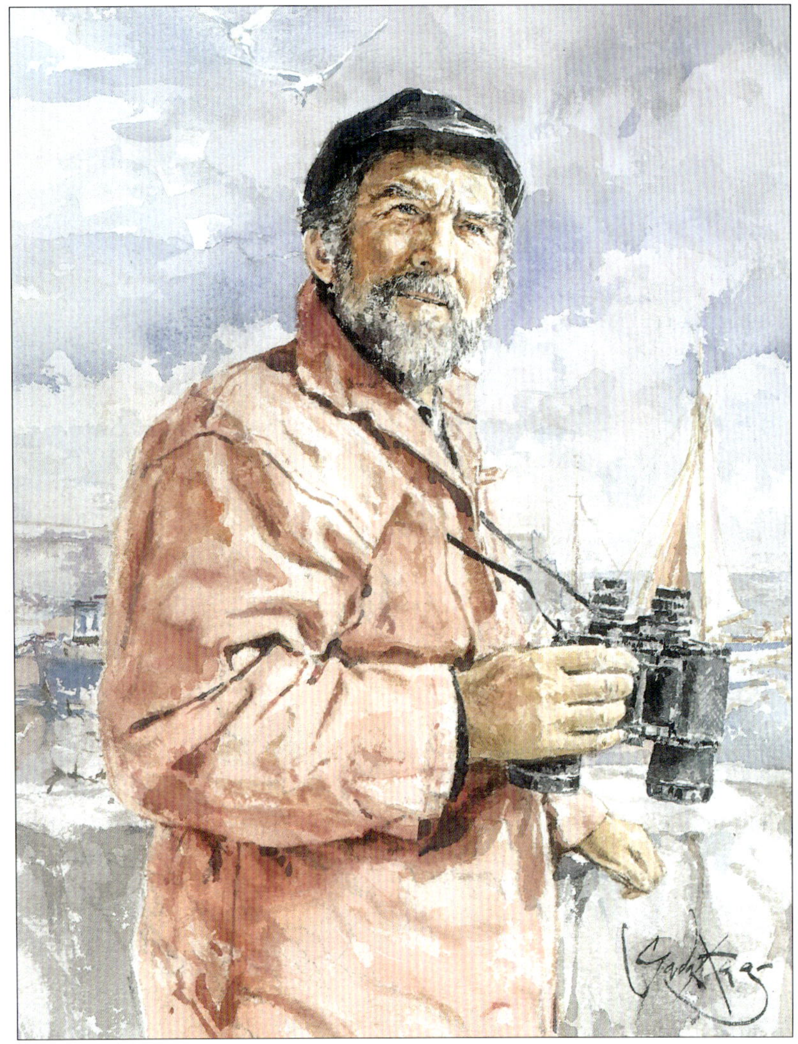

LOOKING OUT TO SEA

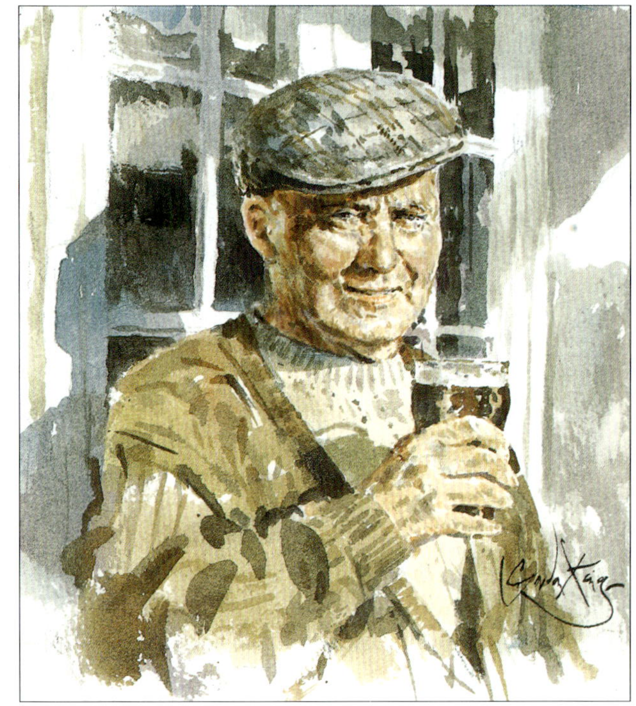

A PINT OF THE BEST

I find painting characters like these lots of fun, seeing a lifetime's experience in their faces.

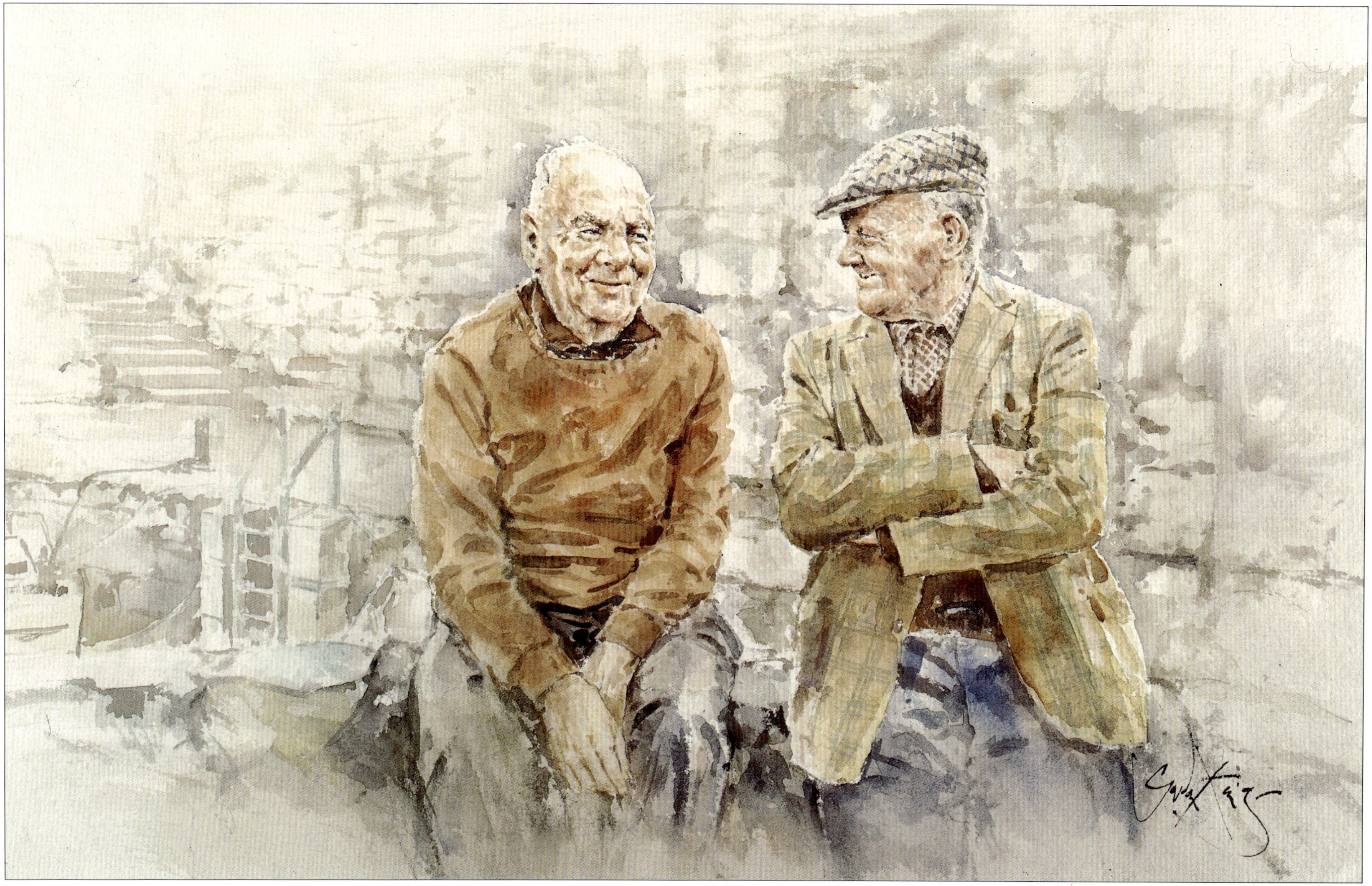

OLD FRIENDS

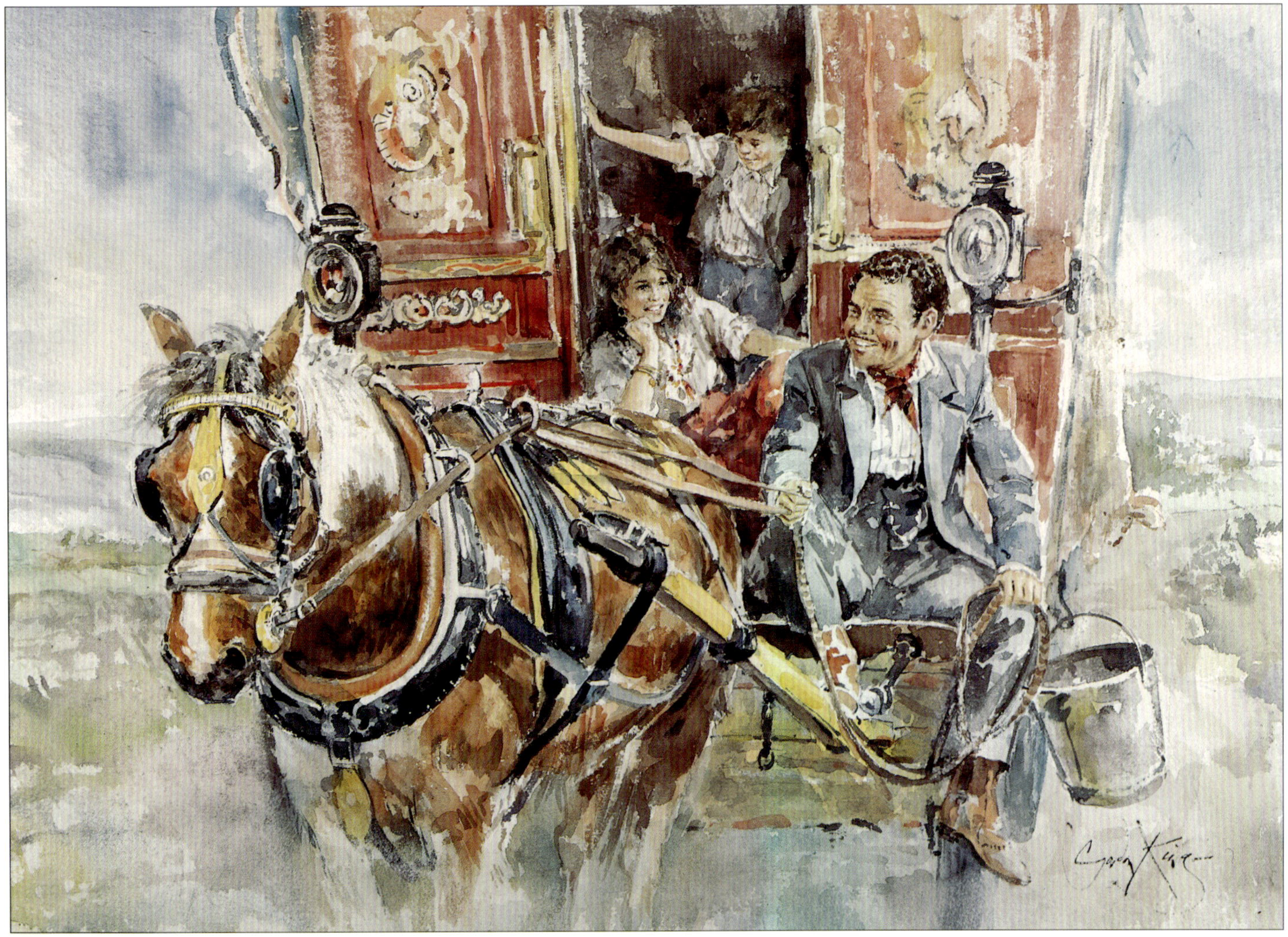

THE OPEN ROAD

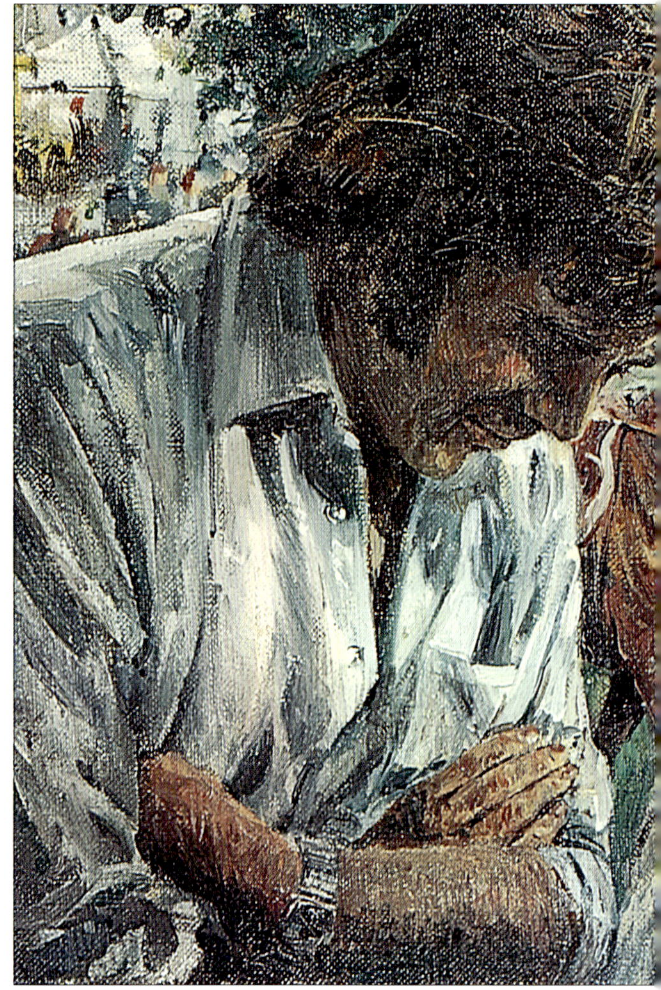

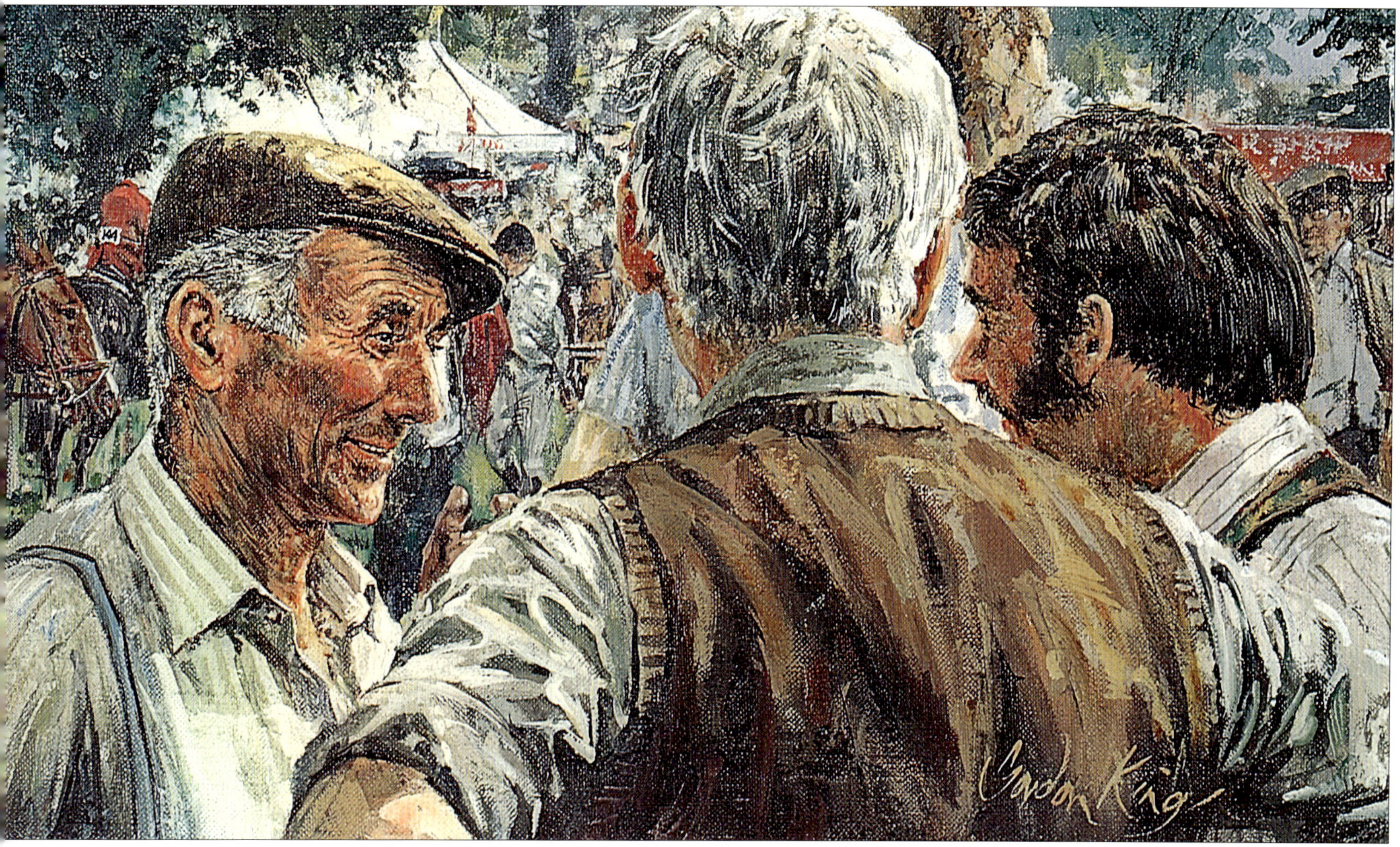

THE COUNTY SHOW

THE MORRISMAN

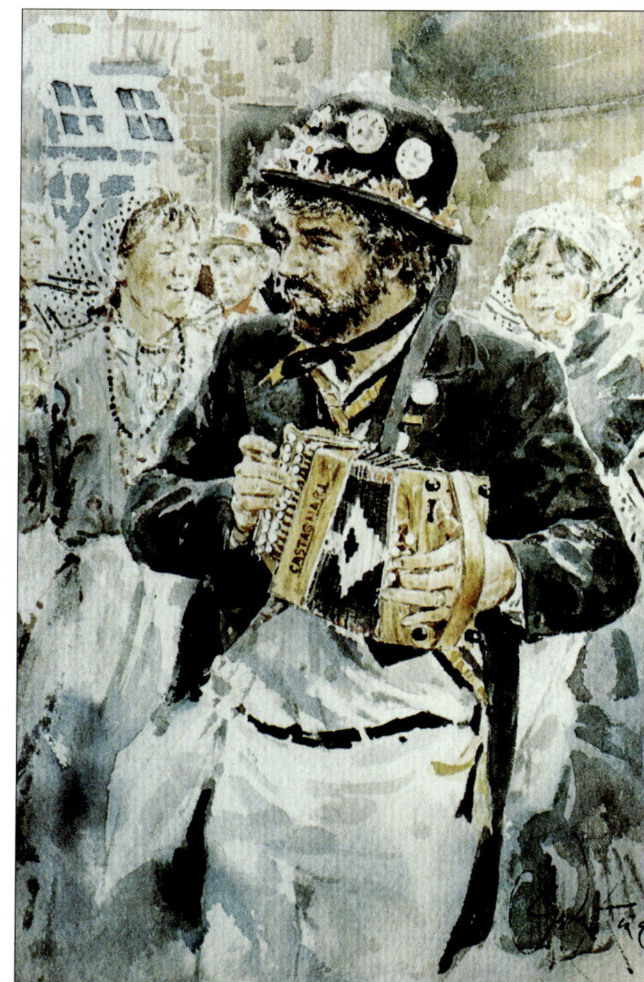

These are all characters I have found in my travels in and around the U.K. following traditional country pursuits.

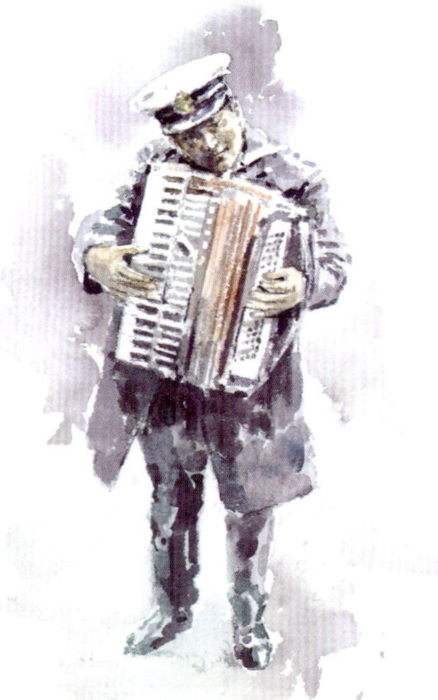

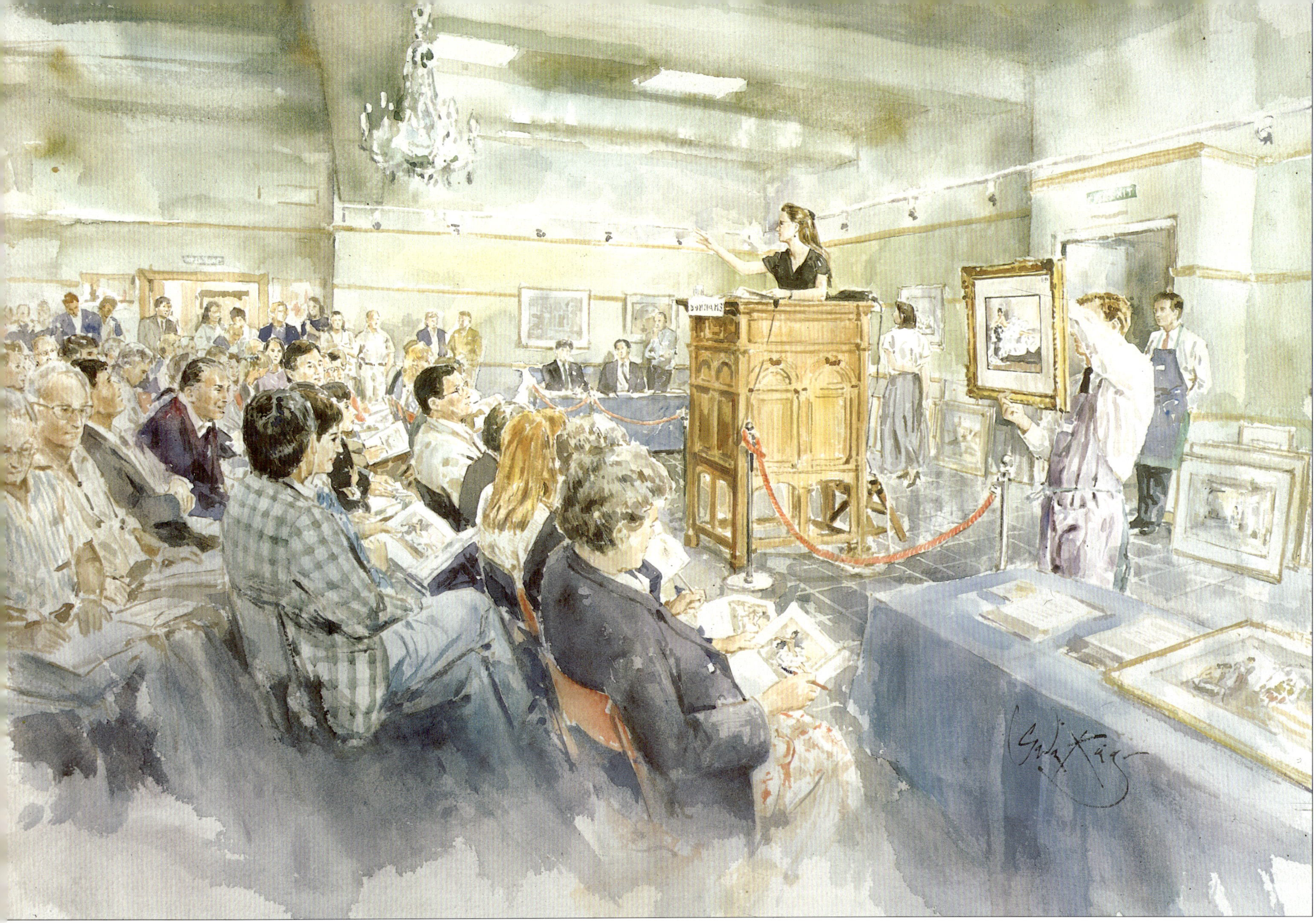

UP FOR AUCTION

Bonhams kindly gave permission for me to do this painting of their auction of work by Sir William Russell Flint held on Saturday, 19th May, 1990. It shows a small watercolour entitled 'Clara Sprott' coming under the hammer for £68,000 which was the highlight of the day.

At their next Flint auction Bonham's put 'Up For Auction' on display beside the auctioneer's stand.

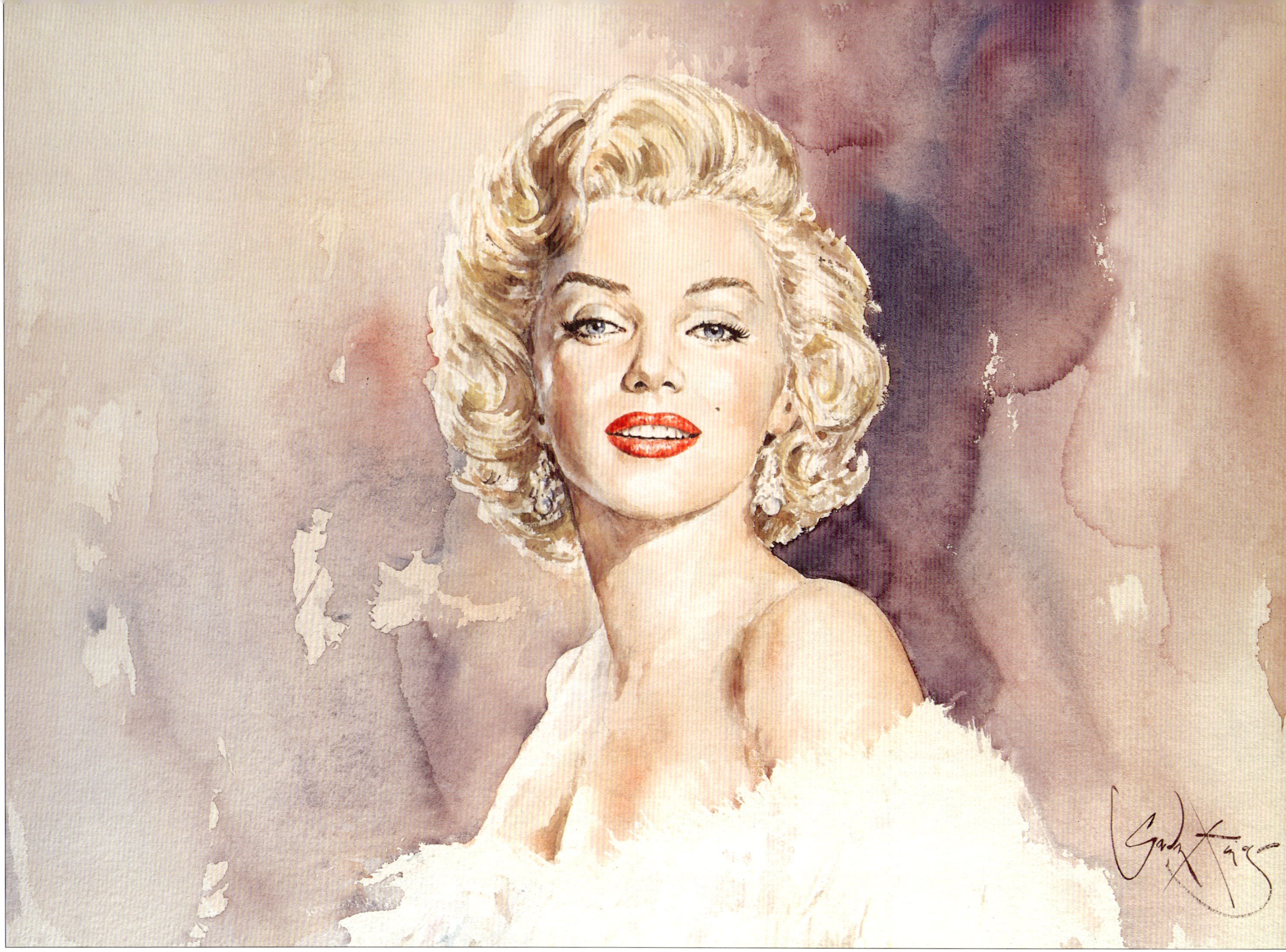

SCREEN GODDESS

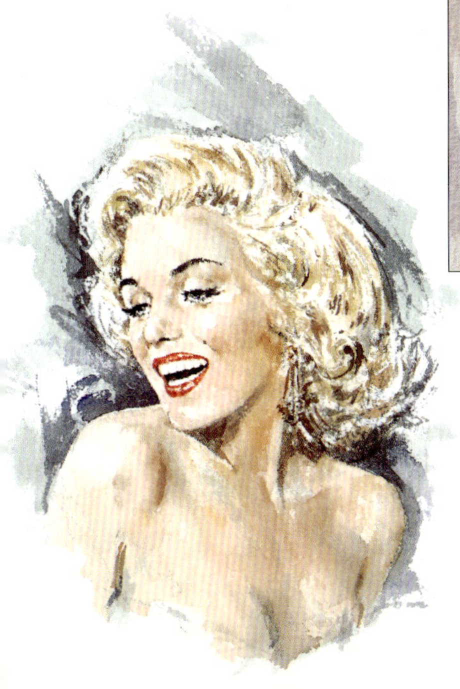

As a teenager I was mesmerised by the Monroe magic. I even made several attempts to catch a glimpse of her while she was filming at Pinewood Studios.

My first painting of Marilyn was done in oils for the London exhibition 'Masters of the Female Form'. In this watercolour I wanted to capture the underlying simplicity and freshness of her appeal together with the aura of glamour which surrounded her.

Being a figurative artist, the question I'm often asked is 'when does a painting become a portrait?' With portraits there is always more emphasis on capturing all the relevant points of likeness and character, giving a sense of knowing the person. I still like to think a portrait will stand on its own as a painting regardless of whether the viewer knows the subject or not.

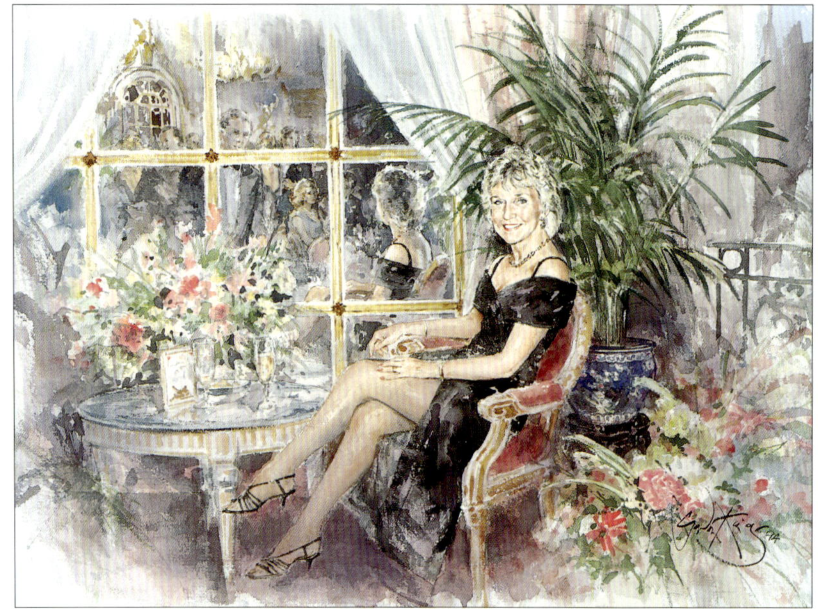

SUSAN PALLETT

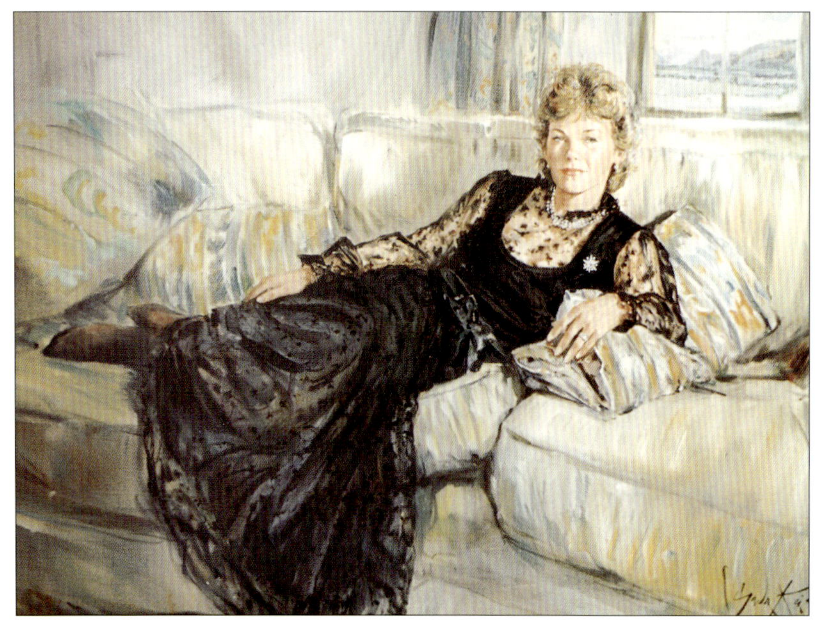

ROO WILLIAMS-WYNNE (OIL)

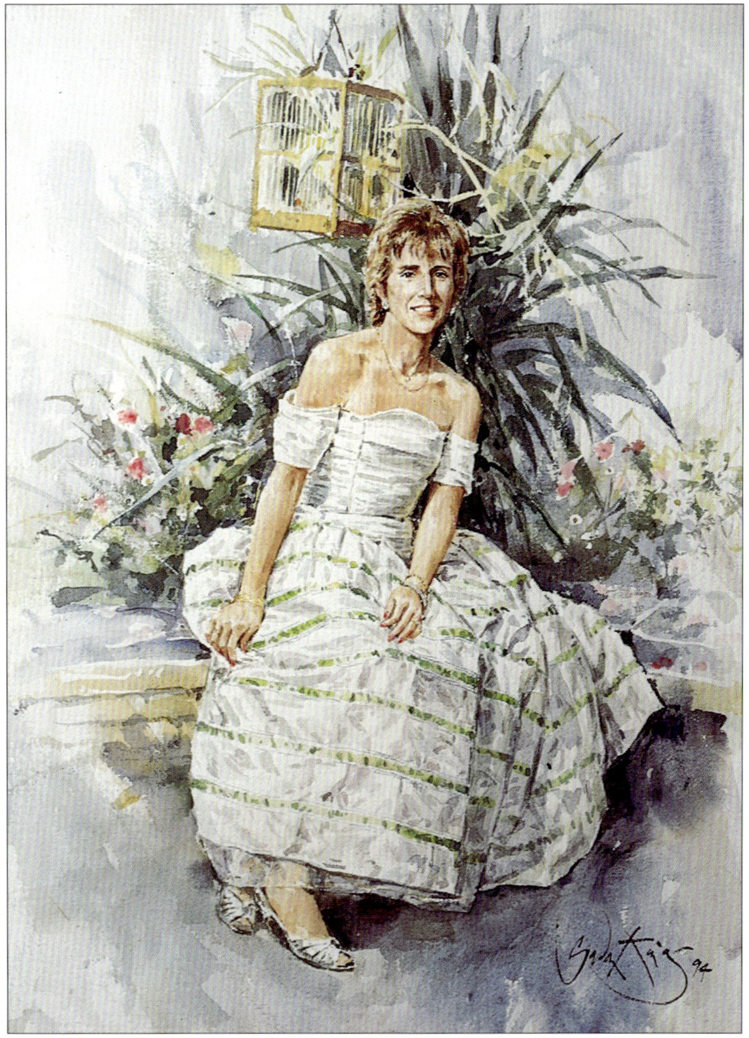

SANDRA KANE

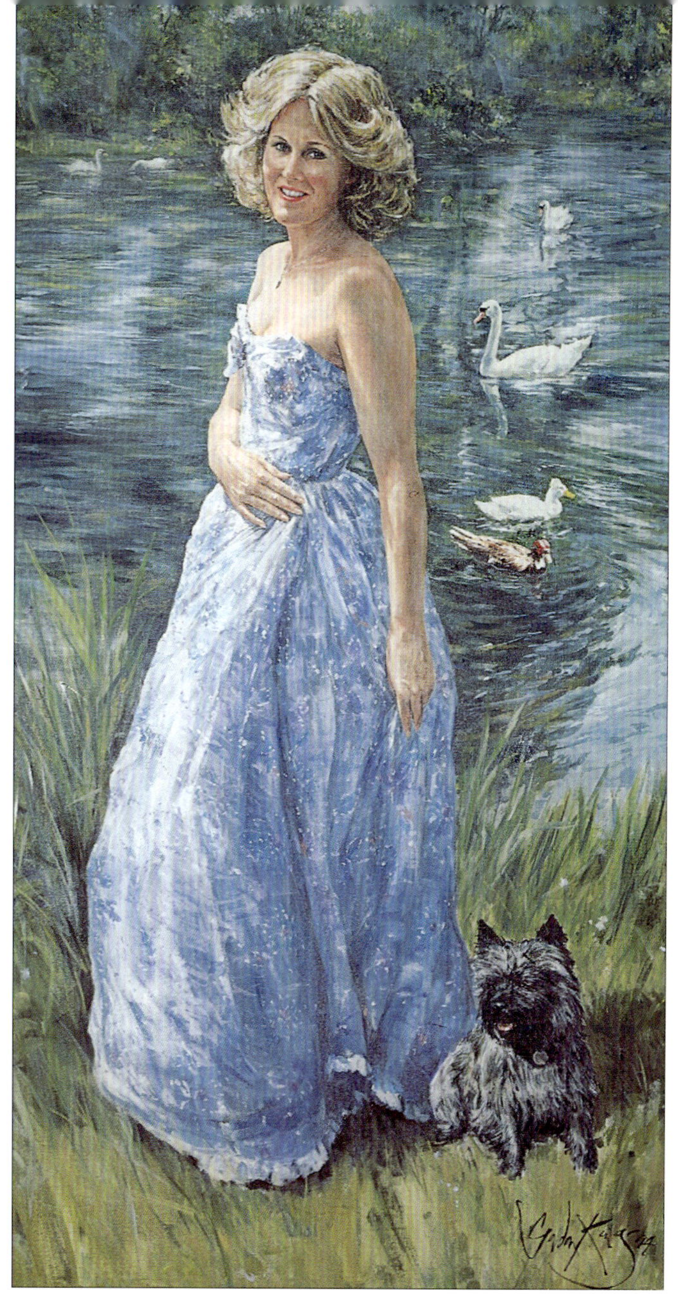

SHARON SHARPLES (OIL)

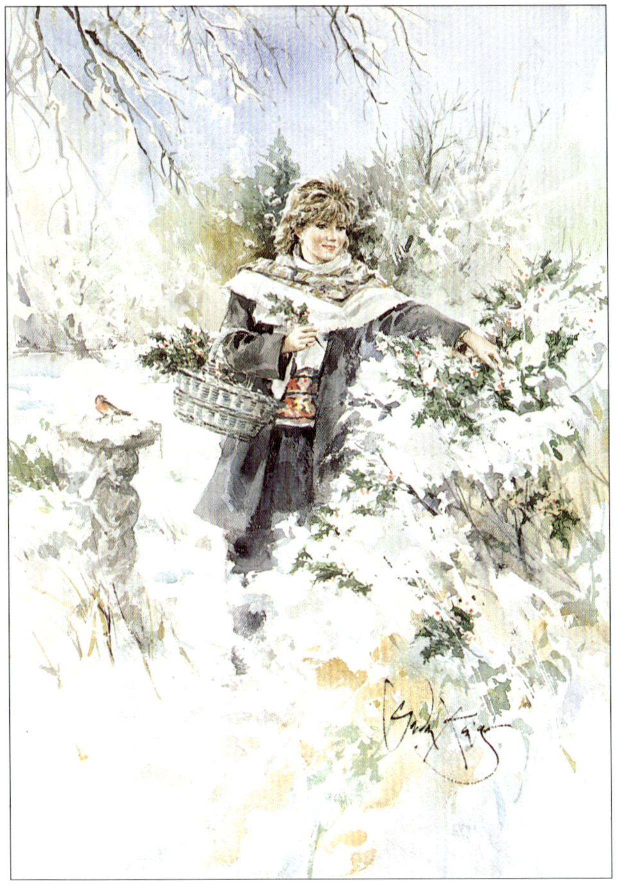

PICKING HOLLY

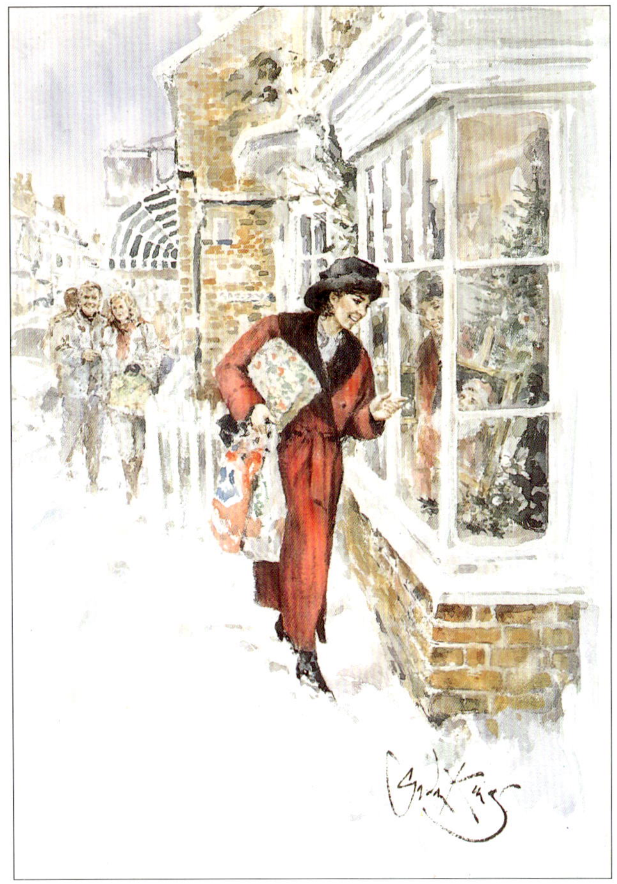

CHRISTMAS SHOPPING

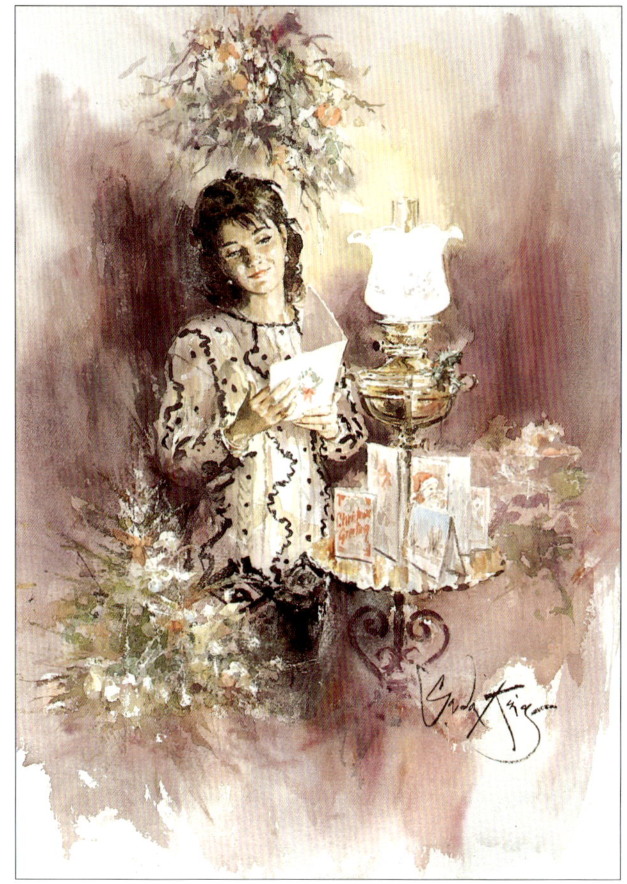

A FAVOURITE CARD

For over a decade I've painted my daughter, Louise for the family Christmas Card. The early cards were subsequently reproduced by Rainbow Cards and the originals collected by the Bell family. More recently the cards have been reproduced in the Polytint Card range.

Each year, when September comes around, I begin thinking of ideas for the next card and fortunately there always seems to be something which triggers off an appropriate image.

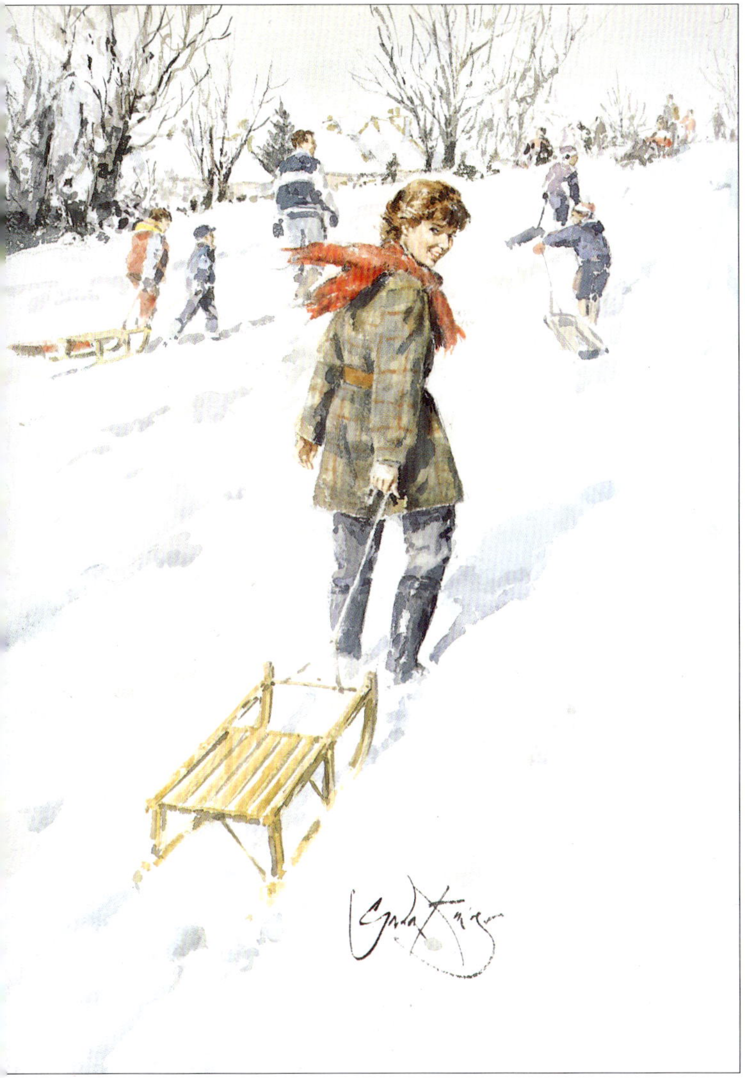

ON GOLD HILL

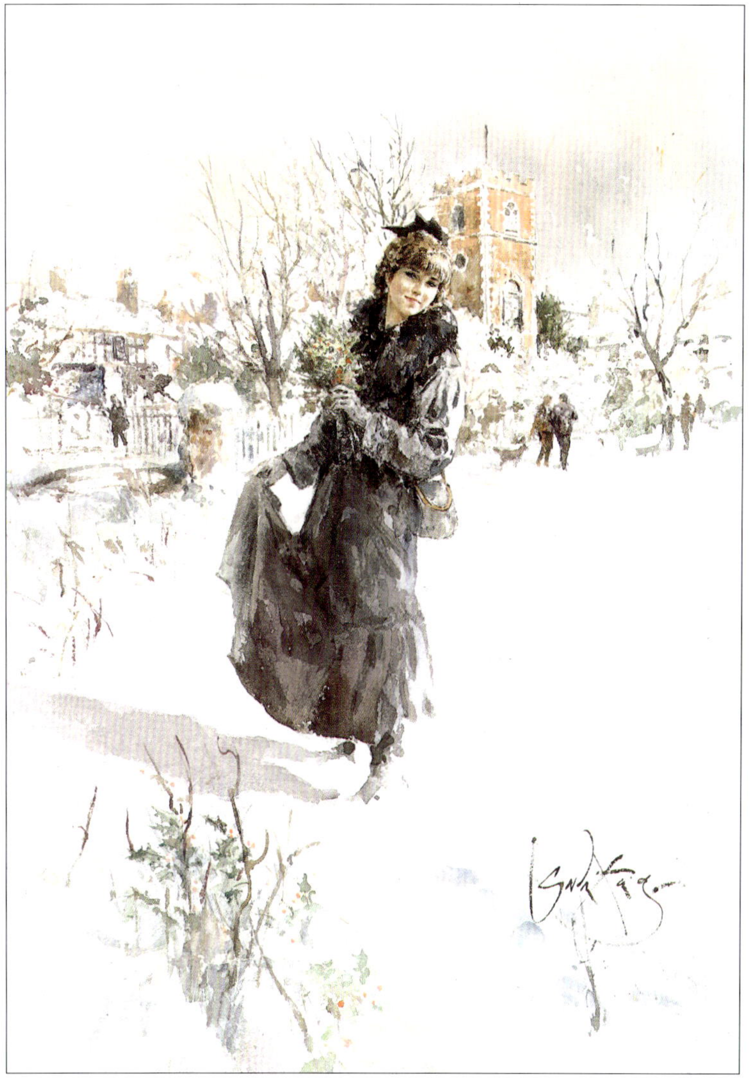

CHRISTMAS SUNDAY

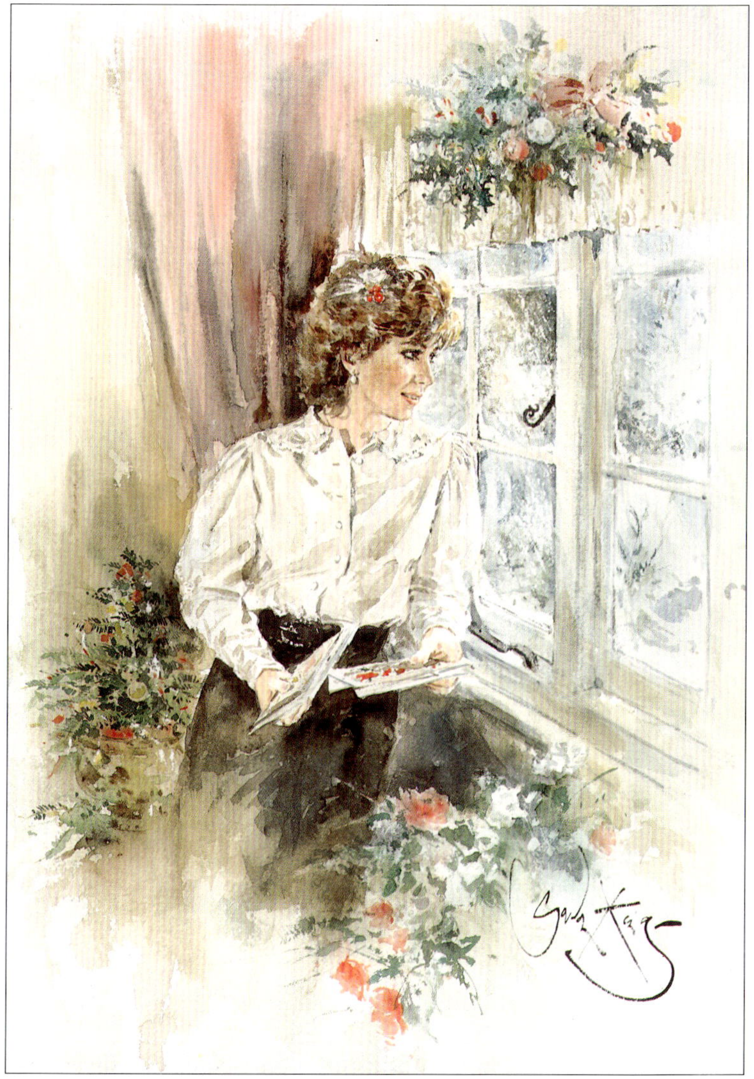

WHEN WILL THAT CARD ARRIVE?

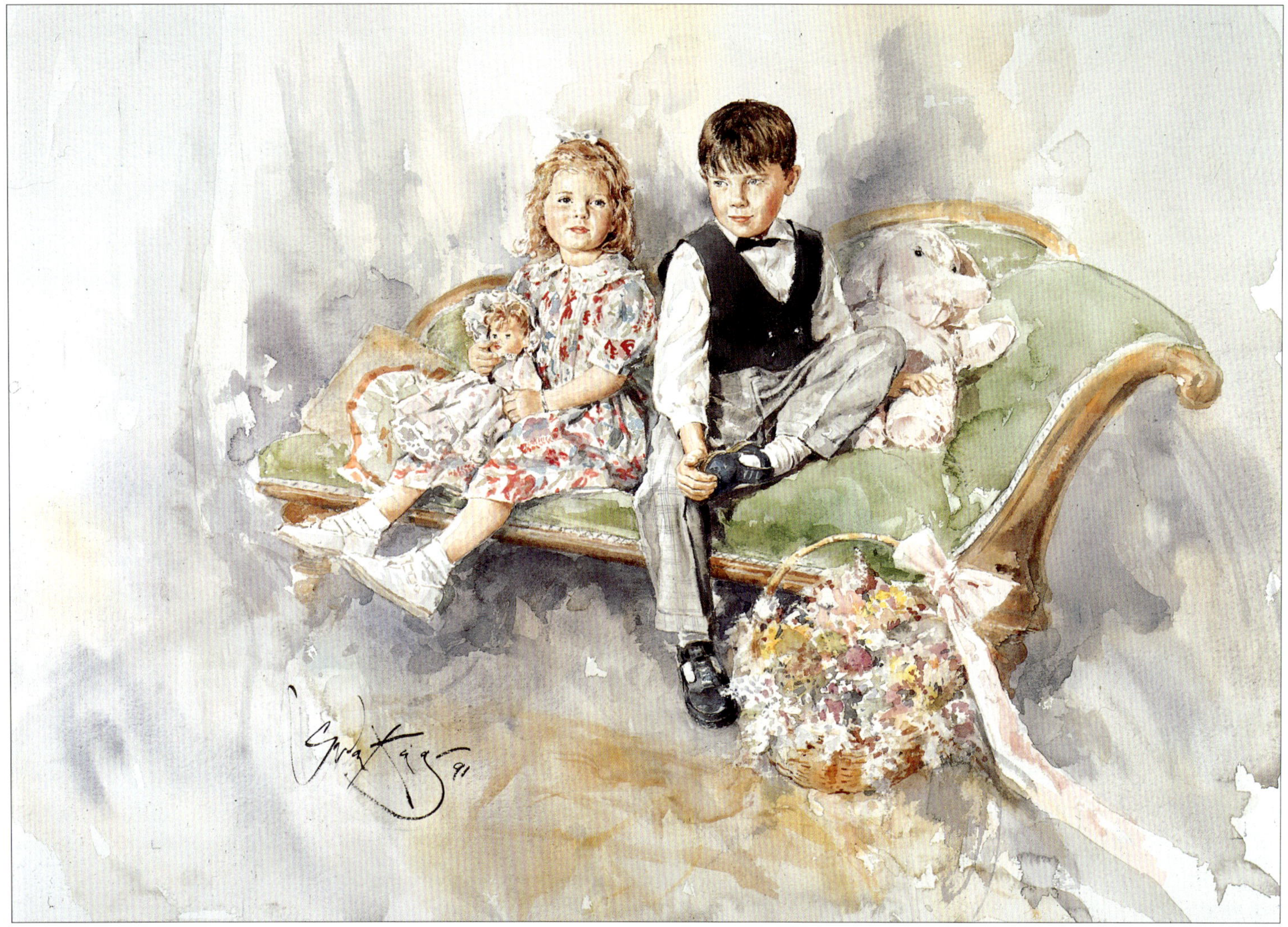

ALISTAIR & ANTONIA
THE CHILDREN OF DR. & MRS IAN WHITE

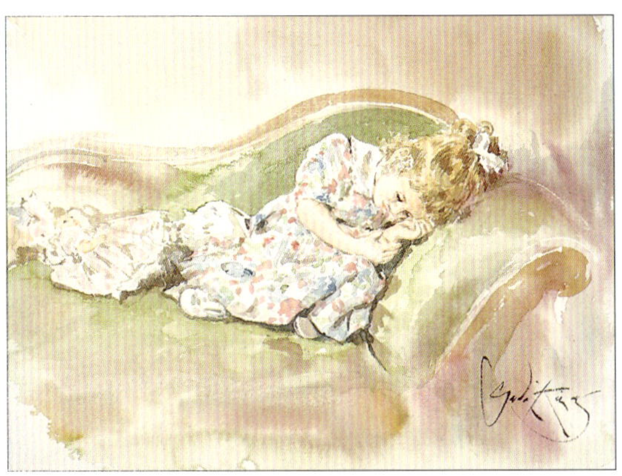

SLEEPY TIME
A SKETCH OF ANTONIA

This is the most recent painting I have done showing Jane, my daughter-in-law with her new baby, Darcy Jane.

THE NEW BABY

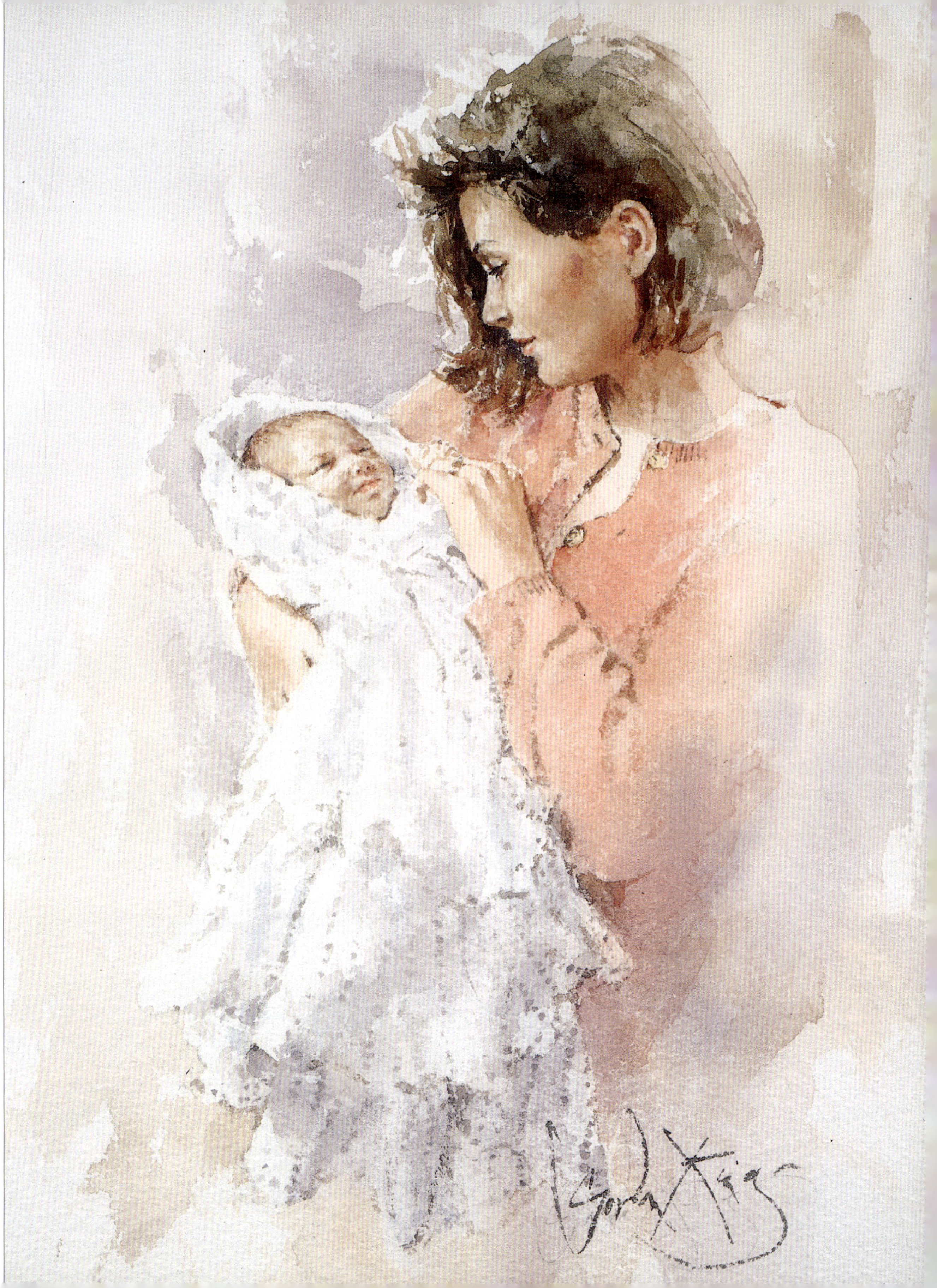

Limited Edition Prints

PUBLISHER:

MICHAEL STEWART

Suzie & Selina
Colette
Fleur
Airs & Graces

PAUL COOPER GALLERIES

Lavender Blue
Henley Girls
Thoughts & Smiles

MAGEE GALLERY

Steady Boy
Grandfather's Tales

WASHINGTON GREEN LIMITED EDITION PRINTS

Camille
The Rose & The Letter
Enchanted Pool
The Fan & The Mask
The Night of The Masquerade
Screen Goddess
Peace & Harmony
Lost in Thought
Nureyev – The Legend
Isabella
Small World
A Flower Market in Venice
Afternoon Shadows
Serena
Between Rehearsals
Ascot Hats
Days of Summer
Footprints in the Sand

SILKSCREEN:
Hidden Thoughts

I would like to take this opportunity to thank all the people who have made their paintings available for reproduction in this book. My apologies go to those whose old favourites may not have been included due to the limited space available and hope they will enjoy some of the new work that has been featured.

I would like to dedicate this book to Mary and my granddaughter, Darcy Jane.

List of Plates